BRAVE THE WILD RIVER

BRAVE THE WILD RIVER

*The Untold Story
of Two Women Who
Mapped the Botany of
the Grand Canyon*

Melissa L. Sevigny

W. W. NORTON & COMPANY
Celebrating a Century of Independent Publishing

For information about permission to reproduce selections from this
book, write to Permissions, W. W. Norton & Company, Inc.,
500 Fifth Avenue, New York, NY 10110

For information about special discounts for bulk purchases,
please contact W. W. Norton Special Sales at
specialsales@wwnorton.com or 800-233-4830

Manufacturing by Lake Book Manufacturing
Book design by Lovedog Studio
Production manager: Anna Oler

ISBN 978-0-393-86823-4

W. W. Norton & Company, Inc.
500 Fifth Avenue, New York, N.Y. 10110
www.wwnorton.com

W. W. Norton & Company Ltd.
15 Carlisle Street, London W1D 3BS

1 2 3 4 5 6 7 8 9 0

For Gia and Sofia—
be curious and be brave.

I know of no more effective way to wreck an expedition than to put in one woman, or worse still, two.

—Roy Chapman Andrews, Explorer's Club, 1932

———

We don't have much truth to express unless we have gone into those rooms and closets and woods and abysses that we were told not to go into.

—Anne Lamott, *Bird by Bird*

CONTENTS

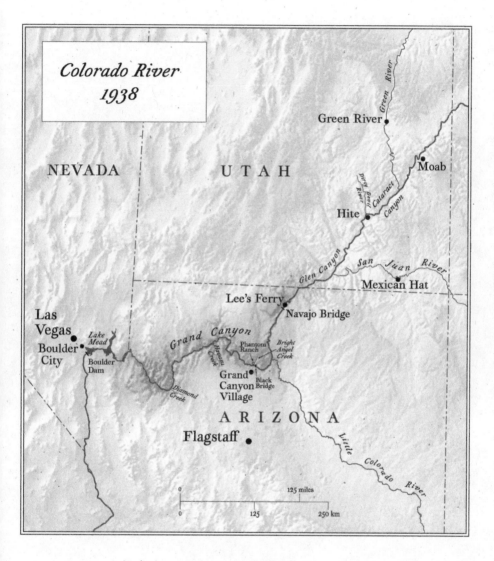

Map by Paul Mirocha

Prologue

STRANDED

THE NIGHT WAS FULL OF NOISES. THE DRIFTWOOD campfire snapped and spluttered, casting a circle of light on the river-rippled sand. Beyond, darkness pressed. Somewhere in the undergrowth a small creature rustled and scratched. The willows fringing the sandbar made a susurration as water rushed round their roots. Over, under, through it all, ran the Colorado River.

It was nothing like the sultry summer nights she had spent as a girl in Michigan, with a chorus of crickets and a percussion section of frogs. Michigan was a world of water, hemmed by lakes and stitched with rivers. Here, in the wilds of Utah, stone and sky prevailed. The high faces of the canyon walls boxed her in. The river, sloshing the shore, resounded as loud as an ocean.

Lois Jotter was alone. She shouldn't have been there—that's what people would say. Certainly not separated from her companions in the depths of Cataract Canyon, the place everyone called "the grave-yard of the Colorado River." The date was June 23, 1938. At the age of twenty-four, she had come, with her mentor and colleague Elzada Clover, to collect plants. The two women, both botanists from the University of Michigan in Ann Arbor, had set off down the Green River in Utah with four companions and three boats. They intended to raft more than 600 miles down the Green and Colorado rivers to Lake Mead, passing through the Grand Canyon along the way.

From above—though it would be decades, yet, before satellites and space travel would show the world this way—the Colorado River's watershed looks like a ragged, many-veined leaf, its stem planted firmly in the Gulf of California. In a wetter climate it might be invisible, hidden by the canopies of trees and overhanging banks of flowers and ferns. But here, in the American Southwest, the river carves and folds the landscape around it as if water holds a weight not measured in ounces. Its headwaters begin in the Wind River Range of Wyoming, a jumbled stretch of the Rocky Mountains, where cold rivulets of snowmelt wake beneath ice each spring to surge into a thunderous rush and pour into the Green River. Jotter and her companions had floated a placid stretch of the Green, 120 miles through the red rock of Utah, where the river loops and doubles back like a dawdling tourist in no hurry to reach the next vista.

Earlier that day, they had reached the confluence where the Green joined another tributary known, until not long before, as the Grand. It, too, draws its headwaters from Rocky Mountains west of the Continental Divide. The Grand was shorter than the Green, but it had won the affections of a Colorado congressman named Edward Taylor. In 1921 he successfully lobbied to rename the smaller tributary after its main channel: the Colorado River. "The Grand is the father and the Green the mother, and Colorado wants the name to follow the father," Taylor said in his persuasive speech to the U.S. House of Representatives, adding as further evidence that the Grand was a much more treacherous river than the Green, killing anyone who tried to raft it.

Downstream from Jotter's campsite, the Colorado River swept on into deepening canyons, one after the other—through Cataract, Glen, and the Grand Canyon, 277 miles long and so deep it exposed the raw bedrock of the world. The Grand Canyon ends near the border of Arizona and the tip of Nevada, where the still-filling reservoir of Lake Mead behind Boulder Dam (now called Hoover Dam) momentarily knotted the river into a lake. Routed ignominiously through hydroelectric turbines, the Colorado then meanders southward, unraveling into a ribbon on the border between Arizona and

California. It gathers one more major tributary along the way, the Gila River, before losing itself in the delta in Sonora and Baja California, Mexico.

The river was an attraction for a botanist, particularly one interested in thorny things. No one had ever formally surveyed the plant life of the Colorado River through the canyonlands, considered by some the most mysterious corner remaining in the United States. Tucked into side canyons, braving what Jotter called "barren and hellish" conditions, were tough, fierce, spiny cacti no one had ever catalogued. This was why they had come: to "botanize" the canyons and discover the plants that thrived in secret nooks and crannies up and down the Colorado's sheer cliffs and shifting sandbars. If they succeeded, Jotter and Clover would bring out a trove of pressed plants for scientific research. The plants would be an essential record of a region that was changing fast. Once filled, Lake Mead would become the largest human-made reservoir in the world; exotic plants and animals had been accidentally or deliberately introduced into the river channel; and more tourists arrived by the day. Jotter and Clover had the chance to do what no one had done before: chronicle those changes through a botanist's eyes.

But just four days into the trip, things had already gone badly wrong.

Earlier that day, the crew had pulled the boats ashore at the confluence of the Green and Colorado rivers. The trip's leader, Norman Nevills, wanted to scout the rapids ahead and plot a careful route through them. The river was high with snowmelt, chewing up whole trees and spitting them out like toothpicks. Then a boat pulled free from its mooring and spun into the current. Jotter heard a shout and dashed to the shore to see the boat sail by, captainless and undirected. Recklessly she followed her oarsman, Don Harris, into a second boat to give chase. Harris rowed while Jotter bailed water with an empty coffee can, hands cut and bleeding from its jagged rim. Battered and breathless, the two swept four miles downstream before finding the lost boat aground. Harris left Jotter there and walked upriver to rejoin the rest of the crew, promising to return. Night fell. Nobody came.

Jotter had plenty of time, as she gathered a fresh armload of driftwood and stirred the coals back to flame, to recall what everyone had told her about running the Colorado River. The few people who had ventured this far told stories of wreckage flung along the rocks, and skeletons tucked into stony alcoves with withered cactus pads clutched in their bony fingers. She had passed, on the journey down the Green, the names of other river runners painted in white on the canyon walls: names made familiar by newspaper obituaries. Locals bragged, with a kind of gruesome glory, that the Colorado was the most dangerous river in the world.

It was not dangerous because of its size or steepness. Its volume was unimpressive: a whole year's worth of water flowing down the Colorado was what the Mississippi delivered to its delta in two normal weeks. The Colorado averaged a drop of nine feet a mile over its 1,450-mile length, and stretches of the river were nearly flat. It ought to have been the most ordinary river in the United States. But the Colorado was an unruly thing, governed by the mad rhythms of a desert climate. Surges of snowmelt, thick with mud, came down each spring, followed by torrents of storm water in summer. Every flood carried a fresh barrage of boulders and debris torn from the land and tossed in the river's maw. This was what made the Colorado so difficult to run: landslides and slurries at the mouth of every tributary, churning the river to a frothy roil with whirlpools, stomach-somersaulting drops, and standing waves big enough to swallow a boat whole.

To make matters worse for travelers, the strength of those floodwaters and the abrading power of the silt had turned the river into a knife. It had sliced the Colorado Plateau into a marvelous maze of canyons in Utah and Arizona. The steep walls added another element of danger. Should something go wrong—if the boats were smashed to smithereens—there would be no help forthcoming, and little chance of escaping by foot up the cliffs and over the desert.

Cataract Canyon, where Jotter was stranded, was only the beginning: their first test, and they had failed. The Grand Canyon still lay ahead. By 1938 only a dozen expeditions—just over fifty men, all told—had successfully traversed the Grand Canyon by boat since John Wesley Powell's journey nearly seventy years before. Only one woman on record had attempted the trip: Bessie Hyde, who vanished with her husband, Glen, on their honeymoon in 1928. Their boat was left empty; their bodies were never found. People said women couldn't run the Colorado River. Well, Clover and Jotter weren't just women: they were botanists, and they were going to try.

Jotter had time to remember those stories and to wonder what had happened to her companions—somewhere upriver, no doubt trying to reach her. But the night stretched on and they didn't come. An unseen fish splashed out on the water. The fire burned to embers. Two rowboats, their fresh white paint showing new scores and scrapes, listed on their sides on the riverbank. Jotter checked the ropes that anchored them, and nervously, checked again. She dragged out the bedding and spread it to dry in the firelight. She unpacked the drenched bags of food, matches, and cigarettes. She stoked the fire with another stick of driftwood, gleaming and polished from its tumble downriver. She put her back to a stone and her face to the flames. She toasted some bread and ate it. The river was rising, and soon she had to move the fire back from the encroaching edge. Stars bloomed in the sky overhead, one great river of stars, a perfect echo of the real river below.

With nothing but stars and the river for company, she had time to wonder if coming here had been a mistake.

Chapter One

ON THE BORDERS OF PRECIPICES

WHEN SARAH AND MAYNARD CLOVER BROUGHT their seventh child into the world on September 12, 1896, they were evidently at a loss for a name. The elder children had been given short, sensible names. The oldest was a boy, Melvin, followed by a bevy of girls: Maud, Alice, Mabel, Bessie, and Vida. But a family friend had urged something quite different for the latest addition to the family: Elzada, after his fiancée, and Urseba, after his sister. Perhaps this outlandish suggestion could have been safely ignored, but the young man had died shortly before the baby's birth. The parents felt they ought to honor his memory. Elzada Urseba Clover she became.

This name proved impossible to pronounce for the littlest boy, Maynard Jr., born two years later (followed by yet another daughter, Cora, the ninth and last child of the Clover family). His baby talk turned the name to Eldoda, shortened to a single syllable, "Dode," a family nickname that stuck.

The Clover farm was tucked into a corner of Nebraska just west of the Missouri River, where temperatures scorched above 100 degrees Fahrenheit in summer and plunged to minus 30 in winter. Farms cut patchwork squares out of the tallgrass prairie, embroidered with narrow bands of oak and willow. Elzada learned to work the fields alongside her siblings, to feel the texture and grain of the limestone soil beneath her fingers and watch the first struggling shoots in spring.

Few professions were open to women at that time. Her mother was a housewife, her elder sister Alice a dressmaker. But Sarah and Maynard taught all their children to read and write and encouraged them to go to college if they could. Elzada had a natural gift for dramatic storytelling and loved to tell jokes. She graduated from a teacher-training course at Peru Normal School—basketball player, member of the Dramatic Society, and vice-president of the Science Club—and took a job at a Nebraska high school to earn money for college tuition.

She became ill with influenza during the 1918 pandemic, the same year a solar eclipse crossed the United States, its path of totality just south of Nebraska. For anyone inclined to believe in signs and portents, the brief, unnatural darkness falling across the country that June might have easily seemed to foretell the end of the world. The pandemic killed at least 17 million people, roughly equal to all the soldiers and civilians who died in World War I, which was still a few months away from ending with an armistice. The disease death toll may have been much higher, as much as 50 million, almost 3 percent of the global population. But Elzada Clover recovered and went back to teaching high school. Her mother had died after a long illness when Clover was seventeen; now, her father decided it was time for a change. He headed west to a town called Mission at the southernmost tip of Texas on the banks of the Río Grande. Clover went with him.

Her heart was given over to the open spaces and fierce beauty of the desert. A farmer's daughter, she knew the joys of growing things, but it was cacti and succulents she especially loved, which needed no encouragement and hardly any water to sprout from the parched ground.

For much of the preceding century, botany had been a suitable hobby for ladies. Indeed, it was the only branch of natural history that qualified. Zoology and ornithology involved the pursuit and killing of animals; geology demanded strenuous hikes and heavy lifting; and as for entomology—pinning butterflies to a board! No, nothing else fit the ideals of white, affluent Protestants of the nineteenth century. Botany alone gave women the freedom to go outside.

By this time botany had advanced into a serious laboratory science in Europe, especially Germany. Scientists there pored over glass slides beneath microscopes, their fingers stained brown with iodine.

They knew that an insect, bumbling into the secret folds of a flower, shook pollen from the slender, yellow-topped stalks called stamens onto the sticky-knobbed pistil to spawn seeds. They rejected the old, mystic idea that a "vital force" caused plants to grow and imbued the soil with fertility. Instead, they began to parse out the secrets of cell formation and division, making sketch after sketch of geometric forms—cells stacked tightly together like a bird's-eye view of the cloisters in a monastery, a nucleus in every one like a monk's head bent in contemplation.

American botanists, meanwhile, lagged behind. With a vast, wild country to investigate, they were still preoccupied with collecting and classifying plants, a branch of science called taxonomy. To name even a single species was a daunting proposition. Exact identification usually could not be done in the field, since it required finicky observations and, often, a microscope. Plus, field guides had swollen to enormous proportions, so were not easily lugged around. Instead, collectors pressed plants, preferably while in blossom, and stored them in "herbaria," usually glued to sheets of paper. Later they consulted all the newest textbooks and publications to see if the species had already been described, and dug through the dusty herbaria of other collectors in search of similar specimens. It could be tedious work, sorting specimens into categories—flowering plants divided from the ferns and mosses, those with fruits divided from those with naked seeds, on and on through all the minute characteristics until at last distinguishing, for example, the nodding trillium from the bashful trillium by its pinkish-purplish anthers. Amateur naturalists had a valuable role to play in all this, sending pressed plants by the bundle to professional botanists at universities, and should the flower in question really prove to be a new species, the pressed specimen in the herbarium offered lasting proof to any doubters.

Often, those amateurs were women. Many had been inspired by *Botany for Beginners,* a textbook published by Almira Hart Lincoln Phelps in 1833, which went through twenty-six printings by the end of the century and sold 270,000 copies. A champion of women's

education, Lincoln Phelps taught science at the Troy Female Semi-
nary in New York. Her publisher wrote with satisfaction that *Botany for Beginners*—part instruction manual, part religious and moral
guide—was taught in several exclusively "Female Institutions."

"The study of Botany seems peculiarly adapted to females," Lincoln Phelps observed in her *Familiar Lectures on Botany,* "the objects
of its investigation are beautiful and delicate;—its pursuits, leading
to exercise in the open air, are conducive to health and cheerfulness."

Botany's virtues were women's virtues: gentility, innocence, and
modesty. Flowers, after all, reflected the qualities most treasured
in women: fragility, purity, and loveliness. One American botanist,
introducing the subject to his daughter in a letter, wrote that he
thought ladies would enjoy it because of the pleasure they took in
trying on beautiful clothing. Boys interested in plant-collecting, by
contrast, were taunted as unmanly. The Secretary of the Smithsonian
Institution teased young naturalists by pointing out that botany was
"the domain of women and children and weak-minded persons." By
1887, the field was so fashionable among women and girls that *Science*
ran an article entitled "Is Botany A Suitable Study For Young Men?"
Its author, J. F. A. Adams, strove to overturn the long-entrenched
idea that botany was "merely one of the ornamental branches, suitable enough for young ladies and effeminate youths, but not adapted
for able-bodied and vigorous-brained young men."

Yet one area remained closed to women. They were not permit-
ted to collect any plant that couldn't be reached on a leisurely afternoon stroll. Female seminaries hired men to gather specimens for
botany classes, saving their students the trouble of tramping through
wet, bosky, rugged places, exposing their delicate garments to dew-
drenched grass and their health to bad weather. "A young woman
cannot safely roam at will in any place and at any distance," wrote
Wilson Flagg in an 1871 article on botany. "She is exposed to many
annoyances and to some dangers . . . [She] must confine her walks to
the vicinity of her own home and to the open fields and waysides, and
in these limited excursions she sometimes needs protection."

Some women, naturally, ignored these strictures. Kate Furbish almost singlehandedly classified the flowers, ferns, and mushrooms of Maine, compiling fourteen volumes of pressed plants and watercolor paintings, and Sara Plummer Lemmon went on a plant-collecting honeymoon with her husband during which they scaled a formidable Arizona mountain. Though often overlooked, women furthered the field of taxonomy by defining the geographical limits of plants and describing species new to Western science. They did the field labor that other, professional botanists synthesized into journal articles and textbooks. Lincoln Phelps subtly egged on rebellious women in lectures she delivered to her mostly female audiences: "It is not a sedentary study," she proclaimed of botany, "which can be acquired in the library, but the objects of the science are scattered over the surface of the earth, along the banks of the winding brooks, on the borders of precipices, the sides of mountains, and the depths of the forest."

Lincoln Phelps was not radical in her efforts at educational reform. She believed women were best suited to be wives and homemakers. Yet under her guidance and inspired by her writings, generations of women learned "a speaking acquaintance with plants." They took to the ditches and hedgerows, newly awake to the beauty of thistles and dandelions. "It is a delightful study," Lincoln Phelps wrote in *Botany for Beginners,* "it presents you with sweet and pleasant objects, the contemplation of which is calculated to render your tempers mild and amiable. It will always furnish you with an agreeable amusement, which is not only innocent, but of a nature to refine and improve your minds."

She probably did not have cacti in mind. Not one page of *Botany for Beginners* showed young ladies how to cut a specimen that tries to cut you back.

THE PLANTS OF THE RÍO GRANDE VALLEY, where Clover lived in her late twenties and early thirties, could not be described as "sweet and pleasant objects." There, clutching the ground with a stubborn refusal to die in drought or succumb to flood, were plants such as *Opuntia,* the prickly pear with its brilliant scarlet fruits; *Yucca,* the Spanish bayonet, no more than a cluster of deadly-looking spikes until it sent up a maypole of pale flowers with as many frills as a flamenco dancer's dress; and *Echinocereus,* squat green cylinders covered in spines with common names like "prostrate hedgehog" and "devil's fingers." Strangest of all was the night blooming cereus, its fleshy barbed arms stretched skyward, waiting spellbound for the rare summer nights when it unfolded an intoxicating white flower to beckon the moths.

A love of plants did not translate easily into a job. For most of the 1920s, Clover worked as a schoolteacher and administrator at various rural schools in Texas. Her résumé indicates that she supervised an "Indian mission school" during this time; this appears to be a garbled reference to the South Mission School in Mission, Texas, a racially segregated elementary school for Mexican Americans. As the principal of South Mission School, Clover must have been complicit in a racist program of instruction that sought to "Americanize" children of Mexican descent and offer coursework "fitted to their needs," which differed from the education white students received. But unlike church-run schools or federal boarding schools for Native Americans, which used violent methods to stamp out Native languages, South Mission apparently allowed its students to speak their native tongue; Clover herself spoke Spanish.

Clover's duties as a school supervisor seem not to have held her attention. In 1929, her father died in a car wreck and she returned to her old college in Nebraska, now called the Peru State Teachers College. For two years she oscillated between Texas and Nebraska, earning a bachelor's degree in 1930 (along with two of her sisters, Bessie and Vida). A college education wasn't all that unusual for women of the era; they made up about 40 percent of the U.S. student population. But college was usually thought of as a stepping-stone to becoming a wife and mother. Only a few hundred women in the United States had earned PhDs. So Clover was an outlier when she enrolled in the University of Michigan to get a master's and PhD in botany.

The botany department in Ann Arbor, housed in a square brick building with evenly spaced, factory-like windows, had a long and distinguished history. A century before Clover's arrival, the University of Michigan established the first permanent paid position in botany in the United States. It was held by Asa Gray, a slight, eager, dark-haired man in his late twenties. Gray had trained to be a doctor, a profession he had picked for its financial stability rather than any interest in it. As a physician's assistant he'd tramped around small villages in upstate New York, taking his pay in pigs and sacks of grain. But his heart wasn't in it. He wanted to be a botanist.

The trouble was, botany as a paying profession did not yet exist. In 1831, Gray flung caution to the wind and quit the practice of medicine, to go—where? "The D—l only knows," he wrote to a friend. He drifted, beginning his first forays into a gargantuan book called *Flora of North America,* which would become his life's work. When the University of Michigan approached him with a job offer in 1838, the job in question was actually "Professor of Botany and Zoology," typical of the time, when all natural sciences were lumped together. But by some happy clerical error, "zoology" disappeared from the paperwork before Gray signed it.

The university at Ann Arbor was still under construction. Gray was fated never to teach a class there. He spent the next year roaming around Europe, supposedly buying up books for the university's library, but really poring over herbaria of North American flora. Almost all the important collections of American plants were housed in Europe. The United States, after all, had no professional botanists, so Europeans felt it couldn't be trusted with its own plants. Plant collectors in the United States, meanwhile, turned around this superior attitude toward Indigenous peoples in every country, including their own, dismissing local knowledge of plants in an eagerness to "discover" species. The field of botany suffered because of racism and colonialism. As Native languages and cultural practices vanished under the U.S. government's systematic eradication efforts, information about plants and their uses also disappeared.

Gray wanted to elevate the United States's reputation in professional botany. He longed to join exploring expeditions, instead of receiving secondhand specimens from men and women who wandered the American West and the Colorado Plateau, then still a part of Mexico, but he was perpetually too busy to go. Instead, through correspondence with collectors, Gray slowly began to compile the definitive catalog of North America's plants.

The University of Michigan was in financial turmoil when Gray returned from Europe. He took a job at Harvard University in 1842, where he spent the rest of his career. Slowly, his introductory textbook, *The Elements of Botany*, began to edge out Lincoln Phelps's book in popularity. This was a significant shift in the field of taxonomy. Lincoln Phelps taught an outdated system of classification created by the Swedish botanist Carl Linnaeus, which grouped flowers according to the number of stamens and pistils. Some complained that a system based on a plant's sexual parts was too "smutty" to teach women, but a more serious criticism was that it revealed nothing about the relationships between plants. Corn and oak were classed together; so were the tasty potato and the toxic mandrake. Lincoln Phelps defended the system as useful and easy to learn. Gray, however, taught the "natural system" of classification which considered the structure of the entire plant. It was scientifically superior but also difficult to do without training.

For Gray, the tedious work of taxonomy opened new questions. Why were species of plants distributed over the Earth the way they were? Did they spread to new locations or stay forever fixed in place? What exactly *was* a species, anyway? Gray's favored definition was "kindred individuals descended from a common stock." Like most of his fellow botanists, he believed plants had sprung into being exactly as they appeared and never altered their form.

In 1855 Gray received a letter from a man he had met, very briefly, during his visit to London. "As I am no Botanist," it read, "it will seem so absurd to you my asking botanical questions . . ." The writer wanted information about the range of alpine plants in North America to help him test a new idea he called "variation." His name was Charles Darwin.

Darwin had a radical notion: species changed over time, adapting to "the wondrous & exquisitely beautiful contingencies" of their environment. Examples abounded in every corner of the plant kingdom. The showy blossoms of orchids had a purpose: they tempted bees into their folds and thereby spread their pollen from one flower to the next. The Venus flytrap took a terrifying opposite approach and learned how to snap shut on hapless insects. Seeds bristling with tiny hooks thrived because they could catch a ride on the fur of animals. The plant (or animal) best suited to its situation survived, and taught survival to its offspring.

Racism and sexism warped the idea of evolution when Darwin and others applied it to the human species. But though a flawed observer of people, Darwin was keenly attuned to the natural world. He made Gray his confidant, unfolding his theory of evolution in a letter in 1857. "I know that this will make you despise me," Darwin wrote with some trepidation, but Gray did not despise him. Gray found flaws in the idea—for one thing, Darwin hadn't shown how species passed on beneficial variations to their offspring—but it also fit some of Gray's own observations. Long before Darwin wrote to him, Gray had observed an odd similarity between plants in North America and Asia. How could related species arise, sundered by an ocean? Perhaps, Gray thought, the continents had once been joined. But then, why were the species only similar and not identical? Darwin's variation offered an answer: they'd diverged, fitting themselves to their separate geographies and climates in a strange, slow, unfolding dance. When Darwin's book *On the Origin of Species* was published in 1859, Gray arranged for an American edition and, as its champion, pressed for it to be given a fair hearing in the scientific community. The revolution had begun.

The patient work of cataloging plants consumed the rest of Gray's life. He took bundles of specimens from far-flung collectors and slotted them into genus and species, knowing the work would never be finished in his lifetime. Like a pointillist painting, each plant species defined and marked on a map added to an emerging picture of the planet's great sweep of life, not fixed but ever-changing, with new species unfolding and others blinking out.

Even as taxonomy took on this new importance, it fell out of fashion. Young botanists, flocking to universities after the Civil War, specialized in new areas such as physiology, the chemistry-laden science of how plants take up nutrients, whisk water through their tissues, swallow sunlight, and breathe out oxygen; or pathology, the study of plant diseases; or paleobotany, the study of fossilized plants. In 1900, the rediscovery of Gregor Mendel's careful crossbreeding of peas provided the missing piece to Darwin's theory. Mendel laid out the rules for how offspring inherit traits from their parents, and the science of genetics was born.

This "new botany" required expensive microscopes and well-equipped laboratories. Botanists could no longer do their work with homemade plant presses hitched to their shoulders and sturdy boots. As the field fractured into specialties, opportunities for amateurs—and therefore women—slammed shut. Professional scientists began to distinguish between the "polite botany" done by female collectors and the "serious" work done by men. They chastised amateurs for wasting their time on collecting plants "not important enough to justify the trouble." The Botanical Society of America, formed in 1893, was open only to those engaged in "worthy work." It had a single female member, Elizabeth Gertrude Knight Britton. Barriers were higher for Black men and women, who found themselves barred even from entering the hotels that hosted botany conferences. By the start of the twentieth century, only seventeen women held PhDs in botany in the United States. Less than half of those held teaching positions in colleges or universities. "We say very pretty things about our woman students," noted one eminent botanist, "and give them good high standings," yet few of them found employment.

Elzada Urseba Clover, circa 1938. *Courtesy of the Elzada U. Clover Papers, Bentley Historical Library, University of Michigan*

When Clover defended her PhD thesis on the cacti of the Río Grande Valley in 1935, at the age of thirty-eight, full-time female professors in the sciences were still a rarity. The number of botany doctorate degrees going to women had stalled out at 12 percent and even begun to decline. Clover was not puzzled by the trend. "This is a man's University," she wrote bluntly, "and women do not always get things." The head of the University of Michigan's botany department, Harley H. Bartlett, admired her tenacity and advocated for her, hoping to find her a position that offered more prestige than her place "at the bottom of a large staff" in Ann Arbor. When he recommended Clover and two male faculty members for a government botany job, Bartlett received this reply: "the job, while largely in the laboratory, might possibly require some very arduous field trips and I would prefer a man." Bartlett wrote back sharply that Clover was quite capable of arduous field work. "In fact," he wrote, "I fear the relative inactivity of office work would pall on her more quickly than on either of the men."

The ideal female botanist, described in a letter between department heads, was attractive, mannerly, a good teacher, "doesn't smoke or drink and looks like a thoroughly fine girl." Clover didn't fit this description at all. Someone once told her that her mysterious first name came from a Spanish pirate ship. This appears to be a romantic fiction (perhaps arising from the American schooner *Elzada,* which sank off the coast of Florida in 1912) but the story suited Clover's personality. She was a tall woman, active, robust, dramatic, daring, perhaps just a little bit wicked. She drank whiskey. She could swim, fish, hunt, and ride a horse. She preferred to describe her own code of behavior as "gentlemanly" rather than "ladylike." She was noted among her colleagues for not bothering to take shelter during rainstorms. Even her research specialty, cacti, were the least demure plants imaginable, all showy blossoms and spines.

The job hunt went badly. "Elzada isn't wanted because she is a woman," Bartlett lamented in his journal. She stayed at the University of Michigan, on the lowest rung of the academic ladder: instructor and assistant curator of the botanical gardens. She was the only woman in the department. She loved to teach: a natural outlet for her gift of storytelling. She could kindle a passion for plants in an indifferent twenty-year-old by the sheer force of her personality. Students who tried to keep up with her on field expeditions collapsed in exhaustion, skin scratched by thorns and puffy with poison ivy. A round-faced, middle-aged academic with spectacles, her dark hair bobbed and pinned, Clover harbored a wild streak. She was a confirmed "bachelor," to use her own description. She told anyone who asked, laughing, that she simply never had time to get married. She was a paradox: a modern woman, educated and independent, yet her scientific interests seemed out of step with the era. She didn't want to be confined to the glare of a laboratory, hunched over a microscope. She wanted to explore.

Some faculty members at the University of Michigan still wandered the globe, bringing back specimens for the botanical gardens from the Rocky Mountains and Mexico. But plant-collecting expeditions were no longer the heart of botanical science. Explorers, almost all men, had already gone west and stamped their names all over the trees: Fremont cottonwood, Emory oak, Engelmann spruce, Goodding's willow, Torrey pine. Clover had been born too late, it seemed, for that kind of adventure, and she'd been born female.

ON AUGUST 3, 1937, Elzada U. Clover added her signature in curly script to the guest book of the Mexican Hat Lodge, adding "Univ. of Michigan Dept. of Botany" beside her name. Probably she drove there over the rutted, unpaved roads. The town of Mexican Hat was notorious (if it was notorious for anything) for being the farthest away from a railroad station of any place in the United States. The road was so little-used that the appearance of a car brought everyone out to gawk. Named for a rock spire that sports a jaunty stone sombrero, the town is tucked into a curve of the San Juan River, a tributary of the Colorado, at the northern edge of the Navajo homeland. "Town" was perhaps not the right description for it then, as the nearest post office was twenty-five miles away, in Bluff. It had half a dozen non-Native residents at the time. Almost all of them belonged to the Nevills family, who owned the only lodge for miles.

Clover had a dream: she wanted to make a field study of all the cacti in the Southwest. The University of Michigan offered no funding for the project, but she got enough money from a private sponsor to spend two weeks in southern Utah with an assistant, Carol Davidson. It was an odd place to look for plants, full of crazy pinnacles raked by a wayward desert wind like a child's fingers on a xylophone, the earth tiled with terracotta-colored stone. Not much grew there, but what did was strange and wondrous. Hedgehog cacti (*Echinocereus* spp.) squatted sullenly in the sand, barely noticeable until they burst into gaudy magenta flowers. Jointed stems of cholla (then considered part of the *Opuntia* genus) stuck their spines into fabric or fur at the slightest provocation and hitched a ride to a new spot. Even the wildflowers bristled with attitude. Prickly poppies (*Argemone* spp.) protected themselves with spines and poison; the yellow center and crinkly white petals resembled an egg left to fry in the glaring heat.

Clover rented a room for two dollars a night. By day she went collecting, with the August heat beating down on the anvil-hard earth, on stretches of road barely better than wagon tracks. By night she returned to the lodge to watch the vivid red sunsets leak away into a cerulean sky. Stars blazed like old-fashioned oil lamps hung on invisible pegs. Summer evenings in the desert meant that crickets convened a fiddle contest every night, each trying to outdo the others without waiting for their turn. Lightning flickered on the horizon, forked tongues of blue and gold.

Clover was used to exploring lonely country roads. She drove like the devil was chasing her, straddling the center while her eyes darted from side to side in search of interesting plants. A black-eyed Susan or a tall clump of mullein was enough to make her wrench the wheel into a U-turn and hurl the car to the shoulder to take a closer look.

But she wanted more. She wanted to collect plants from places she couldn't reach by car.

By chance, Clover shared that itch for adventure with her host at the Mexican Hat Lodge. Blue-eyed and wiry, twenty-nine-year-old Norman Nevills was the son of a prospector and oil driller. As a five-year-old boy growing up in California, he snuck away from his parents and attempted to commandeer a boat tied up in San Francisco Bay. (A policeman plucked him out and brought him home.) Nevills never lost his love of boats and water. His father, William Eugene Nevills, had designed a boat to travel the waterways of Alaska (at this time still a territory) in search of gold. In 1921, W. E. Nevills moved to Mexican Hat to drill for oil, leaving his wife, Mae Davies, and his son in California. They joined him in Utah seven years later, after Norm left high school.

Schemes of gold and oil gave way to dreams of tourists. The Nevills family built the Mexican Hat Lodge between the road and the river out of native red sandstone. Rough timbers held up a flat roof covered with windblown soil, so it seemed to have sprung up directly out of the ground. The lodge had a central living area with two wings and three bedrooms. There was no telephone and no electricity, only kerosene and Coleman lanterns. Water came from three big tanks perched on top of a nearby hill, replenished from the wells in Bluff, because the water from the San Juan River was too alkaline to drink.

Tourists came, though few seemed to share Nevills's love of the San Juan River. In extreme dry years it shrank to algae-slick pools alive with wriggling tadpoles desperate to grow legs. In cold winters it froze into a knife-sharp channel of ice. But mostly it was a lazy, meandering river shaded by silvery cottonwoods. It is one of four sacred rivers that encircle the Navajo homeland, along with the Colorado, the Little Colorado, and the Río Grande. Navajos call it Old Man River and tell stories of a man named the Dreamer who climbed into a hollow log and rode the San Juan to its confluence with the Colorado and then rafted the Grand Canyon, encountering monsters and gods along the way. Hopis tell a similar story, of a youth named Tiyo who

traveled through the Grand Canyon in a sealed drum and voyaged all
the way to the sea. Mojave, Cocopah, and other Indigenous peoples of
the lower Colorado weave boats out of tule reeds. People of European
descent had no such deep history of running the unruly rivers of the
West. They thought it a sport for adventurers or fools.

Norm Nevills now ran the Mexican Hat Lodge with his wife,
Doris. They had an infant daughter, Joan. Nevills hired himself out
to motorists as a guide for five dollars a day, partially deflating the
tires so the cars wouldn't bog down in the desert sand. But his real
love was river trips. For $25, he would take a guest on a day trip down
a serene stretch of the San Juan between Bluff and Mexican Hat, past
boulders pecked with petroglyphs. For $250, he'd take a party of four
on a weeklong journey down the San Juan and Colorado rivers as far
as Lee's Ferry, stopping on the way to see Rainbow Bridge, a natural rock arch sacred to the tribes of the area. But Nevills dreamed of
more. He wanted to raft "the big 'un."

One hundred miles to the southwest as the crow flies, the Colorado
River flowed into the maw of a mysterious canyon that no botanist
had ever explored from head to foot. There's no way of knowing how
the thought of the Grand Canyon first entered Clover's head. Perhaps
it was merely the lure of those unknown plants, or perhaps Nevills
had spoken of his dream one evening at the lodge. A guide would
come in handy, Clover thought. She made a bold suggestion: they
could take mules into the Grand Canyon to collect cacti for research.

A pack train wouldn't do, declared Nevills. They would have to
go by boat.

In a few minutes they laid out the entire harebrained scheme.

Chapter Two

HAVE YOU SEEN THAT RIVER?

CLOVER RETURNED TO ANN ARBOR AND WAITED to hear from Nevills. No letter came. In December, when snow blanketed the campus and the lazy curves of the Huron River crinkled at the corners with the calligraphy of ice, she sent a Christmas card to Mexican Hat Lodge, asking if he still wished to take her down the Colorado. The reply came: yes, Nevills had every intention of going through with their sketchy plan. What's more, he'd recruited two boatmen, plucked from among the many guests who had signed the register at Mexican Hat Lodge the preceding summer. All Clover needed to do was invite two scientists to go along.

Clover went to H. H. Bartlett with the idea. Bartlett had reigned over Michigan's botany department for sixteen years and had served as president of the Botanical Society of America. An expert in tropical plants, he had gone on collecting expeditions to South America and the Philippines. But he did not receive Clover's proposal with enthusiasm. "Of course I can't say she can't," he wrote in his diary on January 24, "but I told her it would be silly to do such a foolhardy thing without proper preparation for genuine work."

Undeterred by this coolness, Clover arranged to meet a professor of geology, Thomas Lovering, and his wife, Corinne, over lunch one January day. Lovering had spent a year teaching at the University of Arizona early in his career and Clover hoped he would have some insights into the geology of the Grand Canyon. Whatever he knew, it couldn't have been much. No one knew for sure how the canyon was formed. The Colorado River had not behaved like a normal river, seeking the path of least resistance to the sea. It barreled straight into an uplift of land called the Kaibab Plateau, instead of going around as any self-respecting river would do. John Wesley Powell theorized that the river formed first and the plateau rose around it—in his metaphor, the river was like a fixed buzz saw and the plateau was like a chunk of timber raised into the blade. That idea had stood for decades, but in the 1930s other geologists began to challenge it, saying the river could not possibly be older than the land around it.

There were other, more fundamental questions to muddy the waters. Geologists still argued hotly over the age of the Earth; estimates ranged anywhere from a few million years to a few billion. They did not yet believe land masses could unmoor themselves and go rollicking around the planet like bumper cars. Alfred Wegener, a German explorer, had proposed the theory of continental drift in 1912, but American geologists still ridiculed it as nonsense.

Botanists, on the other hand, were drawn to the idea. Flowers were found everywhere on Earth, except perhaps the driest deserts or the snowiest tundra. Peculiar clumps of unique species might grow here and there—endemic, or highly localized, to a place—but at the family level, flowers had global similarities unlikely to have come about if the continents had always been separated by vast oceans. At one time botanists imagined networks of land bridges, long since sunk beneath the seas, ribboning Earth like a badly wrapped gift. But continental drift made more sense. Likewise, the great age of the Earth, which so troubled geologists—and which was becoming increasingly difficult to ignore, what with early forays into the radioactive dating of rocks—seemed right to botanists. The Earth had to be old, for evolution to have had time to work.

One can imagine it made for a lively conversation over lunch: the mysteries of the Grand Canyon, the strange plants that might be found there, perhaps a few tips for weathering the rigors of field work in the wilderness. Corinne Lovering could chime in with a woman's perspective, for she had camped in the Colorado Rockies with her husband on field expeditions. Clover listened and learned. She had not yet decided which of her colleagues to invite on the expedition. But she had brought to lunch with her a dear friend, a graduate student in the botany department. Sitting beside Clover at the table, Lois Jotter drank it all in.

$$\Downarrow$$

LOIS JOTTER WAS BORN beneath a paperwork error. On her birth certificate, she was *Mary* Lois Jotter, except a clerk had transposed the A and the R into a mangled first name—*Mray*—that no one could pronounce. The state of California was not particularly concerned with correcting the mistake. It was a dismissal of sorts, an erasure, this clerical indifference. But Mary Lois Jotter was not destined for dismissal or erasure. Her parents managed to correct the spelling on official records two decades after their daughter's birth. By then she was studying biology at the University of Michigan in Ann Arbor and preferred to go by Lois, anyway.

She was born in Weaverville, California, on March 11, 1914. Her mother, Artie May Lomb, was a Southerner who had learned a love of tinkering from her father, an inventor. As a teenager she had won a medal for mechanical drawing and, along with her sister Esther, she learned to forge and weld iron and operate drills and planers. A magazine story about the sisters gushed, "Women can do about everything, and they have begun to find it out." Esther went on to a career in engineering, but a bout with scarlet fever as a child had left Artie weak and fretful. When she was twenty-four, she married Ernst Victor Jotter, a forester from a German Mennonite family. Jotter was an active, outdoorsy man, despite a bullet lodged near his spine that doctors couldn't figure out how to remove (the result of a chance encounter with a drunk cowboy). It was an unusual household for the time: Jotter was quite willing to cook, clean, and raise two children while pursuing his career in forestry. Both parents encouraged, even expected, their daughter, as well as their son, to love science.

A giant sequoia (*Sequoiadendron giganteum*) flourished in the front yard of Lois Jotter's childhood home in Weaverville, many miles north and west of its native range on the flanks of the Sierra Nevada. Her father had planted it there. His employer, the U.S. Forest Service, existed to harvest and sell trees, at a time when most private logging operations followed a "cut and get out" policy that stripped forests of valuable timber and left the rest to rot. Conservation was a new idea. Gifford Pinchot, the first head of the U.S. Forest Service, defined it as "the wise use of the earth and its resources for the lasting good of men." In California, the wise use of sequoias meant cutting them down by the thousands between 1890 and 1925. A single sequoia could equal an acre of northern pine and yield enough shingles to roof a whole neighborhood, with wood left over to put a picket fence around every yard.

But the sequoia had champions. Parallel to the conservation movement arose an ideology known as preservation, which spoke of wilderness in romantic terms, as a refuge and spiritual retreat, values that could not be quantified in board-feet. Preservationists wanted to see picturesque areas set aside, forever protected from what they considered the ravages of logging, mining, and development. The sequoia was their symbol. They rallied supporters with nationalistic language, saying that the solemn groves of Yosemite Valley had no rival even in the Swiss Alps, and outstripped the Gothic spires and cathedrals of Europe in grandeur. They spoke, too, of the value of watersheds and wildlife habitat. In time, they found allies in the business world. It made sense, from a business perspective, to preserve landscapes that were "for all public purposes worthless" and had nothing of value but scenery. Tourism was the new timber.

Yellowstone became the first national park in 1872—intended to be a "pleasuring ground for the benefit and enjoyment of the people"— followed by Sequoia and Yosemite in 1890. U.S. Cavalry troops, including "buffalo soldiers" in Yosemite, protected the parks in the early days, which in many ways remained opened to exploitation. In the parks, the ideologies of preservation and conservation often blurred. Preserving a place for tourism, after all, was another kind of use. Neither camp respected the rights of Native Americans to their homelands. Federal laws treated Indigenous peoples as trespassers in the new national parks: the government forcibly removed Blackfeet, Lakota, Shoshone, and other peoples from Yellowstone just after the park's creation, and this pattern was repeated in other parks well into the twentieth century. Preservationists then praised the wilderness as pristine and untouched by humans, when in truth, the land had been tended carefully by its Native inhabitants for generations.

E. V. Jotter, like his fellow foresters, was a conservationist. He thought of trees as a sustainable crop. But he must have harbored a secret love of the sequoia, a love not satisfied solely by its utility. He must have sensed the beauty and power in the heady forces that sent sap and sugars surging through xylem and phloem from roots to leafy crowns. Hence the sequoia in the front yard of his home in Weaverville, a tree he planted in an out-of-the-way place where no one with a chainsaw would think to look for it.

Lois Jotter grew up beneath that sequoia, a sweet note amid the broken mountainsides and eroded streams of Weaverville, which had suffered from hydraulic mining in the Gold Rush days. When she was seven, the family moved to Madison, Wisconsin, where E. V. worked at a Forest Service laboratory focused on conserving the nation's fast-disappearing timber. They kept up their family tradition of Sunday walks in the woods. On one such walk, E. V. pointed out an unfamiliar tree—a many-branched shrub with pinnate (feather-shaped) leaves—and named it aloud: *Acer negundo,* boxelder maple. Lois was hooked. She decided to become a botanist.

Three years later they moved to Ann Arbor, Michigan, where E. V. took a job as a university instructor. The West was a distant memory; Lois spent the rest of her childhood and teenage years roaming woodlands of maple, oak, aspen, and dogwood, forests alight with creamy white blossoms in spring, a blaze of red and yellow leaves in autumn, and muffled with snow in winter. She delighted in the exotic plants at the university's botanical gardens. Something was nearly always in bloom: plants for medicine and plants for beauty, plants that could thrive in crannies of bare stone and plants that needed coaxing, care, and rich brown earth. Bartlett, who managed the garden, welcomed visits from children. When young Lois expressed an interest in taking home some of the plants, Bartlett explained he could not give them away, but if she would write to her relatives in California for some western plants to add to Michigan's collection, he could set up an exchange. So Lois Jotter's education as a botanist began.

By the time Jotter graduated from the University of Michigan in 1936 with a master's degree in biology and botany, her father had been posted to the Soil Erosion Service (soon renamed the Soil Conservation Service) in Washington, DC. The newly created agency was tasked with ensuring that the Dust Bowl, which was ravaging drought-stricken farms on the Great Plains, never happened again. Botanists, for the first time, became shapers of public policy. On their advice, government programs planted thousands of windbreaks to slow the howling dust storms. E. V. Jotter's faith in trees was justified: they were heralded as the saviors of the nation.

Jotter kept in touch with her parents and her older brother, Walter, in regular, affectionate letters. With her father, particularly, she shared an open-hearted, unreserved correspondence. Early in 1938, she wrote to him to describe the lunch with the Loverings, explaining that Elzada Clover was a "former, and very favorite roommate." The two women were separated by a generation in age, but they were much closer in their academic careers: Clover with a freshly minted PhD, and Jotter just a few years away from earning hers. They had lived together for two years with a group of female graduate students (botanists and zoologists) in an apartment a block away from the dilapidated Natural Sciences Building.

They were not alike. Clover, now forty-one, was a botanist of the old school, devoted to collecting and cataloging plants. Jotter, twenty-three, belonged to the new: her PhD work focused on the cytogenetics of *Oenothera,* the evening primrose. Cytogenetics, the study of how chromosomes relate to cell behavior, was a burgeoning field of science. Only in the past couple of decades had scientists begun to appreciate

Mary Lois Jotter, 1934. *Family photograph*
courtesy of Victor Cutter III

how molecules of DNA called chromosomes carried genetic material from one generation to the next. In the 1930s there was a mania for counting chromosomes, partly because it provided a brand-new characteristic for identifying plants down to the species level. This enthusiasm for counting chromosomes, in fact, may have sidetracked biologists from understanding the nature and functions of genes: there was still no satisfactory theory on how plants inherited traits, and scientists had only recently begun to consider how the environment might influence genes. Still, *Oenothera* was a favorite genus for delving into changing ideas about evolution, genetics, and natural selection.

Their personalities were also different. Clover enjoyed her freedom as an unmarried woman and was uninterested in romantic relationships, while Jotter evidently harbored some doubts about nearing her twenty-fourth birthday without finding a husband; she had a string of beaus and close male friends that made her father fret. (The average age for a woman to marry in the 1930s was twenty-one, and it would remain so for another four decades.) Jotter had little interest in clothes, while Clover liked to dress with snap and style: on rainy days she sashayed around campus in a favorite white suit, violet blouse, and perfectly matched violet umbrella. Most of all, Jotter did not share Clover's adventurous streak. The younger botanist spent her days in the botanical gardens and the laboratory; she described herself as bookish and a bit of a klutz.

Clover had mentioned to Jotter the possibility of collecting desert plants together after Jotter finished her PhD. "Pack-train, guide, water-holes, heat, dust, etc.," Jotter wrote to her father, a succinct and somewhat cinematic summary of her imaginings of the Southwest, "but wouldn't it be interesting. Lots of compensation for not being married!"

CLOVER COULD BE STUBBORN, and persuasive. Two weeks after Bartlett first wrote disapprovingly in his diary of Clover's "wild plan," he changed his mind. "Elzada Clover proposes to join a very venturesome but truly scientific expedition through the canyons of the Green & Colorado Rivers," he wrote on February 9. "After considering the proposal carefully I indorsed it, for it is not as crazy as it seems. I wouldn't hesitate to do it myself, so why refuse my approval for her."

Bartlett's support was, literally, immaterial. He told Clover he wished the university could officially sponsor the expedition, but there wasn't any money to give her. Nobody said so directly, but it's hard not to wonder if university officials were secretly relieved not to have Michigan's name stamped on the sides of boats that very well might sink with all hands.

By this time, Clover had grown anxious for the trip to proceed. It fit perfectly with her dream of cataloging all the Southwest's cacti, but, more than that, it was a chance to make her mark on the field of botany. The Colorado River's canyons had been mapped by surveyors and river runners, but never by a botanist. There were no peer-reviewed papers, no catalogs, no herbaria. Whatever she found would have value: beyond the pure thrill of taxonomy, it was a chance to see how the flora of the surrounding deserts mixed and mingled in the unique setting of a series of very deep canyons. She wanted to go; she would find the money somehow.

With some trepidation, Clover applied for a modest $400 grant from the Rackham School of Graduate Studies. She did not have much confidence in getting it. "I have a difficult time here," she explained to Nevills, "because I have tendencies toward enjoying the more spectacular things." The "hard boiled" men on the grant committee frowned upon anything that smacked of a stunt or gave rise to lurid publicity. Clover wrote her application in the most sedate language possible, but she suspected that at least a few of the committee members thought boating the Colorado River was "a pretty wild thing for a woman to do." They might withhold the money in hopes of dissuading her. To Nevills, she confided, "I haven't told them that I'm going anyway."

The lack of university support suited Nevills. He had always intended for it to be a commercial expedition with paying passengers, something that had barely been tried with Grand Canyon river trips. His willingness to include women was unusual. In 1932, the president of the men-only Explorers Club, Roy Chapman Andrews, announced boldly in a lecture that women were unsuited for exploration. Forced to defend himself against the backlash of indignant women (even Amelia Earhart weighed in), Andrews protested that he had no problems with women who wanted to go on expeditions with their husbands or with members of their own sex. He merely believed they shouldn't be mixed in with men, because they were too sensitive, "unable to stand up under the little daily annoyances" that plague an expedition. Andrews argued, "A leader has enough difficulties in running a big expedition without saddling himself with any that can be avoided." Nevills, evidently, did not agree. He wanted to drum up publicity, and nothing could be better than a female botanist—or two. In his letter to Clover at Christmastime, he suggested she invite a "college boy" and "one more lady" to join, adding (as if Clover needed a reminder) that "no woman has ever lived to make the trip clear thru."

The letter was full of rash promises. Nevills intended to break an unspecified world record for descending the canyons by boat, film color movies, document secluded archeological sites, and offer a nightly radio broadcast. The crew would all share in the monetary rewards of the publicity, which he fully expected to cover the cost of the expedition and then some. Some of this must have sounded like hyperbole to Clover, who responded simply, "The whole thing sounds elegant." She said nothing in reply to Nevills's imprudent guarantee of safety. She expected some risk, but she told the Loverings with her usual dramatic flair that she would rather die doing something exciting.

Clover consulted with other professors at the University of Michigan about her plans: men like George R. LaRue, director of the university's biological station; Dow Baxter, a forest pathologist; and Ermine Case, professor of historical geology and paleontology. "A chance of a lifetime," they all enthused. Professor Case added—notwithstanding the dangers—that he had always wanted to boat the Grand Canyon.

But none of them volunteered, or else Clover did not invite them. Instead, she picked a twenty-five-year-old zoologist named Eugene Atkinson, settling the question of the college boy. He was working on a PhD in paleobotany and had a job lined up as the first director of the Lakeshore Museum in Muskegon, Michigan. Born in Kentucky, Atkinson was a "professional sculptor–taxidermist." He hoped to collect (that is, shoot) specimens of birds and mammals from the Colorado River to sell, and thus defray the cost of the trip.

That left one final slot for a scientist. Jotter half-expected to receive the invitation and felt hurt when it wasn't forthcoming. But Clover hesitated. It was one thing to risk her own life. To ask another woman to endure the hardships of the journey was a different matter. As Jotter put it, she "knew my parents had no spare daughter." But it was hardly appropriate in the prudish 1930s for Clover to disappear into a remote wilderness in the company of only men. Propriety demanded a female companion, so they could chaperone each other and squelch any rumors of immodest behavior. Jotter was studious and dedicated, and, despite her bookish personality, she knew how to "rough it" outdoors. She had spent three summers as a camp counselor at the University of Michigan's biological station, a 10,000-acre property on the shores of Lake Douglas. There, Jotter had learned how to row a boat so she could rescue any kid that toppled into the water.

She also had more backcountry experience than most. She had attended the Yosemite Field School for six weeks the preceding summer, a program designed to train future National Park Service naturalists. Hiring women for these jobs was still a new idea. The first female rangers, Clare Marie Hodges at Yosemite and Helene Wilson at Mount Rainier, began in 1918, and only a handful of women had followed in their footsteps by 1938. This was not for lack of trying on the part of women. From the start, the Yosemite Field School attracted more women than men, which disgusted its organizers. Around 1937, officials in Washington, DC, wanted to bar women from the class, since they did not foresee any field jobs for women in the Park Service. Yosemite's chief naturalist, Bert Harwell, supported limiting the number of women but thought they shouldn't be eliminated entirely. "They keep the men from dropping down to a level of no shirts and plenty of whiskers," was his argument. He settled on fourteen men and six women, including Jotter, for the 1937 class. The Yosemite Field School instilled backcountry skills in its students, though it's less certain they came away with a heightened commitment to conservation. At night, for entertainment, Jotter and her classmates would build bonfires on top of Glacier Point and push the hot coals over the edge. The descent of the flaming embers, trailing showers of sparks, was better than a firework display. "Firefall" would remain a tourist attraction for another three decades, until the Park Service decided the display was an embarrassment.

Clover had one final consideration in choosing her companion. They would be living in close quarters and uncomfortable conditions for weeks on end, with barely any privacy, utterly reliant on each other in situations that could mean life or death. She received several suggestions for female botanists older and more experienced than Jotter, but she didn't want to run the risk of an unknown companion. Better to choose a friend, she thought. The decision was made.

On Valentine's Day, Jotter sat down to write a long letter to her father. She gave a detailed explanation of her spring semester schedule and dwelt at length on a joyous, foggy day she'd spent with friends, hunting for mosses, snails, and bugs near the Huron River. She paid her way through graduate school as a teaching assistant, and Bartlett had asked her to preceptor his class on *Oenothera*. ("Am I scared!" she confessed—she was new to teaching.) "Oh, yes," Jotter scribbled at the end of the letter, almost an afterthought, "Elzada has asked me if I would like to go on the Colorado river expedition. . . . The only thing that stops me is that would cost money—and I don't think I should take the time from my research. But I would love it!"

Two days later, she dashed off another letter with the news that Bartlett had offered to take care of her *Oenothera* project for her, should she decide to go. She wanted her father's permission, written

up in a formal letter to show to Bartlett, who was her thesis advi-
sor. ("He hasn't asked me to do that of course, but it seems like a
good idea.") She also needed to borrow $200 for her share of the costs
of boats and supplies—no small sum in 1938. It equaled a third of
her annual salary as a graduate assistant, or five months' rent for the
apartment Jotter shared with a roommate. "I would like to go if at all
feasible," Jotter wrote apologetically to her father, promising to wait
at home on Thursday evening so he could call and talk things over.
"Let's not say anything about this to remainder of family until it gets
settled," she added.

Her father phoned on Thursday as planned. They spoke about the
prestige of the expedition, which, if successful, would result in scientific publications and public lectures. In the end, E. V. left the decision
in his daughter's hands. But the next day, he wrote a letter to Bartlett
expressing his "mixed emotions" about the opportunity. "Of course,"
he wrote, "I am concerned with the possible hazards of the trip." Jotter, oblivious to his worries, wrote on Saturday to say she had made
up her mind to go. "I think I'll never get such another chance and we
should get such interesting collections," she said. She gave her father
permission to tell her mother and the rest of the family.

The timing couldn't have been worse.

Exactly one week later, on Saturday, February 26, the *Saturday Evening Post* hit the newsstands. The issue included a seven-page spread
about the first successful solo expedition down the Colorado River,
every sentence rife with vivid and terrifying detail. The man who had
achieved this feat was a filling station attendant from Oregon named
Haldene "Buzz" Holmstrom. He had taken a homemade boat from
the river's headwaters in Wyoming all the way to Lake Mead in the fall
of 1937, not long after Clover and Nevills hatched their plan. A photo
of Holmstrom accompanying the article showed a stocky, unsmiling,
sunburned man clutching the oars of his boat on Lake Mead at the
end of his journey, bowler hat cocked at a rakish angle.

Holmstrom hadn't sought any publicity for his attempt before
launching his boat. He had no more than $100 in his pocket and

looked like a "tramp," in his own words. He was afraid some National Park Service official might try to stop him. "He wouldn't know how husky I was," Holmstrom reported, "nor that I'd studied and dreamed about the Colorado until I felt I knew each rapid and rock and eddy. All he'd see would be a wild-eyed Swede with a shoestring outfit, tackling the longest stretch of bad water in the world."

The Colorado (Holmstrom said) was no ordinary river. After leaving Green River, Utah, there were only two places to resupply, Lee's Ferry and Bright Angel Creek. Between these spots were hundreds of miles of rough water where, if your boat smashed, you couldn't clamber out of the canyon, nor follow the river down its banks, since oftentimes there *were* no banks: just sheer walls, straight up. "Every expedition that goes through," Holmstrom added, just to hammer home this fearsome description, "finds traces of some unfortunates, individuals or parties, who have started down and never been heard of again." And every party, he said, had somebody who "cracked" under the constant strain. The article's author, Robert Ormond Case, noted that only Holmstrom's physical strength and manly character had saved him from this fate.

This was bad enough. But Holmstrom had something worse to say, peculiarly relevant to Clover and Jotter's plans. He knew the story of Glen and Bessie Hyde, the doomed honeymooners who had attempted to boat the Colorado in 1928 and were never heard from again. "Women have their place in the world," Holmstrom declared, "but they do not belong in the Canyon of the Colorado."

The *Saturday Evening Post* sold for a nickel. It had the largest circulation of any magazine in the world, more than a million people. Clover could only pray that the members of the grant committee, still deliberating over her application, did not read it. Jotter did not expect to be so lucky. "In case some kind soul," she wrote glumly in her next letter to her father, "hasn't pointed out the article in the current *Sat Eve Post* . . . I hereby point it out. I'm not refraining from telling you that there is danger involved, but to me it seems worth it. . . . Many of the fatalities," she added, "have been due to parties which were so small that if one boat cracked up they were marooned." Since their expedition would have three boats, Jotter saw no danger of that fate.

She was wrong about this. While most of the men who had run the Colorado had survived, deaths (and near misses) did occur, for all sorts of reasons that a surplus of boats would not guard against. In 1869, John Wesley Powell's crew, the first non-Native men to successfully boat the Grand Canyon, nearly starved to death. Three people drowned during the next attempt in 1889, not thirty miles into the Grand Canyon. The survivors of that expedition, clawing their way to the rim, were nearly caught in a landslide. Bessie and Glen Hyde's boat, in 1928, had been found intact. Whatever had befallen the honeymooners, it didn't have anything to do with getting marooned. In fact, the river could be dangerous to people who simply wanted to cross it, not boat it. Men had drowned at Lee's Ferry trapped beneath capsized boats or knocked into the water by a sideways gust of wind. Sheep could be pulled under the water by the weight of the river's red silt, which clogged their wool while they thrashed and labored until they grew too heavy to swim.

Then there were the prospectors, hikers, tourists, park rangers, laborers, and Native residents of the canyonlands who had lost their lives in half a dozen other ways: from heat stroke, hypothermia, or exhaustion; from stepping the wrong way and falling hundreds of feet off a cliff; from flash floods that tore without warning down narrow slot canyons. More than one body had turned up with a bullet hole. One man had been struck by lightning, another crushed by a falling rock. In 1890, an abandoned camp was discovered midway down the canyon, a gold watch dangling from a tent pole and baked bread in the Dutch oven, its tenants gone without a trace. In 1933, a prospector descending the aptly named Snake Gulch startled a rattler. It struck—and missed. The man died on the spot of a heart attack.

Just a month earlier, Jotter's father had gently chided his daughter for an excursion to Detroit to drink cocktails with a gaggle of friends, one of whom was a young unmarried man. Jotter took the reprimand in good heart. Now she was proposing a journey much more danger-ous than a jaunt to Detroit, in the company of strangers.

Jotter's brother Walter wrote from Ohio to throw his support behind the journey. "More power to you, sister," he declared, telling her to go if she had to "beg, borrow, or steal the money" to do it. But Walter couldn't resist adding some brotherly advice. The entire family had read the *Saturday Evening Post* story and, as a result, their grand-mother in Ohio wept "thrice a day" in terror over the idea. "Even though you are bubbling over with enthusiasm etc. about the trip," he cautioned her, "carefully censor all you write to [Mother & Father] about it. To put it mildly what little they have been able to find out about the trip & the rigors thereof have put them slightly up in the air."

In response to this caution, Jotter wrote contritely to her father with an apology for all the worry she was causing. "No need to be lachrymose," she wrote, "because if I weren't almost certain (cheerful thought) that we would get thru OK I wouldn't go."

Concerns from her family came pouring in. Jotter tried to assuage their worries. They had read of people "breaking" on the Colorado River, but that didn't mean anything sinister, she explained: just a slang term for abandoning the river without completing the planned run. Jotter and her companions would have two opportunities to do so, at Lee's Ferry at the head of the Grand Canyon, and Bright Angel Creek halfway down. As for checking up on Norman Nev-ills to make sure this wasn't some kind of scam, though Walter sug-gested she make inquiries through the university or the Chamber of Commerce, Jotter couldn't think of any way to do this. She relied on Clover's good judgment, and Clover relied on her stay with Nevills in Mexican Hat. Jotter assured her family that Nevills had made the trip many times before. This was untrue. Nevills had floated the San Juan and the stretch of quiet water through Glen Canyon, but he'd never entered the Grand Canyon itself, nor run the dangerous rapids in Cataract Canyon. Probably that distinction was lost on Jotter. She had never seen the Colorado River.

As for the impropriety of spending weeks on end with strange men in wild country, Jotter had perfect confidence in Clover to protect her from "familiarities." She wrote to her father, "She has done lots of things in such country, and she is mature enough so that she does the right thing always," even if Jotter herself wasn't always so careful.

Jotter couldn't help adding that Clover hadn't pressured her to sign up for the expedition. She didn't want her friend and mentor to be held responsible for whatever happened next. "But don't you see that this is one of the things to do that I'd hate like anything to miss?" she pleaded. It wasn't the promise of adventure that tugged on her—she *wasn't* brave and was sure she'd be "scared pink" most of the time. It was the science. Every sprig and leaf and twig they collected would have scientific interest, for nobody had made collections in the canyonlands before. "I do intend to bring out as much interesting material as I can, as otherwise, I would not consider going just for the experience," she wrote. "I know that I'm not getting into any lark but you know, that it will be something that I'll always regret not doing, if I don't."

The money worried her, and she resolved to forgo buying a new spring coat. Her friends teased her, with gallows humor, that she needn't bother buying new clothes anyway, since she wouldn't have any use for them after the summer. They wouldn't joke about it if they thought there was any real danger, Jotter reassured her father— and perhaps herself.

In March, Clover sent Nevills photographs and biographies of the two scientists she had chosen. His reply, in hindsight, was alarming. Nevills wanted to know if any of the Michigan crew—naming Gene Atkinson specifically, the only man in the group—wanted to handle a boat "for the satisfaction [he] would gain from it." This was deceptive: the truth was, neither of Nevills's chosen boatmen had any experience with whitewater. Nevills thought Atkinson looked capable enough in his photograph: a solemn young man with a thin, angular face and dark, slicked-back hair. He could substitute as a boatman just fine, Nevills wrote to Clover, assuming he had perfect control of his nerves and wouldn't mind getting a little experience rowing in fast water before June. Clover did not agree. She replied that Atkinson did not have enough experience in rough water and, in her judgment, wasn't ready for the responsibility.

The careful division of the crew—three scientists as passengers, and three boatmen to navigate and row—had already begun to break down. But Nevills assured Clover that there would be plenty of time to do science, in a letter that sounded like a draft of a tourist brochure. "One of the great values we shall have in our work," he wrote to her, "is the fact of being in little known, practically unexplored country. You know the history of the Colorado and its great barrier to navigation, so we are afforded a great opportunity to bring out new facts. The few expeditions before us have been purely interested in getting thru the canyons without the personnel to do geology and scientific work on the flora and fauna."

Jotter forwarded this letter to her father and continued to coax him with soothing details about the expedition: a careful accounting of the costs of the trip, the (exaggerated) experience of the crew, and the greatly improved maps of the Grand Canyon. She even listed the clothes she planned to wear: long-sleeved shirts, fitted overalls, cork helmet, wool socks. She was still trying to convince him, or at least reassure him, well after the plans were laid, the publicity photos taken, the route mapped out, and the June departure date near.

E. V. gave his blessing and sent the $200. If he still had reservations, he kept them to himself. But he warned his daughter: You'll come back changed. The river will change you.

She reassured him on that point, too. "When we come out," she told him, selecting with care the comforting *when* over the worrisome, more accurate *if*, "I'll still be me."

∿

THE COMMITTEE APPROVED Clover's grant, though, perhaps to register disapproval, downgraded the amount to $300. She got the news in May and immediately cut a check to Nevills for her share of the expedition's cost with a sense of deep relief. Her salary at the time, just $1,200 a year, would have hardly covered expenses. But now she could splurge a little bit. She bought a $30 movie camera that had to be wound before every use, and 1,000-plus feet of film. She and Jotter fiddled with it, wasting 100 feet of film for practice. They haunted the mailbox for the next missive from Nevills, arranging and rearranging their gear, eager to be gone. "I'm afraid our minds are far to the west," Clover wrote.

When the spring semester ended, a friend innocently asked Jotter about her summer plans. Jotter explained she was going to boat the Colorado River to collect plants. The friend's mother, overhearing, was aghast. "Have you seen that river?" she asked.

"Yes," Jotter lied.

She hadn't seen the Colorado River, but she'd read everything she could get her hands on about it. The title alone of Clyde Eddy's 1929 book, *Down the World's Most Dangerous River*, might have turned her away, if not the tales of Powell's footsore crew eating handfuls of spoiled flour, or the line drawings of crazy Gothic spires and ominous pinnacles blotting out the sun. But Jotter felt prepared for anything. She'd done her homework; she knew what to expect. There would be discomforts, yes—the heat, the biting insects, the nights spent lying awake in wet clothes. But the plants! The accounts of the artist Frederick Samuel Dellenbaugh, who'd gone down the river on Powell's second expedition in 1871–72, promised there would be plants—though of what kind, or how many, no one could say. It was (Clover and Jotter hoped) a "relict flora" of a kind not seen anywhere else in the world.

The friend knew a journalist at the student newspaper, the *Michigan Daily,* and happened to mention Jotter's summer plans. The story made the Sunday front page: "Faculty Women To Face Danger On Stormy Colorado For Science." Its final paragraph read: "Despite doubts over their venture, Dr. Clover and Miss Jotter assure questioners 'there's no danger in a carefully planned expedition.' And then they change the subject by proudly mentioning that they're to do the explore's [*sic*] cooking."

On Monday the *Ann Arbor News* picked up and rehashed the story, and added a photograph of the three travelers poring over maps of the Colorado River, smiles pasted on their faces. At a surprise picnic that day, which Bartlett had organized in the travelers' honor, Jotter laughed with her colleagues over the description of herself as an "intrepid explorer." But she didn't have time to worry about exaggerated press accounts. They planned to depart the next day. She dashed home, washed her clothes, and went out to eat with friends. The next morning, she still had packing to do, plus a last-minute visit to the botanical gardens to check on her evening primroses, and a few tutoring sessions with her regular clients. Oh, and she had to iron a dress and get her hair done—more publicity photographs were scheduled.

Sure enough, cameramen from the *Detroit News* were waiting in the parking lot of the Natural Sciences Building in the late afternoon of Tuesday, June 7, when Jotter, Clover, and Atkinson loaded up their gear. They staged a last-minute photo shoot—perhaps (though nobody said it aloud) a *final* photo shoot. Then they got into Atkinson's car, shouted goodbye to Bartlett and other colleagues who had come to see them off, and headed for Chicago, westward into the setting sun, like heroes in the final shot of a melodramatic Hollywood western.

Jotter's close friend and roommate, Kay Hussey, had also come to wave goodbye. She was the only person in the world who knew that Jotter had boxed and labeled her possessions for disposition before departing for Utah. Just in case.

Chapter Three

A MIGHTY POOR PLACE
FOR WOMEN

I N THE SUMMER OF 1938, *SNOW WHITE AND THE Seven Dwarfs,* the first full-length animated feature, had lately premiered in theaters. The catchy tune "Whistle While You Work" topped the charts, alongside songs by the Andrews Sisters and Bing Crosby. Superman made his debut in the pages of *Action Comics.* The daring fashions of the flapper era had gone out of style, and women wore longer skirts again. The first-ever federal minimum wage was set at twenty-five cents an hour. The economy had been climbing steadily out of the Great Depression, but now it hit a sudden, sharp decline. Men in the Civilian Conservation Corps (CCC) planted trees and built fire lookouts, working in crews segregated by race. President Franklin D. Roosevelt had just been presented a map that envisioned a network of superhighways, laid out like an enormous tic-tac-toe board from New York City to Seattle, Minneapolis to New Orleans.

At the time, no superhighways existed. It took Clover, Jotter, and Atkinson eight hours to drive from Ann Arbor to Chicago, a journey that today could be completed in half that time. They arrived at their hotel after midnight. The two women vanished into their shared room and collapsed, too exhausted to realize they had left their key stuck in the outer door.

The next day they drove west more than 300 miles to Des Moines, Iowa. Thunderstorms roiled over the flat horizon all morning, their bellies lit by stabs of lightning. Jotter realized she had just missed the chance to see her father: he had traveled through Des Moines for work a day or two earlier. "Just as well no more farewells," she wrote to him, worn out by travel and nervous tension. On to Omaha, Nebraska, where Jotter and Atkinson had a day of rest while Clover dashed seventy miles south to see her family in Auburn. It must have been strange to see the familiar fields unroll outside the car's windows, old homesteads lying abandoned with sightless eyes for windows. A pinkish haze hung over Nebraska, Oklahoma, and Kansas in those days, the sky smeared by topsoil stripped by relentless winds. Experts said overgrazing and overcultivation had contributed to the Dust Bowl, and nothing would do but to plant the land with grass and leave it alone for ten, twenty, maybe fifty years. "A desolate spectacle," one journalist declared, lamenting the homes that had degenerated into "tumble-down shacks."

Unbeknownst to the travelers, the *Michigan Daily* article about their adventure had taken on a life of its own. It had leapfrogged from Ann Arbor to Detroit and into the evening edition of the *Minneapolis Tribune*. "Two Women to Risk Lives for Science in Colorado Canyon," declared the headline in letters higher than the masthead. This version, to spice things up, included a paragraph about the death of Bessie Hyde. "Several men have conquered the Colorado; a woman has yet to do it," the writer declared. Unaware of this uncomfortable twist to the story, Jotter went to sleep alone in her hotel room in Omaha. She awoke abruptly in the middle of the night to the sound of wailing sirens. The bakery across the street had gone up in flames. "I am saved for the Colorado," Jotter noted in her diary as firefighters doused the blaze.

They started before dawn the next day. Sometime around midday, they crossed the hundredth meridian, the invisible line John Wesley Powell had drawn down the middle of the country. Powell's 1869 journey down the Colorado River was now the stuff of legend. For science, it had been a failure. Powell's fragile instruments were smashed beyond repair, his maps torn, soaked, and tattered. The expedition had become not a geologic survey, but a desperate scramble for survival—or, in Powell's words, "a race for a dinner."

But Powell had returned with a hard-won understanding of the American West, a land that would not bend easily to human desires. The desert was vast and the rivers finite. In 1877 Powell stood up at a meeting of the National Academy of Sciences and unrolled a map of the United States bisected by a vertical line down the middle. The line was an isohyet, connecting points that have the same annual rainfall—in this case, twenty inches—and roughly coinciding with the hundredth meridian. West of this line, Powell declared, tallgrass prairie faded to shortgrass, trees disappeared, and conventional crops would not grow without irrigation. Powell believed that the West's aridity demanded new patterns of settlement and agriculture, and an entirely new way of thinking for Anglo-Americans. He did not shrink from displacing Indigenous peoples with white farmers; he only quibbled about how it could be done. He wanted communities to be arranged around watersheds, sharing and conserving water in a common trust. He hoped to halt the rush of westward settlement until accurate surveys could be completed.

Powell's keen vision and precise ecological knowledge couldn't compete with the mirage of manifest destiny. Americans went west anyway, expecting rain to follow like a sheepdog at their heels. They got the Dust Bowl instead. Powell—explorer of the Colorado River, director of the U.S. Geological Survey, savvy politician, and one-armed Civil War veteran—had been dead for thirty-six years. People still hailed him as the hero who conquered the Colorado River, but rarely spoke of his prophecies about the limits of living in a waterless land.

Jotter could see firsthand, as they drove west through Nebraska to Colorado, the ecological shifts Powell had so eloquently described. Her eyes sharpened. The familiar maples and hickories vanished, replaced by cottonwoods following the sinuous tracks of streams. Cornfields and rolling hills planted with grain transformed into sand pimpled with tiny flowers. Then came a long barren stretch with no flowers at all. The Rockies reared before them, an imposing barricade. In the old days, motorists passing through Rocky Mountain National Park traversed a road so steep they sometimes had to ascend in reverse so that the gasoline in their tanks wouldn't slosh beyond the reach of the siphon. But the National Park Service had just completed the Trail Ridge Road, following an ancient route of the Ute and Arapaho peoples. A sleek, modern highway, it was designed so that beautiful vistas opened at every curve like postcards.

At 12,000 feet in elevation, Clover, Jotter, and Atkinson crossed the Continental Divide, the ridge that splits the North American continent. On the east side of the Rockies, water rolled into the vast Missouri–Mississippi watershed, draining to the Gulf of Mexico. On the west side, raindrops plashed into the watershed of the Colorado River Basin, pouring down to the Gulf of California. The travelers got to see this principle of hydrology in action, for a thunderstorm was advancing over the Rockies, dark streamers of virga lifting and twisting off the peaks until finally the skies opened. It rained. Thunder and lightning came together in deafening, blinding claps. Then, without warning, the rain ended. Drifts of snow, pockmarked by raindrops, clung to the highway's shoulder. Shafts of blinding sun came down, and then a sharp patter of hail. Ice gleamed like shards of glass. They descended the winding road, wind-whipped clumps of alpine flowers giving way to spruce, spruce to pine, and pine to aspen trees, until finally fields of blue lupine and white mountain phlox unrolled before them, bright as a stained-glass window.

Alongside the car, they caught their first glimpse of the headwaters of the Colorado River—the upper reaches of the branch once named the Grand. Jotter and Clover thought it looked unusually high—"on a rampage," Clover wrote to Bartlett, out of its banks in places—but they expressed no alarm in their letters home. They drove late that night, looking for a place to stay, and were rewarded with the sight of a full moon rising over mountains behind them, tipping fields of sagebrush in silver. They slept in a tiny town on the upper reaches of the Colorado, their last stop on the road before reaching Utah. It had been a beautiful day, though not without its moments of foreboding. Clover had admired a long black car that passed them on the road and wished aloud that she might take a ride in it. Then she realized it was a hearse.

$$\Downarrow$$

IN MEXICAN HAT, Norm Nevills labored to finish the boats on time. The work was going slowly. He had to use hand tools and contend with the fickle Utah weather, hard wind and sandstorms one day, rain the next. Plus, he was making up the boat design as he went along. He kept a careful log of the process. "Determined procedure for making the difficult angle cuts necessary to fit the ribs in with the triangular piece," he wrote on May 14. "Had much trouble getting joints properly fitted . . . found method of attack was wrong," was the entry the next day.

According to Nevills, he didn't consult other rivermen about the boats; he preferred to puzzle things out on his own. He shared that spirit of inquiry with his wife, Doris, whom he'd met in 1933. She was nineteen then, a tiny, blue-eyed, brown-haired woman traveling through Utah with her family. Nevills recognized her instantly as a kindred spirit. They met exactly three times that summer and got married in October. "This is characteristic of all our decisions," Nevills wrote. "Whatever we do or decide to do we make up our mind quickly."

Doris and Nevills had an idea for their honeymoon: to float the San Juan River. They constructed a boat out of an outhouse and an old horse trough, patched the knotholes with tin, and plugged the cracks with scraps of underwear. In February they took the boat on a test run, wielding oars made from the pump rods from a well. At the first riffle the boat scraped over a rock and all the homemade caulking fell out. Nevills made repairs with scrap iron and the couple set off on their honeymoon not long after. One night it snowed. Another, they woke to find the boat sheathed in ice. Nevills was convinced they hit every rock in the river.

Like other boatmen before him, Nevills had tried to fight the current, powering through rapids as Doris sang out warnings of rocks projecting from the muddy water ahead. The trip was a revelation. He realized he needed to work with the river instead.

Powell, on both his expeditions, had used round-bottomed White-hall rowboats, built for speed and power on flat water. Pulling on oars is more powerful than pushing them, so Powell's men faced upstream, looking over the boat's stern, and ran the river blind, their backs to the hazards ahead. The setup meant they relied on raw power, not finesse, to muscle through the rapids. The technique, and the heavy, lethargic boats, were poorly suited for whitewater. Nearly three decades later, a fur trapper named Nathaniel Galloway ran the Colorado River with one companion in a nimble craft of his own design, the fourth expedition on record to successfully traverse the Grand Canyon. Galloway, too, sat looking over the boat's stern—but he turned his boat backward so that it hit the rapids stern-first. This way, a lone man wielded the oars, facing downstream so he could spot the hazards and (with a bit of luck) avoid them. Galloway relied not on power, but on quick sideways movements through the current to avoid holes and waves.

Nevills claimed he hadn't heard of Galloway, but hit upon the same technique independently. He called it *face your danger,* a phrase he'd heard often from his mother. "I was learning from that great text-book, the river itself," he wrote. He built a new boat, blunt on both ends and shaped like a crackerjack box, and took a group of tourists down the San Juan and Colorado to Lee's Ferry for the first time in 1936. The trip was a success, though he made the mistake of tell-ing the tourists to plan the meals, and they all arrived at Lee's Ferry "plain hungry." Doris took charge of the menu from that point on, acting as a business manager, and Nevills dove with enthusiasm into advertising river running trips. "For myself I must get a reputation," he wrote, one based on a record of safety. He wanted to convince people that river running wasn't a death-defying feat, but the kind of adventure anyone could have for a price.

Early in 1937, a man named Ed Holt came through Mexican Hat. He had gone through the Grand Canyon with Clyde Eddy in 1927, the tenth expedition on record to make it. He jeered at Nevills for sticking with calm water. "You ought to try a real river—the Colorado," he said.

"I'll be running it next year," Nevills shot back.

Nevills had no such plan. But saying the words aloud seemed to crystallize a dream he had harbored all along. He began to talk about the trip with Doris, poring over maps of the Colorado River and devouring every book he could find. When Clover arrived at Mexican Hat Lodge on her plant collecting trip a few months later, he was ready.

Nevills recruited LaPhene "Don" Harris to row one of the expedition's three boats. A laconic twenty-seven-year-old, Harris had grown up on an Idaho farm and came to Utah to study engineering in college. He was stationed in Mexican Hat at the time as a river gauger for the U.S. Geological Survey (USGS). He'd gone down the San Juan with Nevills a couple of times. The timing of the Colorado River trip— unwisely planned for the midsummer peak of high water—was probably chosen to accommodate Harris's work schedule, as he could get a paid vacation in June just before a job transfer to Salt Lake City.

Harris put up $200 for his share of the expedition's costs, and lent Nevills another $235 to cover boat-building materials. Almost everything had to be custom ordered by mail. Nevills made a special order for extra-large sheets of a new material called SUPER-Harbord, a laminated plywood made from Douglas fir pressed with waterproof resin. A single sheet of SUPER-Harbord made up the bottom of each boat, sixteen feet long and five feet broad. More plywood made up the straight sides, reinforced with white oak ribs, and decking covered the boats fore and aft, leaving a kind of cockpit in the center. Nevills added airtight compartments on either end for extra buoyancy. The prow and stern rose at sharp angles from the water (referred to as the rake). On the river, the boats would look something like curled leaves or abalone shells, the ends tipped up into air, the bottom gently curved from prow to stern. Nevills intended for the rocker-like effect of the rake to allow the boats to pivot on a dime.

With Harris's help, Nevills finished the construction in mid-June. Each boat boasted 2,300 screws and weighed 600 pounds. Nevills ordered three oars apiece (two and a spare). The oars were sturdy things, eight and a half feet long and made of ash, three inches thick at the butt. There were also seven cork life jackets in various sizes, unattractively lumpy and pale yellow, "sewed together with government-approved thread," plus 125 feet of rope for each boat. Nothing would be allowed on board that wasn't essential to the expedition's survival. Even the passengers had a tight squeeze. They could cling to the flat deck at the front, holding onto the ropes for dear life, or else squish themselves in behind the oarsman. It was meant to be safe, not comfortable. The boats were *almost* unsinkable, Nevills was careful to say. There was no use imagining they were *absolutely* unsinkable. After all, the *Titanic* had gone down in his lifetime.

🌱

CLOVER, JOTTER, AND ATKINSON reached Green River, Utah, on June 12, and spent a day or two there collecting plants (in Jotter's words, "we botanized lots.") Presumably Atkinson used the time to prepare his hunting gear: he intended to shoot, skin, and tan animal hides along the way for museum specimens. Clover sampled the cactus while Jotter focused on her specialty, evening primroses. She pressed one bedraggled specimen in a letter to send to her mother, saying that the white flowers looked far more beautiful when they bloomed at night. "This collecting business is more than grabbing plants up," Jotter explained.

Ideally, a botanist collected the entire plant—root, stem, leaf, and flower—and pressed it flat between sheets of newspaper, and then added a blotter to whisk away moisture. Stacked on top of each other, these alternating layers would go between pieces of thin wood, cinched tight with straps. There was a delicate art to laying out a specimen, the leaves splayed out separately and arranged as naturally as possible. It was time-consuming work, and that was for the easy plants. A cactus pad had to be sliced in half, lengthwise, without disturbing

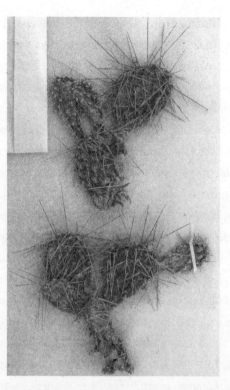

Opuntia polyacanta var. hystricina (plains prickly pear)
collected from San Juan County, Utah. *Catalog #1644420,*
courtesy of the University of Michigan Herbarium,
Clover & Jotter collection, used by permission

its spines, and the pulpy stuff inside scooped out, before it could be flattened and preserved. The plants would be housed in herbaria as a permanent record, and should any prove to be an undescribed species, it would serve as the "type specimen" or point of reference for all future research. Clover kept a lab book to jot down the specimen numbers, followed by the plant's scientific name or a blank space if she couldn't identify it in the field, and a few scribbled notes about the geography, soil, and condition of the plant. The first specimen in the book, a Colorado prickly pear, was numbered 1912. As a point of pride, botanists usually numbered specimens in sequence over their career, so the number implies that Clover had made 1,911 collections prior to this expedition.

The plants collected from the Green River were meant as a basis for comparison later. A theory at the time held that the Colorado River acted as a corridor for plant migration. The canyonlands lay at the intersection of three deserts: the Great Basin, the Sonoran, and the Mojave. Clover was curious to see if plants peculiar to each zone extended their ranges along the river channel. That was one idea they wanted to test. They also knew that plant communities changed with elevation and intended to track those subtle shifts as they descended the river. Lastly, there was the possibility of a "relict flora" tucked away in corners, persisting in place through changing climates as the plateau rose and the river cut down—for example, plants left over from the cooler and wetter Pleistocene that managed to hang on when the climate swung to desert. To answer these questions, it would be necessary to collect plants all the way and get a complete picture of the ecology.

After collecting, the women organized their gear. Sleeping bags existed at the time, but were expensive. Jotter had opted instead to create a gargantuan bedroll out of overlapping blankets wrapped around an air mattress (a gift from her parents) and stuffed into a heavy canvas ground cloth. She squashed it into the smallest possible cylinder. Both women had tried to pack lightly. They were amused to find that Atkinson had not, and ribbed him about his overstuffed duffel bag—"more junk than an old lady could think of," they teased. The three of them finished in time to go to the town's Tuesday night movie. This week's showing was *Heidi*, starring Shirley Temple. The next day they drove nearly 200 miles from Green River to Mexican Hat, the desert rock outside the car's windows burnished red and wrought into fantastic sculptures by the wind. Jotter had an instinctive sense that understanding a place—its plants, animals, and the workings of its weather—lent it a deeper splendor. She tried to put this into words in a letter to her mother, writing that the scenery was beautiful, "especially when one can stop and examine the plants, and know <u>something</u> of them."

Harris and the Nevills family greeted them at Mexican Hat Lodge. The three boats looked neat and fresh in their white coats of paint, the words NEVILLS EXPEDITION in big block letters on their sides. Jotter was dismayed. Ever since the University of Michigan gave them the grant, Jotter had thought of the venture as a scientific expedition under Clover's direction. She knew it wasn't, really. They had no institution to sponsor their work and were paying Nevills to be their guide. It was technically a commercial trip. But this hadn't hit home until now.

The women painted labels onto the cans of food, in case the paper wrappings didn't survive repeated wettings. Then they sorted the cans into watertight sacks, each holding two days' worth of rations. There was canned fruit, canned vegetables, canned meat, and canned spaghetti. Even the butter was canned. They would have Ry-Krisp crackers with every meal, in lieu of bread, and a brand of powdered milk called Klim to drink, stirred into cups of river water. Breakfast included Postum, a caffeine-free coffee substitute made from molasses and roasted wheat bran, which did not in any way taste like coffee. Doris had planned the meals, so there was little danger of them going hungry before they reached the resupply point at Lee's Ferry—unless, of course, one of the boats and its supplies were lost, or some other catastrophe delayed them.

There was one last finishing touch. Clover and Jotter borrowed a can of green paint and added names to the boats' prows. The lead boat was the *Wen,* in honor of Norm's father William Eugene Nevills. The other two boats were named the *Botany* and the *Mexican Hat.* Nevills had played with the idea of christening one boat with his wife's maiden name, the way Powell did on his first and second expeditions downriver, but he decided in the end it wouldn't give the right impression. Her maiden name was Doris Drown.

$$\Downarrow$$

ON SUNDAY, JUNE 19, they left Atkinson's car at the Mexican Hat Lodge, loaded the three boats onto trucks, and drove to Green River. There they met the sixth and final member of the crew, Bill Gibson. He was an architect and amateur photographer from San Francisco whose job was to film movies of the trip. Nevills hadn't bothered to tell Gibson he was also expected to row a boat. The snowstorm of letters between the two men said nothing about rowing or rapids; they were entirely consumed with plans to drum up publicity. Gibson even fronted the money to hire an expensive publicity agent (a friend's uncle), who had promised to get articles about the expedition in "every city, town, village, & hamlet in the country," not to mention radio interviews, magazine spreads, and movie deals. Gibson gushed to Nevills that their publicity campaign would put a presidential election to shame. Ironically, despite Gibson's efforts, nearly all the articles about the expedition so far had come from Jotter's slip to her friend in Michigan.

Green River, a little town of less than five hundred people, was an odd choice for a launch point. Nevills had decided on the route even before he met Clover. They would start with three or four easy days drifting down the Green River to its confluence with the Colorado, then raft through Cataract and Glen canyons to Lee's Ferry, the first layover and resupply point. That ought to take less than two weeks. From Lee's Ferry, they would enter the Grand Canyon. There would be one more resupply stop at Bright Angel Creek, near a resort called Phantom Ranch at the bottom of the Grand Canyon, where a park trail led to the rim. The journey would end at Lake Mead. Nevills expected the whole trip to take somewhere between thirty and forty days.

Some of the local "river rats"—working-class men who lived around rivers and took pride in their knowledge of the desert's capricious moods—thought it a foolhardy plan. It meant going through Cataract Canyon, the so-called "graveyard of the Colorado." This stretch of ominous rapids could be easily avoided. Nevills could have launched at Mexican Hat, going down the San Juan and joining the Colorado in Glen Canyon, through familiar stretches of water. Or he could have trucked the boats to Lee's Ferry and started at the head of the Grand Canyon. Perhaps Nevills hoped to expand his tourist business to the Green River and upper Colorado, or perhaps he wanted to follow in the wake of famous expeditions of yore (Powell and Galloway had gone down the Green). Maybe he just wanted to see the region for himself. What was the use of choosing the safest route, anyway? They'd signed up for an adventure.

Clover and Jotter dressed in their practical brown overalls for the occasion. The overalls were a compromise. Skirts were out of the question, but Clover thought blue jeans looked too masculine, even though Levi Strauss & Co. had introduced a design for women in 1934. They arrived hot and dusty from the drive and were displeased to find a newsman waiting for them. He had come all the way from Salt Lake City to interview and photograph the crew—the women, specifically.

The story of their venture had by now leapt from the local news to the national papers, and the coverage had not been flattering. The day before, a syndicated Associated Press article had publicized James Fennemore's opinion of the trip. Fennemore, ninety years old, was the last living survivor of Powell's second expedition down the Colorado. Fennemore had fallen ill and quit the expedition at Lee's Ferry and never entered the Grand Canyon. Even so, the newspapers wanted his opinion, and he thought the Colorado River was a "mighty poor place for women." Maybe it wasn't quite as dangerous to boat now as it had been sixty-seven years ago. "Still," Fennemore proclaimed, "there isn't any use going down that river just for the novelty."

They weren't going for the novelty, Clover tried to explain. They were going for plants. The Colorado River had never been botanized before; that was the main thing. This was a necessary correction, since the article about Fennemore had referred to Clover and Jotter as archeologists. But the Salt Lake City newsman was not interested.

"Do you think women can do everything a man can do?" he wanted to know.

"No," replied Clover and Jotter emphatically. The question annoyed Jotter. In terms of strength, she probably couldn't do the same work as a man. But her mind, her abilities, and (she hoped) her endurance in the rough country ahead were just as good. Or better.

"What do you think about the riverman's statement in the *Saturday Evening Post*?" came the next question. The "riverman" was Buzz Holmstrom, who heartily agreed with James Fennemore that the Colorado River was no place for a woman.

Jotter smiled at the journalist and replied, "Just because the only other woman who ever attempted this trip was drowned is no reason women have any more to fear than men."

At least, that's what the newspaperman wrote up in his article. In her diary that night, Jotter scribbled wearily that she tried to speak as little as possible, knowing how easily her comments could be misconstrued. To her roommate Kay Hussey, Jotter wrote, "My dear, don't believe anything you do see that's supposed to be something we said because we've been beautifully misquoted out here."

Jotter enclosed a schedule in the short letter to her friend. They planned to reach the first layover at Lee's Ferry on July 4, and the second at Bright Angel Creek on July 15. "Please do not be worried if we don't get there on the exact date," she added, "as we may lay over for a week for high water." This was a sensible caution. The water was very high, and very muddy. Try to bathe in that river and you would come out dirtier than you went in, and when you drank it, you didn't know whether to swallow or chew. Whenever the river doubled in velocity, it quadrupled the size of the debris it could carry. Debris flows—slurries of mud, logs, and rubble—could tear down the side canyons faster than a horse could gallop.

That night, they tested the boats in the Green River. Tethered, the little crafts bobbed in the current like horses straining at the starting gate. Jotter felt relieved. She hadn't been entirely sure they would float. Nevills called them "Cataract boats," but detractors dubbed them "sadirons" because they were shaped like an old-fashioned clothes iron.

So long as they didn't sink like a sadiron, too.

By now an avid audience had gathered: the newspaperman, the residents of Green River, and a crowd of gawkers, at least a hundred of them. Harris's parents were there; they had read the lurid newspaper accounts and driven down in a last-ditch effort to dissuade him from going. Clover was embarrassed by Atkinson's behavior. He swaggered around strapped up with a "regular arsenal"—a rifle, a .22 pistol, and a hunting knife. Clover suspected the locals were laughing at him as a kind of "drugstore cowboy." She and Jotter took him aside and urged him to leave the weapons off until he needed them to shoot and skin game, but Atkinson ignored the advice.

They had a lot of preparations to make before departure, but in the end, they bundled their supplies and gear unceremoniously into the boats' supposedly waterproof compartments. Nobody felt like lingering over the packing under the critical eyes of their audience. "Do you know what you're getting into?" some of the onlookers wanted to know. "Do you know about THAT place on the river? That's a bad place." One riverman later told another that the boats looked "mighty funny" and the hatches were far too small. "Maybe both the ladies are dieting," he joked, "and they won't have to eat much." An old man cornered Harris's terrified parents and growled, "These boats can't make it. You'll never see your boy alive again."

Gibson, irritated, finally spit out a sarcastic comment about the crowd's sure-and-certain prophecies of a disastrous end. But grizzled river rats only shook their heads. It was high summer: a season when broiling heat gave way to black, booming thunderstorms. The Green River was swollen with snowmelt. The Colorado, reportedly, was running at a fearsome deluge of 70,000 cubic feet per second (cfs). That wasn't uncommon for June, when melting snow thundered down the mountains and mingled with early summer rains, but it seemed like madness to try to run it in three handcrafted wooden boats. The floodwater would smooth out smaller rapids, true, but the boats would barrel along at five or six miles per hour on an unpredictable current, waves and whirlpools on every side.

"You couldn't pay me to join them," declared one riverman.

The river itself, and the risk of drowning, was only one of the hazards ahead. The expedition members would also have to contend with heat, hunger, and fatigue; with mosquitoes the size of dinner plates and rattlesnakes the color of dried blood; with wet clothes, sickness, bruises, and blisters, not to mention one another's fraying nerves and tempers. "So they're looking for flowers and Indian caves," an unnamed river runner told a reporter dismissively. "Well, I don't know about that, but I do know they'll find a peck of trouble before they get through."

Nearly everyone had a hair-raising story to share of the wilderness's dangers, and one man, who gave his name as Hunt, was full of sinister hints. He'd heard a rumor about Nathaniel Galloway, that he'd been brutally murdered somewhere along the Green River. He was wrong about this. Galloway had died in 1913 in a small Utah town from a freak accident: he fell across a bar on his wagon, crushed his throat, and suffocated. But Clover did not know that.

"Well," she told the crowd flippantly, "if we don't come back just toss a rose over into the canyon for us."

Nobody laughed. Hunt declared he'd better kiss both women goodbye. He managed to corner Jotter first, then Clover, to do just that. They could smell the alcohol on his breath. (Atkinson, looking on, didn't try to interfere, though he did take a photo.) The two women escaped round the corner of a building to scrub their faces clean. "O, well," Clover wrote philosophically in her journal, "if we don't get thru it will give him something to tell."

The two botanists stayed up late that night writing letters—the last their families and friends would hear from them until they reached Lee's Ferry—and tearing newspapers into strips for the plant press. Perhaps Jotter took a savage satisfaction in shredding the articles that had hounded them so far. The plant press was stuffed into the boats along with the bags of food, life preservers, and Clover's sewing kit. The women squirreled several jars of face cream among the food when nobody was looking, because Nevills had raised such a ruckus about keeping the weight in the boats to a minimum. They had

no sunscreen, which wasn't widely available. As far as medicine—
well, Clover slipped a bottle of Four Roses whiskey into her personal
supplies.

They launched the boats at 9 a.m. the next morning, posing for
last-minute photographs and signing autographs onto people's hats. "A
funeral service could not have been less cheerful," Clover wrote. The
Wen went first, with Nevills and Clover, followed by the *Botany*, with
Gibson and Atkinson, and lastly the *Mexican Hat*, with Harris and
Jotter. A little way downriver, Nevills pulled ashore for a private fare-
well with Doris and his daughter, Joan, peacefully sleeping in the car.
Doris kissed him goodbye, dry-eyed and calm. Nobody made a fuss.

They left civilization behind, which was just as well, since none
of them had to read the syndicated story that ran in newspapers
nationwide that day, June 20. "Two flora-minded women from
Michigan joined four equally adventurous men today in a daring
boat trip down the restless Colorado river's mile-deep gorge," began
the adjective-riddled article. Clover's lecture about the value of their
plant collection hadn't impressed the Salt Lake City journalist. The
"important cacti" and "relict flora" mentioned in the *Michigan Daily*
story, two weeks before, had mutated into "botanical freaks," and
that was almost all the story had to say about scientific research. It
was much more interesting to describe the frail, homemade boats,
the snowmelt-flooded waters of the Green, and the glum expres-
sions of the townspeople. Jotter was reported as saying she and Clover were willing to do their part, but the tasks assigned to them by
the reporter—cooking, setting up camp, rowing the boats, and other
odd jobs—did not include botany.

On the river, sliding beneath the shade of cottonwood trees, the
memory of glum predictions began to fade. Harris let Jotter take a
turn at the oars; Clover envied her skill with the boat. The water was
smooth but the wind strong, and Jotter had to rescue her hat from the
river when it blew off. Thus far, everything seemed planned, predictable, and safe. One evening, Nevills gave the group instructions on

how to run the rapids ahead. Jotter recorded his advice this way: "If you do get sucked in, hit stern first & square, cliff walls current not too strong, quarter up-stream, row against it, always hang on to boat, etc. Finally and so to bed."

Later, Jotter added a wry note to that entry: "I guess I really must not have listened to all this with any sense of responsibility."

Chapter Four

THERE GOES THE
MEXICAN HAT!

"**L**ADY, GET OUT YOUR JOURNAL," NEVILLS TOLD Clover, "and give your last-minute impressions before seeing the Colorado." It was the afternoon of June 23, and they had less than four miles to float down the Green before reaching the confluence with the Colorado River. Clover obeyed, pulling out a pencil and her little leatherbound notebook stamped with the word *Record* in curly script. "I don't feel at all scared yet," she wrote, "altho I know that we will be cut off from any hope of getting out in case of accident, illness, or fright." She was beginning to feel anxious about her decision to invite Jotter and Atkinson on the expedition. What would she say to Atkinson's wife and Jotter's parents if things went terribly wrong?

The journey had gone smoothly since their launch from Green River four days before—"much singing and sitting on sun deck," as Jotter put it. Clover and Harris played duets on harmonicas as the boats floated beneath ancient cliff dwellings and granaries. Early morning light caught the pinnacles at the tops of the cliffs, turning them rose-colored, while the faces remained in shadow. Willows and cottonwoods fringed the river, brushing shoulders with exotic tamarisk trees, a Eurasian species brought to the American West as an ornamental because of its lacy pink blossoms. On still days the trees' reflections stood upside-down in the water, fish slipping among the leaves. The temperature varied wildly, from the chilly forties when Clover and Jotter woke before dawn to cook breakfast, rising to the nineties within hours. By afternoon it scorched over 100 degrees

Fahrenheit. Atkinson made everybody nervous by reaching for his gun whenever he spotted a deer or bird. They now had duck, goose, and venison to stretch their supplies. He had brought down an eight-point buck while hiking with Nevills on the cliffs above the river. Distances were deceptive in the contours and folds of the Utah desert, and stories tended to grow in the telling, but Atkinson said he dropped the deer with a single shot from his .22 pistol at an improbable distance of 125 yards. Nevills added that he nearly dropped dead himself from surprise. "The cooks are baffled with so much meat," Clover wrote, ". . . and no Frigidaire."

They'd had a few mishaps, but nothing serious. Jotter's yellow pith helmet had already saved her life (or at least her skull) when rocks dislodged from a cliff pelted down on her head. Clover got dunked in the river one evening when she was trying to learn how to "line" her boat, a difficult operation that involved attaching ropes to the bow and stern and guiding the boat through the water from the shore, letting the lines out and reeling them in, something like wrangling a rambunctious kite on a windy day. They would have to line the boats whenever a rapid seemed too dangerous to run, at least if there was a shoreline to stand on. From here on, there would be no real river-banks in the usual sense of the word. The shore would be made up of disconnected sandbars—some tiny crescents, others broad beaches—where they would moor the boats and camp at night. Between sandbars they would find loose skirts of rubble, called talus, steeply sloping from the cliffs to the water, and sometimes nothing but bare vertical rock.

The crew was inclined to laugh over the dire predictions and nonsensical newspaper stories—everybody, that is, except Nevills. "I feel certain that none of them realize just what real bad water is like," he wrote in his diary. How could they? Nevills didn't know, either. But he made it his mission those first four days, as they wound down the Green River and got to know the boats and one another, to brace them up with fearsome descriptions of Cataract Canyon.

They braced up the boats as well, literally. Clover rowed while

Nevills added extra screws to the *Wen* in preparation for the rapids ahead. They repacked all the hastily stowed gear, strapping the bed-rolls down tight. The wind was so strong that Clover had to keep one leg thrown over her plant press on the *Wen*'s deck to keep it from blowing away.

Nevills had planned to have the USGS keep the crew informed of the river's level via short-wave radio, but somehow or other he never did add a radio to their equipment. A USGS employee promised to send them word of whether the river was rising by writing the water level on a board and setting it adrift. Whenever they found a curious bit of driftwood, they turned it over in hope of news, but the search proved fruitless. None of them knew quite what to expect from the Colorado River. Nevills told such stories of it that Gibson was now in a knot of terror, half-convinced that waterfalls stretched clear from one end to the other. Some of the crew members tried to relieve their jitters by indulging in gallows humor, shouting from boat to boat: "What kind of flowers do you want at your funeral?" and "Do you have your harp tuned?"

Jotter didn't join in. The feeble jokes grated on her frayed nerves. Harris, too, was quiet. He never talked much: even his journal entries were brief and to the point. "Retire. No mosquitos," was all he wrote the night before they reached the confluence. But early one morning, the beauty of the Green River moved him into an uncharacteristic flight of poetry: "Surroundings so peaceful and quiet it seems they penetrate right into one's soul."

Now, the peace and quiet were nearly over, along with any chance of changing their minds. The river bent sharply around a high, sheer mesa: the confluence was near.

There were days when the Green River was true to its name, its waters a deep emerald hue. Today wasn't one of them. The floodwa-ters tore at the river's banks and muddied the waters to coffee-brown. But as the boats rounded the last corner, they could see a sharp divide where the Green's waters poured into the Colorado. The colors didn't match. The Colorado was red: red as earth, red as blood. The Spanish called it Río Colorado (colored red) because the water was stained with the silt it carried, but various parts of the sprawling watershed had borne many different names. To the Spanish, the first Europeans to explore the region, it had been the river of martyrs, mysteries, and saints. They called it Río de Buena Esperanza, river of good hope, Río de Buena Guia, river of good guidance, and Río del Tizon, river of embers. The river has other, older names. Hualapai refer to the Colorado as a lifegiving spine, Paiute call it Water Deep in the Earth, and Navajo speak of the River of Never-Ending Life. The 246,000-square-mile watershed touches seven U.S. states, two Mexican provinces, and at least thirty Native nations. It encompasses 8 percent of the contiguous U.S. and glances through a dozen different ecosystems on its journey from mountains to sea, including pine forest, oak woodland, chaparral, and three types of desert: Great Basin, Sonoran, and Mojave.

Majestic, Clover thought, her eyes lifting to the cliffs banded in red and white, a few storm clouds scudding above. But Nevills said aloud, "She's a big 'un and a bad 'un." They rowed the boats to the opposite shore and made a precarious landing, quicksand sucking at their shoes, to look over a riffle downstream. Then they set off in the boats to the head of the first rapid, four miles downriver. Both women were surprised by the Colorado's wildness, after their tranquil days on the Green. "The character of the river changed," Jotter wrote in her journal, "and slowly we realized the force of the Colorado." The channel narrowed, choked with boulders; the water picked up speed. Whirlpools appeared. Whole trees whisked by, torn out by their roots. The water level had been rising since the morning of the previous day. Though no stream gauge existed at the confluence to give the exact number, the flow likely topped 50,000 cfs—like watching 185 concrete mixer trucks dump their contents into the riverbed every single second.

They stopped at the head of Cataract Canyon, tied up the boats, and got out. The cliffs on either side of the river were not sheer, but jumbled. Their outline against the thundery sky was sometimes formed of upright pinnacles, rounded by wind, and other times made of great slanted blocks of limestone and sandstone, as if giants or gods had torn up the earth and tossed it any which way. In the river, boulders pummeled by the current's force oscillated tunelessly against one another until the edges wore down and they fit as tightly as cinderblocks. Powell wrote of this place, "The landscape everywhere, away from the river, is of rock—cliffs of rock, tables of rock, plateaus of rock, terraces of rock, crags of rock—ten thousand strangely carved forms; rocks everywhere, and no vegetation, no soil, no sand."

At the head of the first rapid, the crew spotted a boulder with an inscription painted in white on its flat surface. They could just make out the words "Major Powell" followed by a date and some unfamiliar names. The women photographed it, using a handheld Weston light meter to measure the exposure. They held the meter at eye level to take a reading of the reflected light and then manually entered the proper shutter stop into the camera. Tricky enough with a stationary rock. Soon they would have to do it with boats bucking through rapids.

They assumed that John Wesley Powell had left the inscription, but this was incorrect. In fact, a man named William Edwards left those words in 1893. He had briefly captained a steamship called the *Major Powell*, during a short-lived attempt to open the Colorado River to steam-powered excursion boats. "Imagine the calliope piping its stentorian music," proclaimed the *Grand Valley Times*, "through the canyons and labyrinths of this most beautiful and majestic scenic route on a moonlight night." Eager to capitalize on potential tourists, a man named B. S. Ross purchased an open-decked, coal-fired, 35-foot-long steamship and christened it the *Major Powell*. Ross unloaded the boat at the Green River railroad station in 1891 and announced an excursion to the Grand Canyon. They were more than 300 river miles from the Grand Canyon's head, but no matter. On a trial run down the shallow Green River, the boat's twin screw propellers promptly smashed on a sandbar just below town.

Ross tried again in April the following year. Spring floods kept the boat afloat above the sandbars and he made it all the way to the confluence, where the rapids began. Clover, Jotter, and the rest were now standing near the spot where Ross planned to build a grand hotel, possibly even a railroad line to ship tourists around Cataract Canyon to the smooth waters of Glen Canyon below, where another steamboat could pick them up. The dream never materialized. The *Major Powell* consumed so much coal on the return journey upriver that the crew had to abandon it twenty miles from town and walk the rest of the way.

In 1893 William Edwards leased the boat from Ross and made two journeys in it. Edwards overhauled the boiler to burn wood instead of coal, so his crew spent most of the month-long voyages cutting down cottonwood trees to feed it. They made it as far as the confluence, both times, so Edwards painted the ship's name on a boulder and announced he had proven the navigability of the canyon country. Nothing came of it. The *Major Powell* was scrapped for parts the next year, and a flood swept its discarded hull away.

Clover and Jotter knew nothing of this history. They finished photographing the inscription while Nevills and the other men went to look at the river. Nevills guessed the first rapid had fifteen-foot-high waves, and there was barely a break between where it ended and the second rapid began. Boatmen spoke of the river's contours in animalistic terms. There was the lip of the rapid, a smooth straight line that delineated the sudden drop. There was the tongue, a V of gentle billows projecting through the lip and into the whitewater. Nevills would guide the boats straight down that throat, into curling waves that rose, broke, and fell, over and over again, holding their place in the current. His plan was to hit the waves squarely on the boat's broad stern, blunting their impact. At the foot of the rapid was a long, lashing tail, spiked with progressively smaller waves, extending down the center of the river. On either side, eddies forced the river's current backward, sometimes so strongly that an unwary boat could be pulled back into tail waves for a second go-around. In Cataract Canyon, at this water level, there might be a brief respite or no respite at all before another rapid reared its head, and another, hydra-like. Cataract Canyon was forty-one miles long with sixty-two rapids. At flood stage, it was a nearly continuous stretch of turbulent water.

As Nevills studied for the safest route through the rapid, Clover was reading the river in a different way. Tucked here and there, hunkered under boulders or clinging insecurely to scree, were plants that had learned, somehow, to thrive in this place. They wove a thread of pale green around the river's strong blue cord, hitched to the rhythms of drought and flood in ways that botanists had only just begun to perceive.

Ecology was an old science, but the word ecosystem was not yet in widespread use. Botanists at the time were trying and discarding words like formation, association, and biome when speaking about a collection of living things in a particular place. Frederic Clements, an influential Nebraska-born botanist who was then employed at the Carnegie Institution, advocated for the term "complex organism." He argued that, like an organism, plant communities advanced through stages of development to a final, stable stage, which might be forest, prairie, tundra, or desert, depending on the region's climate. This was the "climax community" and the process was called succession.

Standing at the river's edge, Clover's thoughts were influenced by the story of succession. She could see that the steep slopes presented hardly any footholds for plants. It was a place for so-called pioneer species, which crept out and colonized disturbed habitats like tremulous explorers on a lava-blasted Mars. Lichens stuck filaments like tiny pitons into the solid rock and hung on. Given time, they would crumble the stone to an incremental soil, and other things would arrive: grass and cactus seeds blown into precarious pockets by chance, sprouting with just a dimple of rain. Trees, the climax species, would follow—here, perhaps netleaf hackberry or tamarisk. Then a landslide would slice down the slope and scythe everything clean. Patient, the lichen would begin all over again.

In Clements's view, humans stood outside of nature and separate from it, disrupters or destroyers of natural processes. Plant communities had destinies, and disturbance—such as the bitter effects of farming and grazing the Great Plains into dust—was always followed by recovery, in time. Succession was a compelling story in the early twentieth century, even a comforting one. But Clements's longtime friend and rival, the English botanist Arthur Tansley, thought it was just that: a story. It was too simple. It didn't leave room for all the complex biological and physical factors that could influence the makeup of a plant community, everything from the grazing habits of bison, to the regular recurrence of wildfires, to subtle differences in topography, to the chemistry of the soil.

In a 1935 paper, Tansley argued that simply because an individual plant progressed from youth to maturity, always in that direction, didn't mean that collections of plants would do the same. They could suffer abrupt shocks and profound transformations. A host of biological and physical factors swayed their fate. "These *ecosystems*, as we may call them, are of the most various kinds and sizes," he wrote. "They form one category of the multitudinous physical systems of the universe, which range from the universe as a whole down to the atom. . . . [T]hey also overlap, interlock and interact with each other."

A corollary of Tansley's new, expanded definition was that humans no longer stood outside of nature. Tansley and his wife, Edith, also a botanist, toured the United States by train in 1913, following much the same route Clover and Jotter traveled west. They saw remnants of beech and maple woodlands in Michigan, dwindled to lonely patches by logging. In Nebraska and Kansas, they noted cattle and European clover in place of native animals and plants. In Colorado, they saw luxuriant green squares of irrigated farmland replace the tawny prairie grass. Tansley imagined many different types of ecosystems, some greatly impacted by human activity and others less so, but all of them governed by the same fundamental processes. It was the ecologist's job to discover those processes. Why do plants grow where they do? How do they relate to one another and to their physical environments? What makes them thrive or go extinct? These were the topics, Tansley wrote in 1904, "about which we have still practically everything to learn." And it was impossible to develop new theories about ecosystems without first conducting thorough botanical surveys over the face of the Earth.

Rhus trilobata var. simplicifolia (skunkbush) collected near
the confluence of the Green and Colorado rivers. *Catalog
#UT0001749, courtesy of the Natural History Museum
of Utah Garrett Herbarium, used by permission*

Clover, looking out at the shrubs and stubborn clumps of grass on
the talus slope where she stood, did not think of it as an ecosystem.
Probably she had never heard the word. She once wrote in despair
about the confusing English terminology for groupings of plants, in
a 1937 paper that advocated for the use of Spanish terms instead; she
thought the Spanish-speaking peoples of Mexico had developed much
more satisfactory classifications and their intimate knowledge of desert landscapes ought to be integrated into academic research. Though
Clover was unfamiliar with Tansley's concept of an ecosystem, she was
nevertheless doing the work Tansley thought so important. She was
collecting plants. She found skunkbush (*Rhus trilobata*), also known
as three-leaf sumac or sourberry, which looked like a stunted oak tree

poking out fuzz-covered twigs. It grew nearly everywhere west of the hundredth meridian, defying heat and cold alike and sprouting back after fire. The plant was covered in clumps of bright red berries, which tasted like lemonade and made a useful dye. Clover didn't bother to cut a sample; she had already collected it on the Green River. She did take a specimen of rabbitbrush (*Chrysothamnus nauseous*), a gray-green shrub that had not yet burst into its pungent yellow flowers. She also gathered New Mexico desert olive (*Forestiera neomexicana*), a species first described for Western science by the famous Harvard botanist Asa Gray. The flowers had gone, the olive-like fruit was just beginning to bruise blue. It became specimen number 2104 in her notebook. The crisp new spine was already wearing soft from use.

Clover cut samples hurriedly. Jotter, meanwhile, succumbed to exhaustion and found a spot to rest. She woke abruptly. Someone was shouting. Gibson, a little way downriver, was yelling in fright: "My God! There goes the *Mexican Hat*!"

⚜

EVEN IN THAT MOMENT OF ALARM, Nevills couldn't help but admire how beautifully the runaway boat rode the waves with no one at the oars. It entered the lip of the rapid stern-first, just as he'd planned. There was an eddy below: surely the boat would stop there. Nevills turned to Harris. "Go get the *Wen*," he said, "bring it down here, and pick me up."

They would ride the first rapid and collect the lost boat. It would be easy.

⚜

JOTTER RAN TO THE RIVERBANK. It was now 5:30 p.m., and the river's level had risen. The stand of wispy willows where Harris had looped the *Mexican Hat*'s rope was submerged, and part of the bank had crumbled into the water. No wonder the boat had pulled free. Jotter heard another shout and turned. Harris dashed up, having pelted a quarter mile up the shoreline.

"We've got to go after it!" he said, heading for the *Wen.* "Come on!"

Jotter grabbed her life preserver and followed Harris into the *Wen.* They could see the *Mexican Hat* bobbing ahead of them, now swallowed up by waves entirely, now spit out again, its rope trailing uselessly behind it. On the shore, Nevills, Gibson, and Atkinson stood aghast. The *Mexican Hat* had not stopped at the first eddy, and was sweeping wildly through the second rapid. As the *Wen* hove into view, Nevills scrambled frantically down the rocky banks in an effort to intercept them. A greenhorn at the oars!—and whatever had possessed Harris to bring Jotter along? It was too late. The *Wen* hit the second rapid. A sinking feeling in the pit of his stomach, Nevills ran on. He could see the third rapid in the series, and just make out the lip of rapid 4, which Nevills believed was a bad one.

The *Mexican Hat* was gone, and the *Wen,* too, was already out of sight.

HARRIS TRIED TO WRESTLE the boat out of the first rapid to the shore where Nevills was waiting, but failed. "We're going right through, so hang on," he told Jotter. Neither of them had ever seen whitewater like this. They rode up on a wave and broke through a cascade of foam and water, then slipped fast down the opposite side into a gaping trough. Jotter spotted the three frantic figures on the shoreline and just had time to wave. Then cold water overtopped the boat, soaking her to the skin. The *Wen* grew sluggish under the weight of bilgewater.

"Bail!" Harris shouted, his back bent to the oars. The bailing bucket was lashed down tight: no time to retrieve it. Jotter snatched up an empty coffee can, cut her finger on the jagged rim, and began to bail water. Her arms grew leaden; her fingers, numb. Cold, frightened, exhilarated, they rode through four rapids and then Harris managed to pull the *Wen* into an eddy to rest. The *Mexican Hat* was nowhere in sight. Harris muttered under his breath and Jotter realized he was praying.

He turned to her. "Lois, can you pray?"

"I don't know," Jotter stammered. Her Mennonite father and Baptist mother had not prepared her for this particular scenario.

"Do you want to stay here while I go on?" he asked.

"No," Jotter said.

Back into the main current. Waves crashing. Sun going down. The boat spun in the current like driftwood; they hit the sixth rapid prow-first and out of control. Jotter could not keep track—she felt as if they had run through one endless rapid—but Harris guessed they ran six or seven rapids in all, coming four miles downriver. Soaked, chilled, they beached again and climbed shakily out of the boat. They were now on the opposite side of the river from where they had begun. Jotter glimpsed a sandy shore ahead, in the last rays of the setting sun.

If we don't find the boat there, she thought, *we'll never see it again.*

They ran. Every jarring step on the gravelly shore made Jotter feel a little more hopeless. In the last few days, they had lost several items to small mistakes—a bucket, a gallon of tomato juice, the spare life preserver. But now, a whole boat, and all its supplies! Powell had lost a boat two weeks into his 1869 expedition, and his crew had nearly died of starvation.

Then Jotter spotted a flash of white paint along a curved prow—she was almost sure of it. Harris couldn't make it out in the dusk light; he was ready to give the boat up for lost and turn around. She urged him on a little farther. There! The *Mexican Hat* had run aground, all its lifesaving supplies of food, clothing, and blankets still safely stowed, though awash in water. "We tied it in the eddy (precious thing) where it had been caught," Jotter recorded in her diary, "bailed it out, and found everything intact, even Don's rapids[-running] stocking cap."

After a hurried discussion, Jotter and Harris walked back upriver to the *Wen*, and then Harris went on alone. He planned to hike back to deliver the good news while Jotter stayed with the boats. The terrain was rough and rocky, and the light was failing fast.

FOUR MILES UPRIVER, Clover sat morosely by the *Botany*, piling rocks on its rope and holding the end in one hand in deathly fear of it tearing loose. She was alone. It seemed that years dragged by before Atkinson appeared, whistling a jaunty tune. Clover felt an instant of relief, and then Atkinson dashed it. The *Mexican Hat* was gone. So was the *Wen*.

Gibson appeared, under orders from Nevills to bring the *Botany* down a little way. He told Clover to walk. The two men disappeared in the boat, and Clover trudged over loose talus, eyes on her feet in fear of rattlesnakes and hating every minute of it. It would be her fault if Jotter drowned. *This isn't happening*, she kept thinking, over and over. *This can't be happening to us*. Half an hour later, she found Gibson and Atkinson waiting in a little cove, the *Botany* tied up. They had made it through the first rapid without mishap but found no sign of the other two boats. Clover tried to come up with something for dinner. The *Botany* wasn't stocked with any silverware or cooking utensils, so they whittled rough spoons out of bark. Nevills joined them a moment later and did his best to hide his apprehension.

When Atkinson glimpsed movement on the opposite riverbank, his first instinct was to reach for his gun. Luckily, he noticed the figure wore khaki and was waving its arms. The rapid's roar was so loud they could barely hear Harris shouting, but finally they made out the words "Come over!" Quickly, they loaded their meager dinner back into the *Botany* and pulled into the current, overcrowded with four people in the tiny craft. They only had three life preservers. Nevills went without, overriding Clover's objections. She thought *she* should take the risk, because if Nevills died, the rest would have a "devil of a time getting through."

It was pitch-black now, and the short journey eerie and wild. Overloaded, the boat foundered and waves lapped up over its sides. Despite her fears, Clover was impressed by how Nevills wrestled the boat almost directly across the strong current. They landed and

Harris told his story: Jotter was okay; the boat was found. Everyone shook hands and clapped his shoulder in relief. There wasn't time to enjoy the moment, however. Harris was determined to head back to Jotter's camp so as not to leave her alone all night. He wolfed down some peaches from a can, took a flashlight, and headed out again with Atkinson.

They didn't get far. The waning crescent moon had not yet risen, and rattlesnakes seemed to buzz up with every step. They took a few bad falls. When the flashlight guttered and died, the two men gave up and lay down on a flat rock to wait for daylight. Harris was still soaked and wearing only his trousers. He shivered all night, alternating between wearing his damp trousers on his legs and taking them off to drape round his shoulders like a shawl.

Gibson, Nevills, and Clover weren't much better off. They made their beds on a fringe of wet sand near the river's edge, but the *Botany* had hardly any bedding to share between them: just a single sleeping bag and a little piece of canvas, wet from their crossing. *We will probably freeze,* Clover thought, *but we're darned lucky to all be here, so what?* "What say we chuck conventions," Nevills suggested, and so they lay side by side for warmth, using life preservers for pillows. "It may sound shocking," Clover wrote in her journal, "but was in good order & certainly necessary." Nevills had been chivalrous in the matter of the life preserver, but now he took the middle position because he was terrified of rattlesnakes. He told the others he'd prefer it if the snakes had to crawl over their bodies to get to him. Gibson, wearing only his shorts, curled up on one side. Clover lay on the other, fully clothed except for her shoes. Her pajamas weren't among the *Botany*'s gear, and, to her regret, she had neither hairbrush nor face cream.

She slept uneasily. Gibson pulled the damp canvas over to his side, and she had nothing to cover herself against the cold. In the darkness Gibson suddenly screamed, "My God!" and Clover and Nevills sat bolt upright, petrified. Clover's first thought was that the *Botany* had torn loose. But it was only a nightmare; Gibson had imagined the river closing over his head, dragging him down. They lay down again, but it was no use. Clover got up and dug through the *Botany*'s gear, desperately looking for something to use as a blanket.

"Is it morning?" Nevills asked.

"Only midnight," she murmured back.

An hour passed. This time Nevills awoke with a start. The river, still rising, had undercut the bank, and their feet dangled over the rushing water. Everyone scrambled back. They remade their beds farther from the edge. Dawn seemed a long way off. Clover's mind wouldn't rest. She felt almost ashamed of herself; part of her reveled in the uncertainty and danger. She was here at last—damp, cold, bone-tired, but *here*, chasing her dream of botanizing the Southwest. Nevills also lay awake, but his thoughts had taken a more miserable turn. A seed of doubt crept into his mind. He had been brimful of confidence that morning, absolutely convinced of his ability to get the party through. Now he wondered if the day's events were a warning to turn back before it was too late. The river's constant roar sounded full of fury. Nevills comforted himself with the thought: he had prepared for this. He was ready. There was nothing to do but carry on.

$$\downarrow\!\!\!W$$

DOWNRIVER IN A THICKET of coyote willows, Jotter, wrapped in a luxurious amount of bedding, woke for a third time to drag her bed back from the rising river. The darkness stretched in every direction, punctured overhead by stars. To her ears, the river whispered and sang, not a threat but a lullaby. She felt the solitude, but didn't fear it. The Colorado River wasn't so bad. She remembered the *Mexican Hat* whisking down the river without anyone at the oars and smiled. *Who needs a boatman?* she thought.

Chapter Five

A BEAUTIFUL PEA-GREEN BOAT

JOTTER WOKE, ALONE. SHE WASHED HER FACE IN the river and carefully applied her makeup. Then she kindled a fire on last night's coals and settled down to wait. An hour or two after sunrise, Harris and Atkinson came climbing over the rocks to her camp. "There's my river pal," Harris said, relieved to find her safe. Jotter warmed to the compliment when he told her how glad he was she hadn't lost her nerve in the rapids the day before. Ten minutes later, Clover, Gibson, and Nevills beached the *Botany* beside the *Wen*. They had gone a little more than three miles in ten minutes, dodging what Clover thought were fifteen- to twenty-foot tall waves. It had been Clover's first opportunity to experience "big water." She found it exhilarating.

After breakfast (boiled venison), they repacked the gear. Nevills gave everyone a stern lecture about being more careful. Then they set off downriver. Most of the rapids in Cataract Canyon had numbers instead of names, and Nevills took the opportunity to put in some last-minute training as they ran through rapids 7, 8, and 9. Gibson was nervous at the oars now, so Atkinson took over much of the rowing. The oarsman needed strength and quick reflexes to keep the boat centered on a safe channel through the rapids, avoiding boulders and hitting the waves square. Atkinson was inclined to crow about his prowess with the boat, but Harris noted quietly in his journal, "The Colo. has bitten us now and we are ready to have much respect for it."

Around 1 p.m., they stopped at the head of the Mile-Long Rapid. It was peppered with pourovers, deceptively smooth-looking humps in the river where the water ran over a submerged boulder. Beyond each one, they knew, the river plunged into a dangerous "hole" that could pound a boat to pieces. Mile-Long Rapid was really a series of eight separate rapids, but at high water it became one long stomach-churning descent. Everyone except Nevills wanted to run it, especially Clover and Jotter. They were afraid Nevills would make them get out and walk. "But," Nevills wrote scathingly, "I won't let my judgement be swayed by incompetent opinions." He decided they would spend the night there and line it the following day. They moored the boats on a narrow sandbar, with numerous rock crannies where they could curl up and sleep.

Everyone bathed, the men upstream, the ladies downstream. Clover and Jotter washed their clothes in the river. Then the women made dinner: ham, peas, spaghetti, and pears out of a can. They had stopped so early there was still time, after all this, to press the plants they had gathered that day. The plant life was generally sparse, dominated by shrubs, cacti, and clumps of grasses scattered over the talus. Only a botanist would recognize its richness and variety. Their camp had a few gnarled netleaf hackberry trees (*Celtis reticulata*), the first they recorded on the journey, with warty trunks and spreading canopies, aquiver with teardrop-shaped leaves. They took a cutting, then turned their attention to flowers called desert prince's plume (*Stanelya pinnata*) and smallflower sandverbena (*Tripterocalyx pedunculatus*). Next, they cataloged grasses with common names like sand ricegrass, lowly woolygrass, mesa dropseed, and six-weeks fescue (so named because it could feed a cow for six weeks after a good rain). Most of these were adapted to drought and shifting sand, but the redroot flatsedge (*Cyperus erythrorhizos*) liked waterways and ditches, and the alkali bulrush (*Scirpus paludosus*) grew strictly in salty wetlands. Clements had named areas like this an ecotone, the edge where different habitats met and mingled—in this case, river and desert. These borderlands revealed tension, as plants suited to one niche butted up

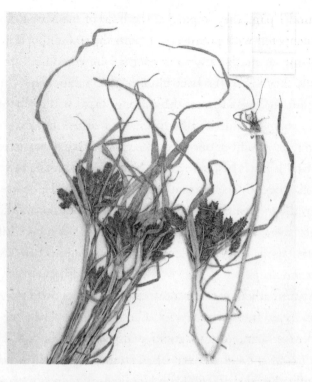

Cyperus erythrorhizos (redroot flatsedge) collected
from Cataract Canyon. *Catalog #1393266, courtesy of
the University of Michigan Herbarium, Clover & Jotter
collection, used by permission*

against their physical limits. Sedges and rushes grew a stone's throw
from the short-jointed beavertail cactus (*Opuntia brachyclada*), with
its flat green paddle-like leaves, and the threespine hedgehog cactus
(*Echinocereus mojavensis*), a tiny stub of a plant so covered in red-and-
white stickers it looked like a firework in the process of exploding.

Some of the plants had stories behind their English names. Earlier in the day, near Jotter's campsite, Clover had taken a sample of
Thompson's woolly locoweed (*Astragalus thompsonae*), a low creep-
ing plant with fuzzy pink seedpods on purplish stems. It was named
for Ellen Thompson, the sister of John Wesley Powell. Thompson
shared her brother's love of exploration. She was married to Almon
Harris Thompson, the topographer who acted as Powell's right-hand

man during his second river trip. Powell had learned something from his first, near-disastrous experience with the Colorado. This time he selected mostly friends and family for the crew and took the journey in stages. Ellen Thompson (who went by Nellie) helped ready the expedition at Green River, Wyoming, in May 1871, and then, with Powell's pregnant wife, Emma Dean, went to Salt Lake City to wait. The women would accompany their husbands downriver only in name: two of the boats were called *Nellie Powell* and *Emma Dean*.

Powell evidently suffered some pangs of conscience, and he left the river in July to visit Emma, returned to run Cataract and Glen canyons, and left again in October to meet his baby daughter, Mary. The expedition broke at the spot that would later be called Lee's Ferry, and most of the men went to Kanab, Utah, to spend the winter. Thompson and Emma joined them in December with the three-month-old baby. Only fragments remain of Thompson's diary, but apparently she spent the next few months collecting plants from the Kaibab Plateau north of the Grand Canyon. Though she was ill much of the time with an unnamed complaint, Thompson gloried in the beauties of nature and joined her husband and brother on long treks through the deserts of northern Arizona and southern Utah. "I never felt more exultant in my life," she wrote after a snowstorm blew over the Kaibab Plateau and turned the world white and glittering. In the course of half a year, she collected more than two hundred varieties of desert plants, sending them by the bundle every few months to Asa Gray at Harvard for cataloging.

In the summer of 1872, Powell and his crew went back to the head of the Grand Canyon to resume the river trip. Thompson went with them and convinced her husband to take her a mile or two downriver through a few riffles, or small rapids. According to Frederick Dellenbaugh, Thompson "enjoyed the exhilaration of descending the swift rushing water." He called her the "most cheerful and resolute explorer of the whole company," but nevertheless, she was left behind when the men set out. (So was her namesake boat, the *Nellie Powell*.) Had she gone, a good portion of Clover's botanizing on the Colorado River would have happened sixty-seven years earlier. At least sixteen of Thompson's plant species turned out to be unknown to Western science, and Clover and Jotter would find several of them, including woolly locoweed, canyonlands prairieclover (*Petalostemon flavescens*), Utah fleabane (*Erigeron utahensis*), and, prettiest of all, the tiny blossoms of froststem suncup (*Oenothera multijuga*), which looked like four-petaled suns rising sleepily from the tumbled boulders.

Clover and Jotter did not have to work in isolation like Thompson, who, according to her obituary, explored wild country for weeks or months without "the sound of another woman's voice." They had so much to collect that they worked well past sundown. Then it was up again at 4:30 a.m. to make breakfast for the crew, moving quietly among their sleeping companions and fumbling at the dishware with cold fingers while dawn pinked the tops of the cliffs and painted them blush and rouge. It was annoying, after all that work, to find the men reluctant to turn out of their bedrolls for a hot breakfast. Clover thought they looked like pupas lined up in a row in their bedrolls. She finally got out her harmonica, more than an hour after sunrise, and blasted a few bars of Reveille, the bugle call used to rouse military troops.

Nevills had not changed his mind about lining the boats around Mile-Long Rapid. Everyone pitched in, bracing the bucking boats from the shore, with the men waist-deep out in the current to wrangle them around rocks. It was difficult work. If they kept the lines short, the boats would bash against boulders. If they let the lines out, the powerful current could snatch them up and capsize them. A misstep on the slippery stones could result in a broken limb. They had to proceed with painful slowness. Heat reflected from the cliffs in palpable waves. Stones bruised their shins. After an hour and a half, they had gone only one hundred feet downriver. After three hours, Nevills reconsidered. They would have to run Mile-Long Rapid after all.

The men left Clover and Jotter with the boats and went down the bank on foot to study the river. The two women set about making lunch. "It is hot as ———," Clover groused in her diary, leaving a long slash in place of a swear word. Finally, Nevills and Gibson returned. Nevills intended to run the *Wen* through, alone. Gibson grabbed his movie camera and walked back to find a vantage point from which to film; Jotter went with him. A sense of dread gripped Clover as she battened the hatches of the *Wen*. Her hands shook as she struck a match to light Nevills's cigarette. "Promise you'll take me on the next run," she said.

Nevills promised.

"Have a good time," Clover said, shaking his hand.

"Be seein' you," he replied, climbing into the *Wen* with the cigarette clamped between his lips. Clover watched him disappear around a bend in the river, trailing white smoke.

It was awful to wait. The hours ticked by: one, then two. No one returned to camp to tell her what had happened. "I have never had such mental anguish," Clover wrote in her journal. After three hours, she decided she had waited long enough. She checked the prow ropes securing the *Botany* and *Mexican Hat,* and, as an added precaution, tied them up by the sterns as well. Then she filled her pockets with peanut brittle and started to walk.

It seemed an age before she found Jotter, fast asleep in the shade of a tree. The two women walked until they found Gibson, who was coming back toward them, lugging his forty-five-pound movie camera and a tripod. They all guzzled muddy river water out of Gibson's felt hat ("tasted like felt hat," Jotter noted). Gibson had a dismal report to make. He had watched Nevills dash through yawning brown waves in the *Wen* and disappear. When Gibson went down to the spot where Nevills planned to land the boat, nobody was there. It did not help anyone's state of mind that Nevills had given to Clover their only river maps, rolled up and tied with a piece of "lucky string," just in case he didn't come back.

"If Norm's dead," Gibson said, "we should abandon the boats and walk out to Moab."

Sixty or seventy miles upriver, on foot, through the mazed and crazy country called the Land of Standing Rocks—wasn't that a cheery thought? Gibson declared they should wait for Atkinson and Harris to return with news. Clover refused and started walking downriver.

Disconsolate, the others trailed after her.

$$\Downarrow$$

MILE-LONG RAPID, as Nevills likely knew, had an alarming history. More than one earlier expedition had met misfortune at that spot. The second expedition to run Cataract Canyon after John Wesley Powell was financed by a Colorado banker named Frank Mason Brown. Brown had a dream: he was going to build a railroad down the length of the Colorado River.

Railroads followed the natural downgrade of lazy, looping rivers in many parts of the United States, so perhaps Brown shouldn't be blamed for this laughable idea. The Colorado wasn't like any river he knew. Even if railroad track could be laid on the narrow (and sometimes nonexistent) land between the river and the cliff walls, floods and landslides would have surely chewed it to pieces. But Brown didn't worry about that. He only imagined a way to deliver valuable coal from the Rocky Mountains to California. In 1889 he hired a civil engineer named Robert Brewster Stanton to survey Cataract, Glen, and Grand canyons, ordered six boats, and unloaded them at the train station in Green River, Utah.

Stanton was a meticulous man with a severe mustache, neatly trimmed beard, and a crippled right arm which made it impossible for him to swim. He had serious misgivings when he saw the boats, flimsy cedar craft so stuffed with provisions there was barely room for the crew. One thing was missing from the supplies, however: life preservers. Fourteen men had signed up for the expedition, including two cooks, George Gibson and Henry Richards, the first Black men on record to attempt to run the Colorado River. "But it was not our purpose to explore the canyons," Stanton wrote later, "or to dash through the rapids, for the glory of its accomplishment." It was a "serious undertaking of a perilous railroad survey," but it turned out to be a far more serious undertaking than Stanton had imagined. The crew limped their way through Cataract Canyon, driving survey stakes and meeting with one problem after another. The clumsy raft that held a third of their food in watertight boxes splintered into bits. A boat broke up and sank at rapid 6. By the time the expedition reached the head of Mile-Long Rapid, much of their food had been taken by the river and they were lunching on three lumps of sugar apiece and a cup of river water. But the Colorado was not finished with them yet. At Mile-Long Rapid, the river smashed one boat on a rock and ripped the floorboards from another. The crew had to cannibalize the pieces to cobble together a floatable craft.

The men emerged from Cataract Canyon demoralized and hungry. The group split; half stayed to survey Glen Canyon while the others went ahead. Stanton, Brown, and six other men entered the Grand Canyon on July 9. The next day, eleven miles downstream from Lee's Ferry, Brown was tossed into the river and sank beneath the churning waves. He never reappeared. Unable to locate his body, the crew scratched an epitaph into the sandstone and went on. Six days later another boat capsized. Its occupants, Richards and Peter Hansbrough, were dragged into the rain-swollen torrent and drowned. Stanton abandoned the ill-fated survey and the missing bodies of his companions. With the four remaining crewmen, he left the boats and climbed up a side canyon toward the rim to escape the Grand Canyon. A thunderstorm caught them halfway. Looking up through the relentless sheets of water, it seemed to Stanton as if the entire upper edge of the canyon had begun to move toward them. Boulders, tossed like dice in the grip of a landslide, shattered into pieces as they passed. The landslide narrowly missed the cowering men, and afterward, a "deathlike stillness" fell.

So much for that trip. Stanton completed the work that winter at his own expense, relaunching in Glen Canyon and boating to the sea, thus doubling the number of people on record who had successfully traversed the Grand Canyon. Just two of the original crew returned with him. Nobody died this time, though the photographer fell from

a precipice and shattered his leg so badly he had to be evacuated to
the rim during a freak snowstorm. Somehow, Stanton remained opti-
mistic about the railroad line: it was "neither impossible nor imprac-
ticable," he wrote, and a whole series of track, tunnels, bridges, and
hydroelectric dams could be completed for a reasonable $51 million.
Nothing ever came of it: the railroad was never built.

Meticulous engineer that he was, Stanton was not immune to the
influence of canyon country. Sometimes it seemed to him, walking
through the weird blue shadows in moonlight or the surreal shifting of lavender and pink in the day, that the canyon walls wanted
to close in overhead and tumble down upon him, crushing his body
to atoms. He confessed he sometimes let his imagination "run riot"
with his thoughts. This was happening to Clover now, as she hurried
downriver in search of Nevills. Her mind was in a wretched state. She
could barely pay attention to where she put her feet. She descended
one rocky gorge and climbed up another, jumping over boulders and
snagging her feet on polished branches of driftwood strewn like a
game of pick-up sticks on the shore. Gibson's dour silence was worse
than his predictions. It was hard not to dwell on his conviction that
Nevills was dead.

Relief filled Clover when she spotted two figures coming toward
them. "You're alive," she shouted. "Sure," replied Nevills, surprised.
He had overshot his intended landing place but brought the *Wen* successfully through Mile-Long Rapid, and now he and Harris planned
to bring the *Botany* and the *Mexican Hat* down as well. Clover
reminded Nevills of his promise that morning: she wanted to go with
him. She couldn't bear to stand on the shore and wait. But Nevills
shook his head, no. He estimated that the current dashed along at
twenty miles an hour, and the waves loomed twenty feet—at least,
it felt that way, and he had landed with six inches of water in the
bottom of the *Wen*. Too wild for the women, he thought. Instead, he
left Clover, Jotter, and Gibson strung along the shoreline at strategic
points to take photographs.

An hour later, Jotter, poised with her camera, saw the *Botany* come bucking through. The boat was tiny in the viewfinder of the camera, and "it most killed me not to see exactly what was happening," she wrote. Harris came next in the *Mexican Hat*, charting his own course instead of following the *Botany*'s line. For a moment, Jotter was sure a wave had swamped his boat. Then they were gone, whisked round the bend. Her exhaustion lifted, Jotter ran downriver after them, jumping from rock to rock. She found them triumphant, all three boats lined up in a row.

"Well, we were very happy to all be together again & unharmed," wrote Clover in her journal. When she watched Harris disappear into the waves she had become violently ill; now assured of everyone's safety, she crept under a bush and cried out of sheer relief. Embarrassed, she told the others it was only the blowing sand reddening her eyes. No one seemed to want to stray too far from the camp. The men huddled over a map of the river, and Clover and Jotter started on dinner ("tired as we were," Jotter wrote): vegetable soup, fruit cocktail, and tea. The water noisily sloshing on the sandbar seemed less like a river's unhurried rhythm and more like breakers on an ocean—but unlike the ocean's long rollers, the waves crested and crashed one after the other without a pause. There was no escaping the cacophony. It seemed amazing that the river could get any higher. It had risen during the day, to nearly 60,000 cfs. But it could get higher, and wilder, as the jam of logs and boulders at their campsite attested. A flood four times that high had come down the Colorado in 1884. (Lee's Ferry had no gauging station at the time, but a cat took refuge from the flood in the crook of an apple tree and an engineer used its perch to estimate the floodwaters at 250,000 cfs.) In the distant past, torrents of 500,000 cfs had come roaring down. This was how the Colorado's canyons had formed: not incrementally, grain by grain, but under the impatient sculpting of massive floods.

The men scrubbed up for dinner. The narrow sandbar had no room for privacy, so Jotter and Clover politely gazed at the river while their companions changed into fresh clothes, Harris with a price tag still dangling from his trousers. "It seems very informal," Clover wrote, "but there's absolutely no feeling of indecency. We are a very compact little unit in a 'wild, untamed, unrelenting world.' People who have not fought with such elements can't realize how petty & trivial are the things 2/3 of us do in civilization."

The women were too tired to collect plants that night. "Sore feet and blind staggers!" Jotter dashed off in her journal by way of explanation, and they dropped into bed.

THE DAYS BEGAN TO BLUR. They ran the river, reconnoitered, and ran again. They had blisters on their hands and feet, and cuts and bruises everywhere. They set up camp on slopes so steep the dishes slipped and clattered off the angled stones, and they had to build balustrades of rock to keep from rolling down to the river in their sleep. Gibson's nightmares continued. The soles of Clover's shoes came off.

Unbeknownst to Clover, Nevills had begun to form his own opinion of their "compact little unit," and it wasn't flattering. "The women are standing up beautifully so far," he recorded, but he had a complaint about every one of the men. Atkinson was sneering and unpleasant, and Gibson in a "blue funk." Only Harris could be trusted to handle a boat in big water, but he didn't follow orders and seemed intent on going his own way.

The women seemed determined never to complain about the hard work or danger. They told no one when a riptide caught them one evening, while they were bathing in privacy around a bend in the river, though it had dragged them beneath the water at a frightening speed. Just as Clover had told no one, some days earlier, when she'd sustained a small injury: she had been gripping the neck of a wounded goose for Nevills to dispatch with a belt buckle, and he missed his aim. She never made a sound, so Nevills didn't know he'd taken a chunk of skin off her knuckles. Evidently, neither woman felt a desire for praise or sympathy from their male companions. If they came to the Colorado to prove their courage, it was only to themselves.

They reached a bad spot on the river, too dangerous to run, too difficult to line. They laid driftwood skids up the steep side of a hill, unloaded the boats, and dragged them. It was grueling work in the frightful heat, with loose stones to dodge and pink rattlesnakes spiraled in the sand, waiting for an unwary heel. Nevills fretted that the women were taking on too much of the "heavy work." Once—just once—Jotter wondered if she had made a mistake in coming down here. Then she thought: *You got yourself into this. Nobody made you come.* They had to portage all the supplies around the rapid, including the eight-point rack of the dead deer, a plucked and naked goose, and a stack of rat traps. Atkinson still intended to collect specimens to taxidermy for his museum in Michigan. The others were amused. No one complained about the smell.

Every night they scooped up a bucketful of river water and left it to settle. Every morning they found three inches of mud at the bottom, and the water not appreciably clearer. Drinking it left their mouths lined with clay and their teeth gritty. Everyone grew nauseous, from the heat or the work or the unfiltered water. Prescription: a shot of whiskey. Jotter crawled weakly from her bedroll one night and vomited into a bush.

After a while, even the rocks seemed to ripple and heave.

"You've no idea how difficult it is," Clover wrote in her journal one day, "to keep the mind on mere plants when the river is roaring & the boats are struggling to get thru." But they had plants to catalog; that was why they had come. They found a lone Rocky Mountain juniper (*Juniperus scopulorum*), less than two feet tall and growing many feet below its typical elevation, an example of the relict flora Clover hoped to catalog. Four-wing saltbush (*Atriplex canescens*) was abundant, with spoon-shaped leaves covered in protective scales, giving it a dandruffy look. Mormon tea (*Ephedra torreyana*) grew high on the talus slopes, a shrub made up of spindly, blue-green stalks, sprouting tiny cones at the joints. Less frequently, there were wildflowers like desert trumpet, a spray of dry-looking twigs that flowered into a galaxy of tiny stars; narrowleaf four o'clock, a riot of purple petals; and prickly poppies, soft and white as a wedding dress but covered in spines. They found Russian thistle (*Salsola kali*), too, lots of it. Known more poetically as wind witch or tumbleweed, it had been accidently introduced from Russia in bushels of flaxseed in the 1870s. Poor Stanton had burned the stuff in campfires while trying to evacuate his wounded friend in the snowstorm. They flared up merrily, he wrote, but offered "little more heat than could be produced from burning a sheet of newspaper."

Clover found tumbleweed everywhere in Cataract Canyon, growing in roundish clumps and still green, not yet dried into their iconic skeleton shapes. The wind would tear up the globe-like structures and send them bouncing across the landscape, scattering seeds as they went. That quirk of their reproductive cycle made them an excellent example of successful evolution, and also a favorite trope of the so-called "Wild West." Gene Autry had starred as a singing cowboy in a 1935 film called *Tumbling Tumbleweeds*. Novelist Zane Grey's romanticized cowboy characters felt their spirits lift at the sight of tumbleweeds driven before the wind.

But the plant that delighted writers and moviemakers worried botanists, so much so that the U.S. Department of Agriculture sent a survey in 1892 to farmers in seven Midwestern states to find out how far it had spread, and whether it was regarded as a "really troublesome weed." The conclusion was that tumbleweed had managed to cover 35,000 square miles in just two decades after its introduction, at a speed that "far exceeds that of any weed known in America." A single plant could weigh as much as a small dog and swell to the dimensions of a large steer, bearing hundreds of thousands of seeds in its hollow belly. It hitched rides on railroads, stowaway seeds tucked into the straw bedding of cattle cars. It crossed rivers on ferries. It crowded out crops, clogged up machinery, and so irritated the legs of livestock that farmers in infested fields took to dressing their horses in high boots or leggings. Tumbleweeds caught fire and bounced over the firebreaks meant to protect buildings, shedding sparks. On windy days they could bust down fences, their sheer numbers more effective than the battering hooves of wild ponies. North Dakota's frosts didn't slow them down, nor did Utah's hot weather. They thrived on disturbance, and there was plenty of that in canyon country. Boulders brought down by floods and landslides sheltered small nooks where plants could take root, at least until the next flood. Tumbleweed, Clover noticed, was almost always the first plant to arrive.

That tumbleweed grew in Cataract Canyon, with few people and no railroads or ferries to help it spread (despite Stanton's best efforts) was a testament to its tenacity and efficient design. It was also a hint that human influence over ecosystems had by the 1930s extended far beyond anyone's intent or expectation. It was not the only such hint they would discover. But Jotter, too, found it difficult to keep her mind on "mere plants." Her journal, like the river, took on a different character now that she was on the Colorado. So full of plants in the early days of the expedition, now it fixated on the novelty of river life: trying to cook; trying to bathe; trying to change clothes in the privacy of her bedroll; all the daily domestic concerns of making camp and breaking camp. Only one topic consumed her more. That was running the rapids.

⩔

THEY AWOKE ON THE MORNING of June 29 to the sound of a landslide in the distance, raising a cloud of powdery white dust. Progress had been slow the past week. They had covered less than fifteen miles since reaching the confluence of the Green and Colorado. But the water level had dropped over the past few days, and in the glow of the evening campfire everyone felt their spirits rise, "and it seems it isn't such a bad world after all," wrote Harris. Then the rain came. The crew huddled under tarps as sheets of cold water came down, plinging into the river's rush with a sound like dropping marbles. Within thirty minutes the flat, square rock where they had curled up to sleep was awash in stormwater. In the wet darkness they got up and rigged a lean-to barricaded with life preservers, which were soon full of charred holes from flying embers.

Rain-swollen, the river began to rise again. They reached Gypsum Creek Rapid around 1 p.m. that afternoon, their tenth day on the river. As the *Wen* approached the lip of the rapid, Nevills turned the boat's nose to the shore, intending to pull aside. Too late. The current dragged them relentlessly toward the rapid's lip. Nevills stood up on the deck to try to read the water ahead. This was something strange: the river seemed to disappear. He could see a deceptive smoothness in the water ahead, and a ripple—and then, nothing. The boat rushed toward that rim and then, all at once, a mushroom wave reared, shedding its disguise. Its top splayed out wider than its base, and its surface was a sinister, oily black. Clover called out in alarm. Nevills made a split-second decision: he rammed the oars into the water and pivoted the boat to the starboard side, where the river dashed against the cliff. They missed the mushroom. Another hole yawned, and the bottom seemed to drop out of the world.

Looking over her shoulder, Clover saw the *Botany* with Atkinson and Gibson enter Gypsum Creek Rapid stern-first and disappear into the mushroom wave. Her next glimpse showed the *Botany* standing upright on the water, flipped end over end. The thought crossed her mind that the boat caught in the claws of the river was a beautiful sight, if only it hadn't been so dangerous. The boat reappeared, upside-down. Atkinson clung to the hull somehow, but Gibson was gone, swept into the river—his nightmare come true.

In the eddy below Gypsum Creek Rapid, Nevills struggled to turn the *Wen* toward the capsized boat. They reached it. Clover, leaning over the edge, caught hold of Atkinson's hand, then grabbed the *Botany's* rope. They swept onward, into the next rapid.

"Whatever you do, Elzie, hang on to that rope!" Nevills shouted.

The shoreline was close, only six feet away. Atkinson clambered from his insecure perch on the hull of the *Botany* into the *Wen,* and Nevills handed him the oars. Then Nevills took hold of the *Wen's* rope and jumped into the water. He intended to swim for shore and anchor both boats, but the rope tore through his fingers and was gone. Horrified, Clover and Atkinson swept back into the current in the *Wen*, the *Botany* bobbing along in their wake. Clover's mind turned in circles. A silly childhood ditty ran through her thoughts:

The Owl and the Pussy-cat went to sea in a beautiful pea-green boat . . .
Atkinson forced the *Wen* into an eddy, but the *Botany* jerked sideways and tugged them out into the current again.
They took some honey, and plenty of money . . .
The stern of the boat thrust into a curling wave and broke through the other side. A waterfall of foam, mud, and river water pounded down on top of them.
. . . and plenty of money, wrapped up in a five-pound note.
Crash! Another wave swamped the boat. Something underwater grabbed one of the oars, a rock or a helical current twisting it with bruising force. The round metal oarlock bent, trapping the oar and rendering it useless. "Cut me the spare!" Atkinson shouted. "Hurry!"
The Owl looked up to the stars above . . .
Clover couldn't find the knife. It had fallen from its place into the bottom of the boat. She scrambled in the bilgewater until she felt the handle. *And hand in hand, on the edge of the sand . . .* The boat tipped, down, down, down into the trough of a wave. Out again into blinding sunlight. Then down again into the next billow. Clover cut the spare oar free and handed it to Atkinson. She began to bail water, one-handed. The *Botany*'s rope in her other hand tugged cruelly at her fingers. *They danced by the light of the moon, the moon . . .*
Clover listened to the river's dull, hollow boom. Her thoughts turned to Dark Canyon Rapid, though it was still miles ahead. It had an ominous reputation: a rapid strewn with boulders and running hard against a cliff, which Holmstrom thought the worst in Cataract Canyon. In that moment, it must have seemed possible they would never get the boat to shore, sweeping on down the river until it swallowed them. Clover's thoughts went numb. *No*, she thought, *no, no, no . . .*

JOTTER AND HARRIS IN THE *MEXICAN HAT* were the last to enter Gypsum Creek Rapid. Jotter felt her stomach drop as they tipped into a hole, slipping down five vertical feet in an instant. Twice Harris lost the oars and recovered them again. It was a fine fight, and Jotter enjoyed it, until she saw the round hull of the overturned *Botany* ahead. Her stomach dropped again, this time not because of the rapid. Someone—she couldn't quite see who—was clinging to the hull, and someone else bobbed in the water, buoyed by a life preserver.

Harris pulled toward the figure in the water. It was Gibson, battered, breathless, and nearly spent from trying to stay afloat, his black stocking cap smooshed into a peak by the waves. Jotter climbed onto the prow and grabbed him, hauling him into the boat. Harris turned for shore. As they landed, Jotter happened to glance up. She thought she could make out the *Wen* sweeping around a curve and out of sight. Was that two people aboard, or three?

On shore, Gibson held onto the *Mexican Hat*'s rope and gradually regained his breath while Jotter scooped water out of the boat. Gibson had nearly kicked his shoes off in the water and was now relieved he kept them on, as he contemplated walking barefoot the rest of the way. Harris went downriver and returned: no sign of the others. They got back into the *Mexican Hat* and headed downriver. Soon they spotted Nevills on the left bank, waving his arms to get their attention.

After jumping into the water, Nevills had spent a frantic ten minutes running down the shoreline after the *Wen*. Two miles down, an impassable cliff stopped his progress. This is where Harris, Gibson, and Jotter found him. With the four of them crammed into the *Mexican Hat* ("felt like a blooming ferry," Jotter thought) they continued downriver, as far as Clearwater Canyon. They would reunite there, Nevills thought. They could camp for the night before tackling Clearwater Rapid. It was now nearly 6 p.m. Soon the light would fade.

They reached Clearwater. Clover and Atkinson weren't there.

🌱

CLOVER'S MEMORY OF THE RIDE, later, would be impossibly hazy. She couldn't be sure what rapids they'd run, or what the scenery looked like. She could hardly spare a thought for Nevills, though somewhere in the back of her mind she worried that she'd never seen him reach the safety of dry land. Even the vague foreboding that she and Atkinson couldn't possibly make it through the rapids alive didn't bother her at the time. Her world had narrowed. Bail water. Hold the *Botany*'s rope. Cling to the *Wen*. Bail. Breathe. Again.

They came through seven or eight rapids in roughly six miles, towing the upturned boat. After Clearwater, Atkinson turned the *Wen* toward an eddy in yet another attempt to reach shore. Clover, determined, stood up on the stern deck of the *Wen* and coiled the boat's rope in one hand. She handed the *Botany*'s rope to Atkinson and said, "For God's sake, hang on to it."

She jumped. She had misjudged the distance from the shore and plunged down into a dark, swirling world; the water closed over her head. Then she broke the surface, gasping, and her hands found purchase on a rock. She dragged herself out of the water and snubbed the *Wen*'s rope around a boulder. Turning around, she saw Atkinson floundering in the water—he had panicked when he saw Clover vanish in the river and jumped after her, losing the *Botany*'s rope in the process. The boat was just beginning to slide out into the current again when Atkinson, groping in the muddy river, located the end. The boats were safe, and so were they.

Exhausted, the two of them sat on the sandbar and contemplated their bruises. Atkinson had a bad gash on his leg. Clover rolled up her pants and found a six-inch purple splotch on her thigh. She couldn't remember how she got it. There was no way of knowing what had happened to Nevills or Gibson, struggling in the river's current the last they'd seen them, or whether the *Mexican Hat* had made it through. "Whoever sees the boat first," Clover bargained, "gets an ice cream soda from the other." They shook on the bet and settled down to wait.

$$\psi$$

JOTTER COULDN'T EXPLAIN WHY, even to herself, but she had a feeling everyone was okay. Nevills didn't share her confidence. He lined the *Mexican Hat* around Clearwater Rapid (he thought no chances whatsoever could be taken now) and then handed the oars over to Harris. Hunched in the overcrowded boat, his thoughts raced. Clover and Atkinson could be dead. Or alive, but badly wounded. Or the boats had been lost, and all their supplies. The river could kill them a hundred different ways—quick by drowning, slow by starvation.

The late light was slanting from the west, shadows deepening, by the time they rounded a bend in the river and spotted the cheerful glow of a campfire. Atkinson, who saw them first and won the bet, jumped up and waved. The *Botany* (still upside-down) and the *Wen* bobbed in the shallows, unharmed. "Much rejoicing," Jotter declared at the reunion, "and Elzie and Gene the heroes of the hour." Everyone crowded round, giddy with relief, swapping stories. But Nevills couldn't join their celebration. His nightmare scenarios haunted him. He had brought a group of greenhorns onto the Colorado River, and everyone wondered what the newspapers would say if an empty boat or two washed up at Lee's Ferry without its passengers. "I sometimes wish I had never gone on this trip, at least as expedition leader," Nevills confided miserably to his diary that night. He couldn't shake the feeling that his career as a riverman was over.

Chapter Six

DELAYED

THE 1871 BOOK IN WHICH EDWARD LEAR FIRST published "The Owl and the Pussy-Cat" contained, along with nonsense stories and poems for children, several pages of "nonsense botany." It's easy to imagine a young Elzada Clover poring over those pages, delighting in the elegant, whimsical line drawings of fictional plants: *Bottlephorkia spoonifolia,* with its cutlery-shaped blossoms and leaves, or *Piggiwiggia pyramidalis,* a tall stem stuck over with blossoms shaped like miniscule piglets, or *Fishia marina,* sprouting fish-shaped flowers.

But Lear's nonsense plants could hardly be stranger than the botany Clover was now cataloging on the Colorado River. There were zombie grasses that lay dead and brown all through the heat of summer, only to spring up greenly in fall. There were parasitic plants that drew water and nutrients from a host, such as the clump of desert mistletoe clinging to a tree, or the innocent-looking Indian paintbrush which sent sneaky root tendrils underground to steal from its neighbors. Plants here knew how to deal with droughts that lasted months and floods that tore through in moments. They staved off browsing animals with acid and spines. They handled too much salt by stuffing it into small liquid-filled sacs. Four-wing saltbush (*Atriplex canescens*) could change its sex (swapping pollen for ovules, the structures that develop into seeds, or vice versa) and some plants of this species found this so much to their advantage they did it every year. Porcupinegrass (*Stipa spartea*) planted its own seeds by dropping javelin-shaped awns headfirst into the dirt, where they spun counterclockwise like an auger, a rare form of reproduction known as geocarpy. These were the "endless forms most beautiful and most wonderful" Darwin had described. He might have added "most bizarre."

The morning after their misadventure in Gypsum Creek Rapid, they spread out the food and bedding to dry in the sun. Perhaps the hatches were not so waterproof, after all. The matches were soaked, and so was Gibson's movie camera, which added to his misery. He repaired the camera's smashed shutter as best he could with a screwdriver and a rock. Nevills was jittery. Atkinson and Clover nursed their scrapes and bruises. Only Jotter and Harris had survived the events of the previous day without any shock to their spirits. Nobody felt much like heading downriver to get a good look at Dark Canyon Rapid. Instead, they decided to lay over for the day.

The canyon was now fringed with exotic tamarisk (*Tamarix gallica*) and coyote willow (*Salix exigua*), and the river's edge was thick with hackberries, Western redbuds (*Cercis occidentalis*), and tall broomlike shrubs called seep willows (*Baccharis emoryi*). Singleleaf ash (*Fraxinus anomala*) grew nearby, its round leaves poking up above the brush like vivid green flags. Less common, horsetail or scouring rush (*Equisetum praealtum*) made dense thickets of upright green spears. It was an ancient plant whose ancestors had dominated the Jurassic, with hollow green stems you could pull into pieces. Clover took copious notes, as usual, but apparently collected no specimens here. It was a day of recuperation and "minor odds & ends," as Harris put it. Jotter tried to swim in the slackwater, but a beaver, resenting the intrusion, chased her back to shore. They all crowded into the shade of a big hackberry tree to rest and doze through the worst of the heat. Clover read aloud from Clyde Eddy's book, *Down the World's Most Dangerous River*.

It was not a story calculated to raise their spirits. Eddy had run the Colorado River in the summer of 1927 with a crew of college students, an Airedale dog named Rags, and a bear cub named Cataract. He'd gone to make a movie—a documentary of river running—funded out of his own pocket and, ominously, by the company that made a topical antiseptic called Mercurochrome to treat cuts and bruises. Cuts and bruises there would be aplenty, or worse. By Eddy's count, twenty-nine people had died in Cataract Canyon since Stanton went down the river in 1889, and nine expeditions had wrecked there. Nobody in Eddy's crew died, though they had more than one "narrow squeak," in his words. When they tried to line the boats around Dark Canyon Rapid, one got away and dragged a man underwater. Later, a taut boat line caught another man round the neck and almost strangled him. The men jettisoned equipment as they went, leaving, strewn on the rocks behind them, items that had once seemed essential for survival and now were reckoned as dead weight. Worst of all, Eddy woke one night in Cataract Canyon to see the boats pounding against the rocks and the kitchen dishes floating away. The crew hauled their gear out of the flood's path, just in time. Unsurprisingly, three men abandoned the expedition at Lee's Ferry. A fourth literally jumped ship just a few miles into the Grand Canyon and ran away, not even pausing to pick up his duffel bag.

Eddy never made the movie, but he did write a book about his adventures. He was a superb storyteller and a master of embellishment, unfortunately for the little crowd listening to Clover read aloud. "Danger crowds upon danger," Eddy wrote. "Every move is a menace, nearly every breath a strain—and not to move means disaster." How could they not apply Eddy's words to their own circumstances? They had to go slowly, and yet could not go slowly. Too long on the river and they would run short of food. They set out again on July 1, running down to the mouth of Dark Canyon Rapid and then (like Eddy) lining the boats around it. Jotter kept thinking about her brother Walter and his fiancée, Virginia, who were getting married in Ohio that day with all the Jotter family in attendance—everybody except her. Jotter didn't know it, but Walter had intentionally planned his wedding date to coincide with his sister's river trip. He hoped it would distract their parents from the danger she was in.

The distraction turned out to be necessary, for they were due at Lee's Ferry on July 4, and they weren't going to make it.

Atkinson, riding with a nervous Gibson in the *Botany*, took over more and more of the rowing. They moved through a world of water and stone. Blooms of sacred datura unfurled white trumpets, intoxicating, heady. Cicadas droned monotonous lullabies from hidden perches, like an orchestra with nothing but cellos. Mule deer came down to the river in groups of two or three, and bighorn sheep perched on ledges above, buff-and-brown pelts almost indistinguishable from the cliff walls. Enormous horns curled back from their soft, delicate heads. Clover and Jotter saw not "the wild sheep of God," in the writer Mary Austin's words, but seed-carriers for plants. Fat cactus seeds, not suited for wind transport, fell into the canyon from the high walls and moved from place to place via the hooves or dung of animals. They took root. Too close to the river's edge, floods washed them out. Too far from the water, they scorched in the sun. Withering and dying cacti proved that even the toughest plants sometimes failed to adapt.

They spotted the names of travelers who had made it this far painted on the canyon wall. BUZZ HOLMSTROM still shone bright and fresh, an unwelcome reminder of his declaration: "Women do not belong in the Canyon of the Colorado." Eight miles below this point, they found another precipice inscribed with names: THE EDDY EXPDTN, badly faded, and HYDE with a date below: November 1, 1928. Bessie and Glen Hyde had not lived to see December. While the others laboriously unloaded and lined the boats around a rapid, Atkinson took a can of white paint and added NEVILLS EXPEDITION to the cliff, with all six of their names below. Jotter winced at the defacement, but didn't voice an objection.

Were they inscribing a record of accomplishment, or an epitaph?

They camped that night at the mouth of the Dirty Devil River. The jumbled, pale, sloping walls of Cataract Canyon broke abruptly here. Tomorrow they would enter Glen Canyon, with rounded sweeps of red sandstone to guide the boats the last 170 miles to Lee's Ferry. Harris, sitting by the campfire with Nevills, expressed doubts about the

Sclerocactus parviflorus (smallflower fishhook cactus) collected from Glen Canyon. *Courtesy of United States National Herbarium, Smithsonian Institution, used by permission*

journey for the first time. His job transfer to Salt Lake City started on July 28. If the expedition continued to muddle along with no more momentum than driftwood, he wouldn't make it in time. They had gone just forty-seven miles since the confluence of the Green and Colorado rivers, in the span of ten days.

Nevills was worried. If Harris broke at Lee's Ferry, he would lose his best boatman. Gibson hated to row, and Atkinson had suffered from nosebleeds ever since the bad run of Gypsum Creek Rapid. At this rate, with the long hard work of portaging around rapids in the Grand Canyon ahead, they would reach Boulder Dam three weeks behind schedule.

They all took the time to spruce up a bit. The men bathed and shaved the stubble from their chins. The women did their laundry and hung it to dry on a massive log washed up on the sandbar. Clover had taken to carrying a can of tobacco and a box of matches in her pocket for the benefit of Nevills, whose temper was frayed. "The men depend on Lois & me for so many little things," she wrote in her diary. "Mirrors, combs, finding shirts, first aid, etc. Just as men always have since Adam." They had dinner to cook, and botany to do. Slender lip-fern (*Cheilanthes feei*) leaned over the river's edge as if trying to catch its own lacy reflection. Southwestern false cloak fern (*Notholaena limitanea*), too, grew in cracks among the rocks. They sampled it all, and made note of the Gambel oaks (*Quercus gambelii*) with their glossy green acorns, and the stubby clumps of skunkbush. Climbing over a perilous ledge, Clover came across a squadron of squat hedgehog cacti, at least two hundred of them. They had curious orange spines. *Echinocereus coccineus,* she wrote in her journal, and then crossed it out and tried several other names, before adding a question mark and the notation: "possibly new." She dug up a specimen, roots and all. It would be best to get a living sample back to Michigan.

The light faded. Darkling beetles scuttled over the sand, rumps raised skyward. Antlions lay concealed at the bottom of tiny sand-pits, pincers at the ready, waiting for the unwary ant to stumble into the trap and become dinner. Everywhere a pageant of life and death played out, on a stage no bigger than a sandbar. All day they'd run the river beneath a cloudless sky, the cliffs rising ocher and mauve around them. All night the river rose by inches, as if drawn mothlike toward the moon. *Beautiful country,* Clover thought. Others thought so, too. The whole area—the lower Green River, Cataract and Glen canyons—was under consideration to join the national park system as a monument, an area set aside for its historic and scientific impor-tance. But not everyone who had come here admired the beauty, or the plants. There were some who were determined, one way or another, to transform that muddy river into gold.

WITH ITS QUIET WATER and secretive tributaries, Glen Canyon was the sweet one, stuck between the scowling big siblings of Cataract and Grand. The river was slow here, even sluggish. It curved and bent around sandstone spires, wearing long trailing shawls of cottonwoods and willows on its shoulders. Scrub oak grew higher on the terraces. Springs of clear water ran down sandstone jeweled with moss. Glen Canyon had a rich and storied human history. Ancestral Puebloans had built stone houses there and tended crops of maize, squash, and beans. They carved roads into the steep rock walls—pathways made of hand- and footholds, no more than four inches deep. Later, Navajos and Paiutes deepened those staircases and added trails for their stock. White fur trappers came and stripped the river of its beaver and otter. Mormon settlers crossed and recrossed the river, finding traction for their wagon wheels on the most unlikely clefts of stone. At one time, Glen Canyon even had a town of sorts, a place named Hite that sprang up in advance of a brief and busy gold rush.

You could cross the river at Hite—at least, if you knew how to swim. Where the river came out into the open, a great fin of sandstone thrust up on the right, like the bony backplate of some primordial monster making its way so slowly through the crust of the earth that birds had time to build nests in its wrinkles. Briefly, the river wound through a sheltered bottomland, all mud and willows, before it plunged into the canyon again. In 1883, a white settler named Cass Hite, guided by a Navajo chief called Hoskininni, found fine flakes of gold near this place, really just powder washed down in the glacial sediment that tumbled from the Rocky Mountains during the last Ice Age. Within a decade, several hundred people had rushed to the spot, loaded down with panniers, tin pans, and hope. One of them was Robert Brewster Stanton. He hadn't found any willing investors for his railroad scheme, so now he returned to the Colorado River to make his fortune another way. Stanton was a big dreamer: no scrabbling in the mud with tin pans for him. He wanted to build dredges. Maybe dams, too: a whole series of dams to generate electricity to power the dredges. He expected to make millions in gold.

Stanton hauled the pieces for his first dredge by wagon to Glen Canyon and assembled it. It began operating early in 1901. Dubbed the *Hoskaninni,* the dredge was over one hundred feet long and looked something like a floating hotel, with a double-storied row of windows and forty-six buckets on a kind of conveyor belt. The buckets plunged into the river and came up bearing loads of gravel and rock. They dumped their contents through a screen and then onto tables coated in mercury, which trapped the fine gold. Next, the mercury would be heated and vaporized, leaving gold dust behind. The dredge cost Stanton's investors $100,000 and, after three months of work, yielded exactly $66.95 in gold. Bankrupt, the whole company sold for a measly $200 less than a year after work began. Miners stripped the dredge of its lumber to build rafts and shacks or burn in bonfires. Its skeleton remained in the river to rust.

Hite faded to a ghost town during World War I, nothing more than a few ramshackle buildings made of driftwood and rapidly turning back to driftwood again. But in the 1930s a Mormon named Arthur Chaffin settled there with his wife, Phoebe, with the idea of bulldozing a road to the place and opening it up to tourists in motorcars. It was a difficult place to reach on foot and the Chaffins could hardly have expected many travelers to come by river. They must have been surprised one sunny July morning to see four hungry-eyed men and two women come walking through their cornfield, their shoes worn to tatters.

A skinny brown dog came wagging up to Jotter in delight. The Chaffins greeted everyone kindly and filled their canteens with fresh, clean water, sweeter than ambrosia after so many days of choking on grit and sludge from the river. The six travelers lingered so long that, eventually, the Chaffins issued an invitation to lunch. Atkinson was annoyed. He thought Nevills had delayed on purpose, long after they should have gone, in the hope of scoring a home-cooked meal. This was true, though Nevills may have had their fast-diminishing food supplies in mind. At any rate, nobody complained when lunch was served. Clover helped make it, perhaps unable to stop herself after so long in charge of the cooking. There were tomatoes, lettuce, and onions from the garden, corn canned from last year's harvest, tinned beef, cheese, and coffee. Best of all, homemade bread slathered in grape preserves, a welcome change after weeks of rye crackers. They fell on the food "just like pigs at a trough," Jotter wrote, "except we didn't shove—much."

It was late afternoon when they said farewell to the Chaffins and climbed back into the boats. Jotter took the oars of the *Mexican Hat* so Harris could sit on the stern deck and spread out their supply of Grape-Nuts to dry in the sun. The cereal had turned into unappetizing brown clumps after their upset at Gypsum Creek Rapid five days before, damp in the center and starting to mold. They couldn't afford to throw it away, so it had to be redried and pounded into bite-sized bits. Jotter was sick of the stuff.

They had come too late for the redbud bloom, magenta flowers so gaudy no interior designer would ever choose the color. But the heart-shaped leaves of the redbud trees looked lovely against the rosy cliffs: deep green with a hint of blue. Canyon wrens tipped their heads skyward and sang, starting high and descending low in a tumbling cascade of notes, as if trying to stir up the still water with a musical cataract. There were cottonwoods here, big ones, silvery bark furrowed and runneled with age, leaves constantly moving with a sound like polite applause—the first cottonwoods they'd seen since leaving the Green River. *Populus fremontii* grew in long gallery forests along western rivers, threatened by floods yet also dependent upon them. A dioecious species, some trees are born female and others male. Pollinated by wind, the female catkins split into tiny seeds borne aloft by a tuft of cottony fluff. They set sail in March and April like flurries of warm snow. It takes the annual spring floods to trigger the bloom, after snowmelt scours the sandbars and makes space for seeds to take root.

The cottonwood might have learned to embrace the rough rhythms of life in canyon country, but people did not much care for the river's big floods. "It is plain to any thinking mind," wrote Frederick Dellenbaugh in the introduction to Eddy's book, "that the river must, sooner or later, be brought under control." The Colorado was "fierce, unrelenting, and demoniacal." In dry Januarys it sulked along at a scanty 5,000 cfs or less, a skinny stream with a ribcage of rock and a bellyful of mud. Then spring floods thundered down, tore up the banks, and tossed boulders everywhere. It was always too much water or too little. The politicians and hydrologists agreed: something had to be done to control the Colorado.

In 1921 and 1922, the USGS sent expeditions through Cataract and Glen canyons to search for places to build dams. The chief engineer was a hydrologist named Eugene Clyde La Rue. Forty-two years old, he was a gruff and single-minded man with a small black mustache and, often, a pipe clamped between his teeth. He was afraid of the water, an unfortunate situation for someone in his line of work. Cataract Canyon must have been terrifying; one of the flat-bottomed rowboats flipped in Dark Canyon Rapid. But La Rue was undaunted. He plotted, measured, and mapped. He labelled the rapids with numbers, as if trying to eliminate their mystique in the most humdrum way possible. Numbers—that's what was needed, not Powell's romanticized and terror-inducing names. La Rue was all about numbers. He dreamed of a comprehensive plan for development in the watershed, a "heel-to-toe staircase" of dams and reservoirs that minimized evaporation, maximized hydropower, and controlled floods.

It wasn't going to be easy. Some years earlier, La Rue had explored and discarded the idea of building a dam at the confluence of the Green and Colorado rivers. He built a drilling platform there and dug more than one hundred feet into the riverbed, but never found bedrock: just deep sand and rubble. Debris from a summer storm tore the drilling platform to pieces. Glen Canyon was more promising. La Rue identified eight locations there suitable for a dam. His favorite site was four miles upriver from Lee's Ferry. The sandstone walls seemed to him a testament of the rock's stability: hadn't they stood untouched for thousands of years? A dam in Glen Canyon would back up water into a long, many-branched reservoir, drowning Hite, burying the redbud and cottonwood trees, and flooding the cliff dwellings. "Such slack water would not impair the beauty of the canyons," La Rue wrote. On the contrary, he believed a reservoir would allow people to explore by boat a region that was now only accessible "at great expense and danger."

The Colorado River had resisted every other effort to exploit its treasures. It had snuffed out romantic visions of steamboats stuffed with tourists and killed the dream of a railroad. The gold hunters went away unsatisfied. Dams were different. Dams would change everything.

THE CREW FLOATED FOURTEEN MILES before dusk—just floating, barely stirring the oars—and landed the boats at Ticaboo Creek, one of the places where Cass Hite had found gold. There was no handy sandbar to lay out their bedrolls; they had to haul all their gear some distance up the skirt of talus to find a flat spot to camp. Clover held her tongue, but Jotter joined Atkinson, Gibson, and Harris in mutinous muttering. "I do not like the attitude all but Elzada has taken," Nevills wrote. "Lois is obviously a trouble maker."

All the next day, and the next, they floated downriver. The water was so still and quiet that Jotter and Harris put the *Mexican Hat* in tow and climbed into the *Botany* with Gibson and Atkinson, so the four of them could gossip and gripe. Without the Colorado as an adversary, they had very little to unite them under Nevills's leadership. Lining and portaging the boats had slowed them down, and they chafed under his caution. Harris worried about making it to Salt Lake City in time. Atkinson complained bitterly that no time had been allotted to collect specimens; he needed to hunt and trap animals for his collection, and probably also skin game and salt hides to preserve them, none of which could be done quickly. Jotter, too, was frustrated by Nevills's approach to the expedition as a commercial venture, not a scientific one. ("Everything had to be hyped!" she wrote.) The women had their "housekeeping" duties in addition to botany, and Atkinson, the zoologist, now had a boatman's work. To add to her injured feelings, Jotter had thought the six of them had put up equal shares in the expedition's expenses when, really, they were paying Nevills to be their guide. Nevills was barely breaking even on the cost of the boats and supplies; he'd pinned all his financial hopes on selling the story to magazines and radio shows. But Jotter did not know this. The money rankled, and so did Nevills's authoritarian attitude. Banded together by dislike, the four of them drifted behind the *Wen*. They joked that the birds wanted to join in their mutiny: *gripe,* the birds called from the bushes, *gripe, gripe, gripe . . .*

The whispering did not go unnoticed in the lead boat. "It is the most miserable feeling in the world," Clover wrote in her diary, "to know something is wrong and not to know just what or why." She and Nevills spoke in low tones, endlessly discussing what to do when they reached Lee's Ferry. Nevills was adamant: he wouldn't continue downriver unless he could recruit different boatmen. The truth was, he'd been thinking about quitting since the difficult portage job in Cataract Canyon. He had complaints about every one of the crew except Clover, whom he referred to as "the best man of the bunch." Still, he couldn't help questioning her judgment in human character because of her choice in crewmates—even though he wasn't any happier with his own selections. He didn't trust the assurances of the others that they were "game" to go on. "They hate to admit that the water is too rough for them," Nevills sneered in his journal.

Clover, bewildered and hurt, tried to soothe all these ruffled feelings. She thought stubbornly that she would go on to the Grand Canyon alone if it came down to it. "I am having a wonderful time," she wrote, "and would always feel that I had left something undone."

They met a group of Japanese miners working on a sandbar, who showed them handfuls of gold powder so fine a small sneeze would scatter it. The miners told Clover of a spot with writing on the wall. *Pictographs!* she thought. But when they got to the place, there was only a cross etched in the stone with the date "1860" below. The two women laughed at the joke. Later, however, they stopped to explore one of the Ancestral Puebloan houses, tracing their fingers over the black soot that still stained the ceiling from long-ago fires. There were a few sherds but no intact pots. Jotter was relieved. She did not trust her companions to leave them alone, though the American Antiquities Act of 1906 made it illegal to remove them.

Pictographs and petroglyphs did adorn the cliffs: bighorn sheep with curling horns, the zigzagging lines of snakes, and human figures dancing, hunting, or holding hands. The pictures were etched into desert varnish, a mysterious substance painted in vertical stripes down the sandstone, black on red. Microbes lived in this shiny coating, windblown travelers who alighted in a hostile world of rock and dew to cultivate tiny gardens. Varnish made a good canvas for art. Stanton, when he passed this way, found a map of the Colorado River carved into the rock, one long looping line, like a cursive signature. Jotter and Clover had no time to search for these drawings, but they did spot survey pegs driven at regular intervals into the sandstone, and they marveled at the remains of Stanton's gold dredge, lodged in a pile of driftwood in a tangle of rotting wood and rusty gears. Glen Canyon was full of half-hidden secrets: grottoes and ferns, yes, but also wheels, buckets, flumes, and cables. Natural history and human history collided here until it was hard to tell one from the other.

Sitting round the campfire one evening, Nevills and Clover idly discussed the possibility—a daydream, really—that the Smithsonian Institution would want to display one of their boats alongside the *Spirit of St. Louis*. Charles Lindbergh had made the first solo transatlantic flight in that plane in 1927, and, in a lesser-known adventure, made the first aerial archeological survey of the Colorado Plateau and the Grand Canyon with his wife, Anne, as the pilot.

Atkinson sneered. "The Smithsonian," he interjected sarcastically, "will certainly make room for all our boats by removing Lindbergh's plane."

Atkinson had grown surlier as the quiet days stretched on. He had neglected the open gash on his leg and it grew infected; Clover finally forced him to let her treat it. Privately, she thought he was cocky and cynical. He crowed about his skill with the boat and fussed about the quality of the food, and his sullen attitude seemed to infect everyone else. "Of course he has not been well," she added lamely in her journal. Nevills was less understanding. One by one, he interrogated the others about their intentions to keep going after Lee's Ferry, disbelieved their assurances, and finally lost his temper and announced he would recruit two more men no matter what they did. He told Clover in confidence he had no intention of taking Atkinson the rest of the way. He was none too pleased with Jotter, either. Secretly, he wished he could leave her, too.

At midday on July 5, they passed the mouth of the San Juan River. Nevills was now on familiar water: he had taken tourists down this stretch of the Colorado before. He had always intended to hike the six miles up a side canyon to see Rainbow Bridge National Monument, and their lateness wouldn't change his plans. They woke early on July 6 to a dismal breakfast of Grape-Nuts, battered into submission with a rock. There was no canned fruit left to sweeten it.

Rainbow Bridge had formed millions of years before, when the Colorado Plateau first began to rise in the same tectonic upheavals that formed the Rocky Mountains. A little creek had dashed up against a fin of sandstone until it wore a hole through the rock. The archway was nearly three hundred feet tall and almost as wide, a sweep of sandstone tucked into a jumbled, craggy country, with Navajo Mountain blue in the distance. It's a sacred place to Navajo, Hopi, Zuni, Paiute, and Ute peoples. Diné speak of a male and female rainbow joined in perfect union, and medicine people conduct ceremonies there for protection, blessing, and rain. They consider it a shelter in times of danger. When Kit Carson tried to force the Diné off their homeland in 1864–66 with the might of the U.S. military behind him—a brutal act of deportation referred to as the Long Walk—some fled to the sacred landscape between Rainbow Bridge and Navajo Mountain. The cavalry never found them.

Navajo tradition forbids walking under the archway without the proper blessings. Clover and the others either did not know or did not respect this prohibition; Harris and Nevills climbed to the top of the bridge while the others explored below. "It is like being in the pres-. ence of the supernatural to stand under that structure arching more than three hundred feet above," Clover wrote, but Jotter, tired and irritable, declared herself "not terribly impressed." They all signed their names in the guest registry set there by the National Park Service. Rainbow Bridge had been a national monument since 1910, but it had hardly any non-Native visitors. Few tourists made the difficult fourteen-mile trek overland, and even fewer came by river. Nevills noted that just 2,640 people had signed the guest registry before them. The engineers who wanted to dam Glen Canyon thought that bringing more visitors to Rainbow Bridge would be a side benefit. La Rue pointed out that the reservoir would allow people to access the spot easily in motorboats. Nobody consulted the Navajo medicine people, who feared the spiritual damage tourists would inflict.

Jotter soon tired of exploring and found a quiet corner with Atkinson to talk. Nevills assumed the two of them spent the time napping and disparaged Jotter's laziness. "Anemic, probably," he wrote, "tho she looks big and husky." Evidently, he had forgotten that both women woke before dawn each day, cooked breakfast, stowed their bedrolls, and sometimes even collected and pressed a few plants before any of the men opened their eyes.

Nevills assured the others he had permission to raid a food cache, stashed at a nearby campsite for tourists who made the overland trek. Jotter felt uneasy when he broke the padlock to get inside. They opened and devoured can after can—olives, applesauce, Vienna sausages. Clover made a batch of biscuits, and everyone ate them piping hot from the Dutch oven, then unwisely lingered long enough to cook a second batch and eat again. That meant stumbling wearily down the trail to the river after dark without the aid of flashlights. Nevills almost stepped on a rattlesnake, which was, luckily, equally startled and did not strike. To Clover, the sense of the supernatural lingered, but now the corners buzzed with snakes and the moon-cast shadows seemed "grotesque." She fell once or twice on the uneven footing, and called for the others to wait in a panic. What if she sprained an ankle and had to discontinue the trip at Lee's Ferry? What if she fell, hard, and no one heard, and they went walking on ahead and left her there, alone in the night . . . ? It did not seem, anymore, as if she walked down slickrock steps which human feet had traced for millennia. The sun plunged down behind cliff walls and the canyon turned primeval. Every algae-slick pool hummed with an uncanny chorus: *brri-brri-BRRING* sang the male toads to their potential mates, while the females blinked demurely from the water, eyes like gibbous moons. Rock-colored, blotchy-skinned, canyon treefrogs spent the hot summer days hiding in crevasses, indistinguishable from lumps of stone, but they made up for it after sunset with ear-splitting orgies of music and sex. The ancient chorus rose, claiming sand, water, and stone. Nothing here belonged to humans, not now. A summer night, a desert river: this was the kingdom of cold-blooded things.

REPORTERS IN THE WORLD ABOVE had seized upon the expedition's non-appearance at Lee's Ferry to speculate, with ghoulish glee, about their fate.

FEAR IS FELT FOR THE SAFETY OF 2 WOMEN, 4 MEN ON ROUGH TRIP

read the inch-high headline on July 5. Beneath this, in oversized font, screamed the highlights of the story:

OVERDUE AT LEE'S
Fourth of July Comes, Goes Without Word From the Party

The Trans World Airlines (TWA) flights that departed four times daily from Los Angeles deviated from their usual routes so the pilots (and all the gawking passengers) could peer out the windows and look for the boats—or rather, the wreckage. Two USGS employees stationed at Lee's Ferry reported (hyperbolically) that the river was cresting at its highest level in a decade. They stoked a bonfire and started a twenty-four-hour vigil to keep watch. "I won't say that they probably have met with disaster," a local riverman told the press, "but if they haven't they can thank their lucky stars for a miracle." Journalists took every opportunity to remind readers that no woman had ever "conquered" the Colorado River.

Page-turning prose for the public, to be sure, but absolutely terrifying for the friends and families of the expedition members. In Ann Arbor, Bartlett received word through an overzealous reporter that the party had safely reached Lee's Ferry. "Hurrah! Hurrah!! Hurrah!!!" he wrote in his diary. "I wish it were the end of the trip, but at least one stage is over." A day later, Bartlett wrote glumly it had been a false alarm. Inundated by telegrams and telephone calls, he started talking to the U.S. Coast Guard about sending a search party. He tried to reassure questioners that his staff members were probably just busy collecting plants, but he was rattled by insinuations that he ought to have stopped the women from going. "I didn't really think Atkinson should have gone," he wrote cryptically, "but have no criticism of Elzada & Lois."

Jotter's family felt even more wretched. Her mother, Artie May, was still in Ohio visiting Jotter's grandmother, who was confined to a wheelchair with crippling arthritis and wracked with worry. Jotter's parents were little better off. "Nothing much that I can say about Lois," E. V. wrote to his wife from Washington, DC. "I know a deep and growing realization and conviction of personal responsibility. . . . No use to tell you not to worry. You will and so do I." In the absence of news, journalists clamored for quotes from men who had successfully boated the Colorado River. James Hogue, who had gone down the river with Stanton, was happy to explain the "unimaginable difficulties" of the trip and condemn the expedition for being "thoroughly unplanned." He fervently wished the women had asked his advice before setting off, "but," he said, "I guess they wouldn't have listened." Other, unnamed sources believed the party was "drifting helplessly" on the river "or already smashed to bits on the jagged rocks."

It was only a matter of time before a journalist located Buzz Holmstrom, the hero of the *Saturday Evening Post*. He had quit his gas station job in Oregon and moved to Boulder City, Nevada, to work as a tour guide with Grand Canyon–Boulder Dam Tours. He wasn't very good at it. Instead of regaling tourists with stories of his adventures, he showed up ragged and shirtless and barely opened his mouth. When someone could coax him to speak about the Grand Canyon, he went on at length about the moon shining on the water, the cheerful crackling of a campfire at night, and the stark beauty of the rosy cliffs at sunrise. What was this? The tour company finally exiled him to Pearce Ferry, a bleak dock on the edge of Lake Mead, where Holmstrom scraped paint and sopped up bilgewater from the tour boats. The only excitement came from occasional landslides, triggered by the reservoir's rising waters.

Holmstrom drove to Las Vegas one day to see what he could find out about the lost Nevills Expedition. A journalist told him there had been no news. Holmstrom shook his head. "I am actually worried about their safety," he confessed. On a scrap of paper, he sketched the squiggling line of the Colorado River and traced the distance from Green River to Lee's Ferry with a blunt, weathered finger. Holmstrom had covered that distance in two weeks the previous year. Nevills had been gone almost three. If the boats had wrecked and the party tried to walk out in the scorching hot weather, Holmstrom said, no man or woman could survive. "I'm glad I'm not on that trip," he told the journalist, "but I certainly hope they get through all right."

Holmstrom could speak eloquently on the river's dangers but was curiously silent on the subject of female river runners. At least, he didn't say anything the journalist was allowed to put on record. No matter. Plenty of other people were more open on this topic. "Experienced river men around Boulder City," the journalist wrote, "unwilling to be quoted directly, have stated that they consider the presence of the women in the party as one of the hazards, as they are 'so much baggage' and probably would need help in an emergency."

The story appeared on July 7. Holmstrom went back to scrubbing out bilgewater. But he couldn't get the Nevills Expedition out of his head. He had a boat—a Galloway-style craft hand-hewn out of an Oregon cedar log. He had a car—an eleven-year-old Buick he'd bought for twenty-seven dollars. It would only take a day or two to drive to Green River, Utah.

⋎

EARLY ON THE MORNING OF JULY 7, a plane flew over the Colorado River. Jotter saw it pass overhead and laughed privately at the nonsensical notion that it was searching for them. But that evening, as they made camp on a willow-fringed sandbar, a different plane appeared, smaller than the TWA flight she'd spotted earlier. It circled the little group, humming. White scraps of paper fluttered down like snow.

The group scattered, each person trying to catch one. Nevills and Harris scrambled up a cliff; Gibson climbed a willow tree; and Clover found herself slogging through quicksand. Jotter stayed where she was, because she was cooking dinner. Atkinson stayed with her. They were rewarded when a thin scrap of paper landed nearby. It read:

WE ARE A U.S. COAST GUARD AIRPLANE, LOOKING FOR A PARTY OF GEOLOGISTS FROM THE UNIVERSITY OF MICHIGAN WHO ARE OVERDUE AT LEES FERRY. IF YOU ARE THAT PARTY WILL YOU PLEASE GIVE THE FOLLOWING SIGNAL: EVERYBODY LIE DOWN THEN STAND UP AGAIN . . . . IF YOU ARE IN NEED OF FOOD, EVERYBODY SIT DOWN . . . . IF YOU ARE ENTIRELY ALL RIGHT, EVERYBODY HOLD HIS ARMS HORIZONTALLY OUT FROM HIS SIDE. IT IS MOST IMPORTANT THAT WE DETERMINE WHO YOU ARE, SO PLEASE IDENFITY YOURSELVES BY GIVING THE FIRST MENTIONED SIGNAL <u>FIRST</u>.

Jotter and Atkinson went through the necessary gymnastics, and after Gibson returned and joined in, the plane dipped its wings and departed. Gibson couldn't think of any way to signal for a resupply of cigarettes, and Jotter, presumably, couldn't figure out how to correct "a party of geologists" to "two botanists, a zoologist, and their boatmen." She wondered why their little expedition rated a search by a Coast Guard plane. Everyone was puzzled. They didn't know about the frenzy stirred up by their lateness, or that Bartlett had spent the last few days snowed in by urgent telegrams. "Imagine," Clover exclaimed, "they were planning to rescue us while we were sitting at Rainbow Bridge consuming vast quantities of biscuits!"

The moment seemed to break the tension in the group. They'd had a brief brush with the outside world, and perhaps the message would get through to the loved ones waiting for news. They ate supper, washed the dishes, and climbed back into the boats to float downriver by the light of a gibbous moon. Cliffs rose around them, high and white, and the river was smooth as glass. The boats skimmed on their own reflections, upside-down in the water. Above, the Big Dipper pivoted around its handle, like a butterfly net aimed at stars instead of fireflies. Clover and Harris played harmonica as everyone else sang "Moonlight on the River Colorado," making up the words when they couldn't remember the wistful lyrics exactly.

Harris knew it would be his last night on the river.

Chapter Seven

HELL, YES! WHAT RIVER?

REPORTERS HAD BEEN HAUNTING LEE'S FERRY for days, waiting for the appearance of the expedition. Nevills made a fuss about getting the three boats in formation for their grand entrance, midmorning on July 8 after they drifted the last fifteen miles, but the effort was wasted. The journalists were all tucked into a car on the riverbank, fast asleep.

For more than a hundred miles upstream and two hundred miles below, Lee's Ferry was the only break in the continuous cliff walls where one could easily drive a wagon or a car down to the river. Here, the crew would leave the quiet waters of Glen and enter the Grand Canyon, at a point dubbed Mile 0 by the unimaginative engineers who had surveyed the Colorado for dams. Their destination, Boulder Dam, was still nearly three hundred miles farther downriver.

Assuming, of course, they continued the journey at all.

They had been floating all day between walls of red sandstone. Nicks and hollows marred the smooth sweeps of stone as if, like unfinished sculptures, they still bore the marks of the potter's hands. The river reflected the colors of the world around it: pink stone, blue sky, and, here and there, dashes of the deepest green, captured and magnified back to the seep willows on the sandbars, their pale leaves transfigured to emerald in the water. Abruptly, the cliffs broke. It seemed as if the sky finally woke, stretched, and shouldered them aside. The river bent to the left, and they could see in the distance

After a delay on the river, the six members of the
Nevills Expedition arrive safely at Lee's Ferry in the
midst of a nationwide media frenzy. *AP Photo*

the Vermilion Cliffs, their layers etched in chalky pastels. To the right, a notch in the rocky landscape made a gentle slope down to the river.

Nevills stood up in the *Wen*. "Church is out," he bellowed. "We're here!"

The journalists, jolted awake, came tearing down to the river's edge, too late. The weary crew had to drift back upstream in an eddy and float down again, smiling for the cameras. Then one of the reporters, unwisely, cut open a watermelon. Jotter, Clover, and the rest sat on a handy driftwood log and devoured slice after slice, too consumed by delight to answer any questions.

The two USGS engineers stationed at Lee's Ferry offered to take everyone up to Marble Canyon Lodge in their car, where the hotel's owner had issued an invitation to lunch. It was just as well: the expedition had floated into Lee's Ferry with nothing left but three cans of soup, a box of crackers, and half a can of Klim. Halfway to the lodge, they met a sputtering Ford sedan that crashed to a halt and disgorged a red-faced man loaded down with a movie camera. His name was Jack McFarland, and he worked for Pathé News, the American branch of an international company that made black-and-white newsreels about everything from the destruction of the *Hindenburg* to ladies' hairstyles. The brief, dramatic snippets ran twice a week, every week, in cinemas around the country.

McFarland had, literally and figuratively, missed the boat. Nevills promised to bring everyone back to Lee's Ferry to stage their arrival for a third time. They went on to Marble Canyon Lodge and gratefully sat down to bowls of soup while reporters swarmed round like mosquitoes. The rustic stone building had a spacious dining room and an adjacent seating area with a big fireplace on one end. It must have felt luxurious after their time on the river: Jotter noted rapturously that the table was set with real linen. She was just as hungry for news from home as a meal served on a tablecloth. She had letters waiting from her friends and family, and a piece of her brother's wedding cake—by now, no doubt, a little stale. She ate it anyway.

After lunch, they went back to the river to sort through their gear and reenact their arrival, again. "Silly," Clover noted in her diary, bored with the autograph hunters and the newsmen. Jotter became jumpy under the constant clicking of cameras. Reluctantly, Harris packed his bag. He had decided he couldn't risk losing his USGS job by further delays in the expedition's schedule. Gibson resolved to go on, perhaps to his own surprise ("he's scared to death," Nevills wrote, "but he's man enough to say so") and neither Clover nor Jotter wanted to quit. Atkinson was still making up his mind. His cocksure swagger had, at one point or another, annoyed every one of his companions, except possibly Jotter. But he had a valid complaint: he, Jotter, and Clover had joined the expedition with the understanding that it was a scientific venture. If there had been little time to collect plants, there was even less to properly shoot, skin, and tan animal hides. He'd counted on getting good-quality zoological specimens to sell in Michigan and make up the costs of the trip, and that hadn't happened.

Jotter sympathized. As she put it, "plants stand still and let you catch up with them." Atkinson had the harder task in killing animals, and in her opinion Nevills hadn't allotted enough time to collect anything. Clover, however, was impatient with Atkinson's bellyaching. She and Jotter had made the best of the situation, waking before dawn and working with cold, clumsy fingers long after sundown to collect plants. Under the worst possible conditions, the two women had managed to catalog more than a hundred specimens. She thought Atkinson could have made more of an effort. Not that it mattered much. Nevills was sorry to lose Harris, but he had already decided to leave Atkinson behind no matter what the zoologist wanted to do.

It wasn't the only difference of opinion between the two women. Jotter wrote to Hussey about her exasperation with Clover's response to the press—"eating it up," as Jotter saw it, and making comments about "the eyes and ears of the world being upon us." Jotter took this to mean that Clover had absorbed Nevills's obsession with publicity. This was probably an unfair assessment. Several months earlier, Clover had used almost the exact same phrase to describe the sour old men in Michigan watching her career with critical eyes. She had more at stake than any of them, except perhaps Nevills. If she returned to Ann Arbor with few plants and a lot of histrionic publicity, it would hurt her struggling reputation in the botany department. Clover couldn't stop the newspapers; her only hope now was to redirect the narrative toward science and convince her companions not to make any embarrassing blunders in front of the press.

The crew concealed their unhappiness as best they could from the reporters. It wasn't clear whether the trip could continue, with Harris leaving and the rest of the expedition members at odds with one another. Somehow, they had to recruit two new boatmen at a moment's notice if they intended to go on. Nevills wanted to get to Mexican Hat as quickly as possible, to see his family and start making inquiries among rivermen there. Clover insisted on going with him. She worried that Nevills, left to himself, wouldn't go through with the plan, or would fail to persuade anyone to join them. A man named Jack Stockwell agreed to drive them. Harris went along, and so did Atkinson, to collect his car as he dithered about what to do next. It would take them all night to make the journey, on a road that went miles out of the way through the windswept Arizona desert, south to Tuba City, before turning east and north to the Utah border. "The car is a decrepit affair," Nevills noted, "and I am afraid it won't stand the trip." The five of them ate a hasty dinner and, well past nightfall, squeezed into the Ford and set off into the desert.

⋁

LEE'S FERRY WASN'T JUST a geological quirk in the landscape. It was also a political dividing line, cutting the Colorado River watershed in half. Upriver, the water legally belonged to Wyoming, Colorado, Utah, and New Mexico, collectively called the Upper Basin. Downriver, it belonged to Arizona, Nevada, and California, known as the Lower Basin.

When these seven states decided to settle their squabbles over the

Colorado River in the 1920s, they first tried to divvy up the water according to how much cropland each state would one day irrigate. Boosters believed the arid landscape could be transformed into "smiling agricultural plains" and "vast and rich gardens." This is what "reclamation" meant: reclaiming the desert for farmland. It was an idea so beguiling, so entrenched in the colonial expansion of white settlers into the West, that some local newspapers found they couldn't express it in prose and turned to poetry: "Stretches of desert?—Aye, but they bloom / Watered by reservoir, ditches, and flume!" went one ditty in the *Arizona Republican*.

Negotiations soon sputtered to a halt. Western water law centered on an idea known as "first in time, first in right." The first person to divert water from a river and put it to "beneficial use" had the priority claim. By this logic, California—already queuing up plans for ambitious canals—could take everything it wanted from the Colorado River before the Upper Basin states had even gotten in line. In the end, Herbert Hoover (then the U.S. Secretary of Commerce) proposed a solution. Instead of trying to sort out each state's allocation, they would simply split the river at Lee's Ferry. The Upper and Lower Basins divided the rights to 16 million acre-feet of water annually, roughly in half, though the Lower Basin got a bit more. (An acre-foot is the traditional measurement of water in the West; it's the amount required to cover one acre one foot deep, about 326,000 gallons or half of an Olympic-sized swimming pool.)

Signed in 1922, the Colorado River Compact was meant to "provide for the equitable division" of water. By "equitable," the delegates did not mean Native tribes or Mexico. Nor did they give any thought to securing water for the river itself. There were no river rafters yet to champion for a free-flowing Colorado, no laws to protect rare plants and animals. It did not occur to them to set some water aside as insurance against drier times. They thought the river had plenty of water: 20 million acre-feet annually, at least.

This optimism would prove a grave mistake.

Eugene La Rue, the man obsessed with numbers, had published the first estimates of the Colorado River's annual flow several years before the Compact was signed. From a stream gauge near Yuma, Arizona, he calculated that the river averaged just 16 million acre-feet a year. This was considerably less than the common belief, but La Rue thought the number was still too high. He knew the Colorado River Basin had experienced times of deep drought—droughts that lasted decades or centuries, the kind of drought that shriveled sagebrush and gave the cacti sunburn. In fact, the 1880s and 1890s had been unusually dry. But no stream gauges existed at that time, so La Rue was forced to find other ways to estimate the river's flow through a drought period, such as interviewing crusty old pioneers whose yarns about the old days tended to be less than trustworthy. It was easy for anyone so inclined to dismiss La Rue's attempts at reconstructing the past and focus only on the streamflow data collected in the early twentieth century.

The result, intentionally or not, was to craft a vision of the Colorado River's average flow based on some of the wettest years the river had seen in centuries. Armed with an unrealistic vision of the river's abundance, the U.S. government set about building the infrastructure of what it called a "vast desert empire." The Compact was signed; now it was time to build dams.

$$\downarrow\!\!\!\!\!\downarrow$$

CLOVER DOZED IN THE RATTLING FORD, trying to ignore the strange sounds and funny smells coming from under its hood. Just before midnight, Nevills declared that they would have to stop in Tuba City and find a more reliable ride. A friend of his, Ed Kerley, ran a trading post there.

Luck was with them. Kerley had a brand-new Chevy coupe. Better still, he had a twenty-four-year-old cousin named Lorin Bell, who had grown up on the Navajo Nation and was recently returned from adventures in Tahiti. Blond and lanky, Bell was a madcap, foul-mouthed, freewheeling soul with aspirations to become a writer, though at the moment he worked as a sheepherder, "buried in wool," in his words. As Clover told the story, Nevills shook Bell awake and asked, "Do you want to take a trip down the river?"

"Hell, yes!" Bell replied sleepily. "What river?"

They left Bell to pack, climbed into Kerley's Chevy, and drove northeast to Kayenta, where Kerley transferred them into a pickup and, yawning, headed for home. The moon was waxing and nearly full, but the reds and golds of the Navajo land outside the truck's windows were lost in darkness. Clover scrunched down in the front seat, worrying about wearing a hole in her trousers as they jounced over the unpaved roads—"washboard" roads, they were called, because the texture under the tires was something like corrugated sheet metal. She felt sick from lack of sleep. The sun rose as it does sometimes in the desert, all in a hurry, flooding Monument Valley with a warm rose light that rubbed and burnished the barren stone to a similar hue. Only the westward faces of the great bluffs and mesas clung to their somber blue shadows.

In Mexican Hat, a local woman took one look at them and burst into tears. The newspapers had made the most of the "missing" expedition, and at least some people back home had given them up for dead. Rumor had it that Clyde Eddy was gearing up to rescue them. Lost women generated more newspaper stories than bear cubs or Airedale dogs! Clover went straight to bed and snatched four hours of sleep before she woke to eat breakfast and wish Harris goodbye.

Harris had a "hangdog air," Nevills noted sourly. During the long drive, Nevills had tried to make Harris promise to stay on the expedition at least as far as the second layover, at Bright Angel Creek, where he would be able to hike out of the canyon on a Park Service trail. Harris refused, though not without some doubts. "Glad to be leaving in a way," was the last line in his journal, "but wish I were going on when I view it in another way."

Atkinson took his car and drove back to Lee's Ferry. Nevills hadn't told him yet that he had no intention of taking him downriver. Bell would replace Harris, but who would take Atkinson's place? He and Clover still had to find one more boatman crazy enough to join them.

JOTTER AND GIBSON, left behind at Marble Canyon Lodge, had a leisurely breakfast that morning. The stone building had only a few tiny rooms, but they opened onto a wide veranda with a stunning view of the Vermilion Cliffs. It was a short walk to Navajo Bridge, a graceful steel arch built to carry automobile traffic over the Colorado River. It was the highest bridge of its kind in the world when it was finished in 1929, though it did not hold the title any longer. From the lodge, the river was hidden, tucked into the canyon's cleft and invisible in the desert's deceptive folds. The bridge seemed to span from nowhere to nothing. They were supposed to repaint the boats while they waited for the others to return, but neither of them felt much like walking five miles down an unfriendly road to Lee's Ferry under the July sun to freshen up boats they might not use. "May not continue trip, but keep that quiet for the present," Jotter wrote to Hussey. If Nevills and Clover couldn't find two recruits, the journey would come to an inglorious end.

Journalists had sent their copy to New York City by plane the night before, so newspapers around the nation now carried front-page stories about the "six death-defying adventurers," complete with snarling beasts, foaming rapids, and dwindling food supplies. "The two women are to be complimented on their courage," wrote one reporter, but not many compliments followed in a story all about the expedition's close calls and presumed failure to collect scientific data. "GIRL LEFT ALONE," screamed one headline, telling a harrowing tale of Jotter stranded "on the turbulent river's edge while wild animals howled." Nonsense, Jotter scoffed in her letters home. The only animals she'd seen or heard all night were ants, a few packrats rustling in the brush, and pink rattlesnakes, which (she explained) were rather cute and didn't growl at all. She related the whole story to her mother and added, "I had a lovely time."

Other inaccuracies peppered the newspaper accounts. The *San Francisco News* ran a photograph of Atkinson sitting in a boat with two pretty young ladies in long skirts. The caption named them Miss Elzada Clover and Miss Lois Jotter, though in fact they were two tourists who had charmed Atkinson into posing with them. The real pictures of Jotter and Clover in their dirty, travel-worn overalls weren't so flattering or feminine. Jotter wrote to her mother, "Apologies to all my relatives for the way I undoubtedly look in the pictures which have been shot." She had diligently applied makeup every day at the start of the trip, but soon gave that up as useless. It was galling to discover that the newspapermen printed unflattering descriptions of Clover and Jotter every chance they got. Articles depicted "Miss" Clover as a forty-year-old college professor, plump and bespectacled, while Jotter was rawboned, freckle-faced, and nearly six feet tall. Jotter was indignant. She was only five feet, seven and a half inches.

Jotter and Gibson were still dawdling around the lodge when an old Buick pulled up outside, hauling a handcrafted wooden boat on a trailer. They looked up curiously. A man got out: a stocky, blue-eyed, weatherbeaten sailor in threadbare clothes. Buzz Holmstrom, the man who had declared the Colorado River no place for women, had come to see if he was right.

Holmstrom had first gone to the town of Green River with the intention of putting his boat in the water and chasing down the lost Nevills Expedition, only to learn that they had arrived safely at Lee's Ferry. He turned his car around and drove to meet them, curious to discover whether the two women were going to put a "crimp" in his secret plan. He intended to boat the Colorado River again that autumn, this time with a cameraman named Amos Burg. Burg would make color movies of the adventure to show at the upcoming World's Fair in San Francisco in a money-making scheme. Holmstrom didn't care much for publicity, but he was habitually broke and sent whatever he could spare from his salary back to his mother in Oregon. The *Saturday Evening Post* had paid him $450 for his story; color movies might pay even more.

The Nevills Expedition worried Holmstrom. If rafting the Colorado River truly became a commercial enterprise—the kind of thing even women could do!—then who would want to watch a movie about Holmstrom's exploits? The era of derring-do on the Colorado River, his era, was ending. Soon anyone with money to spare would be able to pay a guide to take them down the Colorado. People had begun to boat the canyons in all kinds of strange contraptions—Burg planned to do it in a newfangled rubber raft—"& as if that weren't enuf trouble," Holmstrom wrote to his mother, "now these women are in the canyon—if they make it I guess it will be time for me to go & hide somewhere."

Jotter knew Holmstrom only by reputation. Like the classical hero of Greek myth, he had plunged into the underworld and returned a changed man. One radio announcer described him as a "He-Man's hero," and another dubbed him "a modern young Viking." These descriptions did not prepare Jotter for the man who stepped out of the rundown old car. He was small in stature, shy, funny, and self-deprecating.

"I brought my boat with some idea of going hunting for you," he told Jotter and Gibson. Jotter thought there was a trace of embarrassment in his manner when he looked at her. "'Course, I thought it would be good publicity for me, too," he added.

His frankness disarmed Jotter. The trio spent the day together, long enough for Jotter to realize that Holmstrom wasn't exactly the bold, manly adventurer depicted by the press. His mother, Frances Holmstrom, was a poet, and something of her romantic soul had rubbed off on him. Everyone painted him as the hero who "conquered" the Colorado River, but Holmstrom didn't enjoy the label. In his diary, near the end of his 1937 trip, he had scribbled a hymn to the river's indifferent beauty: "It has never been conquered—& never will I think—anyone who it allows to go thru its canyons & see its wonders should feel thankful and privileged." An interviewer once asked him how he kept his sanity on his fifty-two-day solo journey. "It may sound funny to you," Holmstrom replied, "but after weeks of being alone with the river I began to think of it as a friend—as a companion." Out there, he said, "with nothing but the roar of the river, and the stars at night, and the canyon walls I began to see things in a way I never had before." The Grand Canyon humbled him. One man mattered little in the face of that immensity.

Jotter and Gibson told Holmstrom of their difficulties, and he, in turn, described the rapids that lay ahead in the Grand Canyon: Soap Creek, Sockdolager, Grapevine. He had no qualms admitting he had been terrified on his solo trip. One night in Cataract Canyon, he had woken in the darkness and stumbled down to the river to cling to the bowline, in a cold sweat at the thought of his boat tearing away downriver without him. But it had been worth it. What Jotter felt about plants, she realized, Holmstrom expressed in a kind of rough poetry about the Grand Canyon. "The spell of the canyon is awfully strong and it holds something of me I know it will never give up," he once told an interviewer.

Night fell, bringing blessed relief from the heat. Atkinson returned from Mexican Hat. They all ate dinner together in the dining room at Marble Canyon Lodge, Holmstrom's treat, though he couldn't have had much money to spare. Reporters, by now, had caught wind of the departures of Harris and Atkinson. Atkinson seemed to have made up his mind; he told the journalists he planned to leave because the expedition's scientific goals had already been fulfilled, a transparent lie to save face. He added sourly that he felt he could do more research on foot, "and we are inclined to agree that he can," a reporter wrote, in a subtle sneer at Atkinson's courage, or the expedition's goals, or both. Jotter wondered how Clover was faring and whether, after all their troubles, the trip would come to a humiliating end. "Gosh knows how it all turns out," she wrote to Hussey, "but I feel stubborn about finishing now."

CLOVER, STILL AT MEXICAN HAT LODGE, complained that she felt like a "monkey in a zoo." Strangers kept showing up to goggle

Grand Canyon National Park superintendent
M.R. Tillotson with Elzada Clover and Norm Nevills.
Grand Canyon National Park Museum Collection #00772

at her, and she was embarrassed when the cowboys rose from their chairs respectfully whenever she entered a room. The morning of July 10, she woke feeling rested for the first time in days. She dashed off a few letters to her friends and family to let them know she was alive, a little ashamed that it had taken her so long.

Nevills and Clover had made several unsuccessful attempts to find another boatman. At last, they extracted a promise from a forty-four-year-old prospector, woodcarver, and jack-of-all-trades named Dell Reed. A soft-spoken, bowlegged man with webbed fingers, Reed lacked Bell's rough-and-ready enthusiasm. He couldn't swim, had no experience with whitewater, and honestly didn't believe he would make it through the Grand Canyon alive. Clover must have shared that worry in some corner of her mind, because she left her journal in Mexican Hat for safekeeping—she would start a new one—and also arranged to ship the plant press back to Michigan. She felt sure she had collected one previously unknown cactus species in Glen Canyon. No matter what happened next, some record of their accomplishments would survive.

They didn't go straight back to Lee's Ferry. Instead, Clover, Nevills, and Reed drove to Grand Canyon Village on the South Rim in an unsuccessful attempt to borrow a short-wave radio to take down the river. The detour added another hundred miles to the drive, but at least they got to meet the superintendent of Grand Canyon National Park, Miner R. Tillotson. Clover thought his manner cold and unfriendly. Tillotson disapproved of river running. "The National Park Service discourages this as a pleasure trip," he wrote in his travel guide *Grand Canyon Country*, "and urgently recommends that it be attempted by none except those making it in the interest of science, accompanied by experienced river men, and provided with the best possible equipment." Apparently, Tillotson did not think the Nevills Expedition met those criteria.

The idea of river running was so new that Nevills hadn't thought to ask permission from the Park Service until Jotter urged him to do so, acting on information from her Yosemite contacts. In reply to Nevills's April letter, Tillotson explained that he had no legal authority to prevent river trips. Only Dr. Clover (to whom Tillotson referred with a masculine pronoun) would have to get a permit, for collecting plants within park boundaries. "However," he added, "because of the dangers involved, especially to inexperienced boatmen and adventure seekers, we naturally do all in our power to discourage such trips." He told Nevills bluntly that the Park Service would not render any kind of assistance if they got into trouble on the stretch of river within the park.

Pressed by reporters, Tillotson had been forced to eat those words and promise to help if necessary. No wonder Clover thought his manner was stiff and chilly.

Jotter, meanwhile, passed the time writing letters and reading "terrible accounts of our suffering" in the newspapers. She dismissed all the press reports as a "terrific lot of untrue ballyhoo." Her family didn't feel the same way. Alarmed, her father sent a telegram with the words: "BE CAUTIOUS CONTINUANCE TRIP," asking Jotter to phone him to consult about her plans. The message was printed in the nearest telegraph office and delivered by mail, so Jotter didn't receive it until the next day. She wrote a letter in reply, explaining that she couldn't call because the nearest phone was forty miles away. Unaware of his terror for her safety, she wrote blithely, "About my own ideas of continuing—I'm all pepped up; would really like to do it." She could say nothing definite about her plans until Clover and Nevills returned, but promised her father that she would make no rash decisions. She told him the newspapers exaggerated the danger. Reporters had made much ado about the "untried, home-made, motorless boats," but Jotter pointed out they *had* to be homemade: you couldn't buy Cataract boats made in a factory. Also, she hadn't actually spent the entire time cold and hungry. "Really most of the stuff written has been absurd," she concluded, "and so wrong that the only right thing was the date-line."

The newspapers obsessed over the expedition, especially Clover and Jotter's role in it. "Women, Too, Dare This Gorge," ran the headline in the *Chicago Herald and Examiner*. "A Woman's Place may be in the home," read one photo caption, "but here are two who sought adventure and found it." The *Evening Star* described the two botanists as anxious to restart the journey. "I'm not worried," Jotter supposedly said. "The trip's been exciting and swell. It looks as though Dr. Clover and I will be the first women to conquer the Colorado."

"Hooey," Jotter wrote in her diary in disgust. To Hussey, she explained the only accurate part of that quote was the word "swell," which she had let slip by accident.

Holmstrom was still there. He had spent the night at Marble Canyon Lodge and lingered long enough the next day to treat his new acquaintances to lunch. They all walked out onto Navajo Bridge to say their farewells. The river, five hundred feet below, was a deep unfathomable green, deceptively calm from this vantage point. The canyon caught the sunlight and its striated walls flashed vermilion. Gibson took a photograph of Jotter and Holmstrom, relaxed and easy, leaning against the metalwork.

Jotter couldn't help asking him, "Do you think we should go on?"

It wasn't really in Holmstrom's best interest for them to succeed. But there was Jotter, open-hearted, candid, eager for his advice. "Yes," he told her. "You should."

He gave Jotter a good-luck charm to carry through the Grand Canyon: his waterproof match case, containing a "burning glass" and a compass, which he had carried on his solo trip the year before. Jotter was pleased and flattered. She told her father in a letter that she accepted the souvenir as a representative of the crew, but evidently took it as a sign of Holmstrom's tacit approval. "We practically wept at parting on the bridge today," she wrote to Hussey, joking that they "laid deep plans to be lost on the next stretch so that he could come look for us." To Hussey, she described Holmstrom as a "big brother-ish" person, but privately thought it was a pity she was taller than he was. She didn't like to date anyone shorter than herself.

CLOVER AND NEVILLS RETURNED to find Lee's Ferry abuzz with speculation and rumor. Jotter and the others had not been discreet, and the press had caught wind of their "mutiny." One paper reported that dissension was tearing the expedition apart. Another said that Holmstrom had been invited to join the crew and had refused on account of the women. Nevills scoffed at the reports. "We've come this far," he said. "There's no sense in staying here."

The boats remained unpainted, and Jotter, Gibson, and Atkinson weren't even there to account for their laziness. They had hitched a ride to Flagstaff, a hundred miles south. A logging town of five thousand people, Flagstaff boasted one pool hall, two nightclubs, and seven places to buy liquor, but as nobody had any money, Jotter found the night "less than exciting." They returned, red-eyed and bleary, by the 6 a.m. bus the next day. Unkindly, Nevills had waited for this moment to tell Atkinson that his presence was no longer required. Atkinson balked, now that he knew for certain the others were going on. He said he wouldn't leave if Jotter needed him. Nevills replied sharply that Jotter didn't have any problem riding with the new boatman, Bell, and borrowed money from Clover to fund Atkinson's journey home. "I believe he is really glad to go home," Clover comforted herself in her journal. "He is certainly not a river man."

Their five days ashore had been so hectic, Clover hadn't had time for more than a cursory look at the plants. But now she made a hasty collection of wildflowers: honey clover (*Melilotus alba*), mountain peppergrass (*Lepidium jonesii*), wild licorice (*Glycyrrhiza lepidota*), and the tiny white blossoms known as Mexican devilweed (*Aster spinosus*). Tamarisks were common, and two kinds of willows. The sandbars were thick with arrow-weed (*Pluchea sericea*), which grew in dense thickets of tall, bendy stalks covered in silvery leaves. The plants would change from this point on—Upper Sonoran giving way to Lower Sonoran—and so would the river, moving swiftly ever deeper into a cleft of earth. Ahead lay a series of deep granite gorges and sandstone canyons, split by faults and riven, now and then, by geologic convulsions that shoved the cliffs aside like sandcastles. Clover expected to find the walls oppressive, the shadows gloomy. That's what everyone said about the Grand Canyon. Geologist Clarence Dutton warned that lovers of nature would "enter this strange region with a shock, and dwell there for a time with a sense of oppression, and perhaps with horror," finding the colors tawdry, the shapes grotesque. Oh, well. She and Jotter had decided to continue, against all the advice of family and friends. They had no choice now but to brave the wild river.

The Colorado was still at flood stage, but under 25,000 cfs at Lee's Ferry and dropping fast. Late in the day on July 13, they loaded into the boats and shoved off.

✲

IN BOULDER CITY, Holmstrom got a jolt of surprise when he read an article saying he had gone down the Colorado River with the Nevills Expedition. He wrote to his mother, "I thot I was here all the time till I read that now I don't know what to think—maybe I am drowned by now."

He went on with a warm description of his visit with Jotter and her companions, filling his letter with the characteristic dashes he liked to use in lieu of punctuation. "They are all fine & I hope they go thru O.K." he wrote charitably, "tho it would probably be better for me if they didn't." He added, "The women on that party are really doing better than the men." He hadn't met Clover, but Jotter impressed him. She was "very strong" and "works like a horse helping portage & trying to get specimens & a good sport—never complaining." This was generous, as Jotter had spent a good deal of her time at Lee's Ferry complaining. Evidently, even her complaints were charming. Holmstrom had a sinking feeling he was going to regret ever saying a word about women on the Colorado River.

Jotter, meanwhile, had sent her own commendation of Holmstrom to her family and friends. In her diary she confessed, "I've never felt quite so much like a hero-worshipper."

Neither of them mentioned Holmstrom's now-famous comment in the *Saturday Evening Post*. But Jotter made the same cheeky bet with Holmstrom and Gibson before the expedition departed Lee's Ferry: both men owed her five dollars and three marriage proposals if she made it to Boulder Dam.

Chapter Eight

PARADISE

THEY ENTERED, AT LAST, THE GRAND CANYON. Pale, water-pocked ledges of Kaibab Limestone rose out of the river, laid down 270 million years ago when the desert was a sea. Before they had gone five miles, the limestone was a vertical escarpment above them and the Coconino Sandstone had emerged beneath it, five million years older, great buff blocks of stone glinting with shards of quartz, stone born of a vast dune-filled desert and still rippled by a wind that no longer blew. Between the two layers lay a rubble slope, the Toroweap Formation, sea-formed sedimentary rock mixed with softer shales and mudstones, which eroded and caused it to slump. This is what gave the Grand Canyon's layers a stepwise appearance: hard limestones and sandstones in vertical cliffs, resting on softer layers that crumbled into talus skirts. Inside the rock, pressed thin as paper, tiny fish were forever frozen midswim. Here and there, tracks left by strange four-footed creatures purled the sandstone, the imprint of five padded toes splayed for balance in the mud. Had they been geologists, they would have marveled at their plunge into the past, each river mile eating away another chunk of history, ten thousand years with every splash of the oars. There were secrets to be told here: about past climates, warm shallow seas, the inexorable work of uplift and erosion, and the catastrophic clawing of landslides and floods.

But Jotter had come to find plants, so she dismissed the entire spectacle of stone as they passed under Navajo Bridge with the scribble, "nice clouds and red cliffs."

A crowd gathered on the bridge to watch the boats embark, cars lined up as tiny as toys. Jotter craned her neck to stare from beneath the brim of her sun helmet. She had stood up there with Holmstrom just two days before, when he handed her his match case. She felt momentarily lonely at the thought of leaving Harris and Atkinson behind. Bell now wielded the oars of the *Mexican Hat,* and Gibson rowed the *Botany.* Gibson didn't particularly want to handle a boat, but he didn't have a choice. Technically he had more whitewater experience than Reed, who shared the *Botany* with him—three weeks more experience. Two guests had joined them for the day. The Pathé newsman, McFarland, rode in the *Wen* with Nevills and Clover, clutching his movie camera. He wanted to go a little way downriver to film the boats in action. Bell's cousin Kerley was also along for the ride, crowded in with Bell and Jotter in the *Mexican Hat.*

They could hear the rapid before they saw it, a low reverberation that settled in one's chest behind the breastbone, building to a roar. A straight white line appeared, cutting off the plunging V of the river. No hint of what lay beyond except for the white curls of water that leapt up from behind the brink, dolphin-shaped, and dropped down out of view. The current slowed, flecks of foam swirling on its surface, and then, as if released from its hesitation, leapt forward over the edge. This was Badger Creek Rapid, eight miles downriver from Lee's Ferry. The tongue cut off abruptly and the river plunged between two deadly-looking holes, so Nevills, despite avid watchers on the canyon's rim above them, decided to line it.

They left two boats at anchor, attached lines to the *Wen,* and dragged it through the first big drop. Then they hauled their duffel bags to a sandbar below the rapid to make camp. McFarland, relieved to be on solid ground again, filmed Jotter cooking dinner and Clover powdering her nose. As dusk fell, everyone divided up into twos and threes. Clover sat with Kerley, watching the brilliant moonlight streak the opposite canyon wall in silver. Reed and Gibson talked in one corner about art, of all things. Jotter sat with Bell, her new boatman. She liked him. He was courteous and kind, though he swore like a sailor, unperturbed by the presence of the ladies.

It was a relief to almost everybody to be rid of Atkinson, whose sour attitude had been contagious. "This is a swell gang," wrote Nevills, "and we're going to town!"

The next morning, they brought down the other two boats. Nevills ran the *Botany* through the rapid with McFarland to give him a chance to film. A wave slapped Nevills back into his companion's lap, who was pale with fright. "The Pathé man thought he'd been places and seen things," Clover wrote superciliously, watching from the shore. At the foot of Badger Creek, McFarland and Kerley said goodbye and began the hike back to Lee's Ferry. Later, McFarland would make the most of his little adventure, telling a journalist that an eight-foot wave had nearly swamped the boat and only Nevills's "daring skill" had saved them from drowning.

The rest set off into Marble Canyon, the upper reach of the Grand.

Marble Canyon wasn't really marble, of course. Powell's account of the Colorado River was peppered with hyperbole, and he had chosen names for romance rather than accuracy. What was needed now, in the wake of the Colorado River Compact, was an engineer's eyes: dependable maps with numbers instead of names. The USGS had already surveyed Cataract and Glen canyons for this purpose and identified all the spots that could possibly support a dam. Now nothing remained but to figure out how to plug up the Grand Canyon, too.

Clover and Jotter must have known something of these plans to dam the canyons and change the Colorado's ecology forever; perhaps that foreknowledge lent urgency to their plant collecting. They were carrying river maps made by a group of USGS surveyors who had boated the Grand Canyon in 1923, led by Colonel Claude Birdseye, a forty-five-year-old topographic engineer and veteran of World War I. La Rue was the crew's hydraulic engineer and chief photographer.

Birdseye's expedition was the ninth on record to successfully boat through the Grand Canyon, but the public still saw the Colorado River as an uncharted, unruly place. "They were in a blind maze," reported one newspaper, "never knowing what was just around the corner." Birdseye set to work eliminating the river's mystery. He charted its contours, labeled its rapids, and marked the mileage (beginning with zero at Lee's Ferry), noting that all previous travelers had exaggerated both distances and drops. He located twenty-nine sites for dams between Lee's Ferry and Black Canyon. The thought of drowning much of the Grand Canyon's spectacular scenery did not appear to worry him. Birdseye only mentioned his concern that Phantom Ranch, the rustic resort at the bottom of the canyon, remain above water once the dams were built.

The expedition encountered the usual hardships: thunderstorms, sandstorms, capsized boats, broken equipment, scorpions, snakes, arguments, delays, people threatening to quit, people actually quit-ting. The crew came to gauge a boatman's skill in a rapid by whether La Rue could keep his pipe lit all the way through. Seven weeks into the journey, a flood raised the river's level by twenty feet in the span of a day, delaying the expedition. Predictably, the newspapers caught wind of this and reported that the crew members were probably dead.

They made the journey safely, however. La Rue now had the last piece in place for his comprehensive vision of damming the Colorado River. In 1925, he appeared before a House committee in Washington, DC, to present his plan: a string of thirteen dams down the length of the Colorado, right through the heart of Cataract, Glen, and Grand canyons. The free-flowing river would become a series of placid ponds. He fought hard for this plan over the alternative proposal: the single, massive Boulder Dam. La Rue believed that a string of small reservoirs would more reliably control the wild river, while minimiz-ing water loss from evaporation. The committee members were not startled by the idea of damming up a river that ran through one of the most well-known national parks in the country. They were, however, extremely surprised by La Rue's claim that the Colorado River didn't have as much water as everyone believed.

By now, other hydrologists had joined La Rue in his call for caution. The members of Congress had a report in hand correctly stat-
ing that the annual flow of the Colorado River at Lee's Ferry was
only about 14 million acre-feet a year—not enough to fulfill the big
promises of the Colorado River Compact. Legally, the seven states in
the watershed had divvied up more water than the river carried. But
the juggernaut of Western water law rolled right over this bleak picture, and right over La Rue, as well. Three weeks after receiving that
report, Congress voted to authorize Boulder Dam. The first piece of
the "vast desert empire" would soon be in place, built of concrete,
steel, and stone. Never mind that the foundation was a mirage.

The 1923 topographic maps, notched with all the potential dam
sites that, for now, had been rejected, were the only trustworthy guide
for people who wanted to boat through the Grand Canyon. Jotter
had received copies from Birdseye himself, now sixty years old and
struggling with ill health. She had met him in Washington, DC, several months earlier, while visiting her father. Birdseye had given her
the maps (which weren't widely available) and a copy of his diary, but
first he tried to dissuade her father from letting her go at all. A young
woman, he said, should not attempt such a trip. Jotter had argued
with him until he wore down and retracted his advice.

Nevills kept the maps rolled tightly in a waterproof case and tied
to the splashboard of the *Wen*. Three miles after Badger Creek Rapid,
they would hit another big one: Soap Creek. New layers came fast, not
so much a matter of the cliffs rising but of the river sinking deeper.
The Hermit Shale appeared, a rust-colored slope of crumbly rock,
and the broken blocks of the Supai Group began to emerge from the
water. All at once, the river seemed to dash straight into a giant stone
promontory, but really it wheeled to the left while a tributary poured
in from the right. This formed Soap Creek Rapid, which, Clover
wrote, "is supposed to be frowning upon us." She meant that it had
a nasty reputation. A raft had wrecked there in 1872 and tossed ten
unlucky prospectors into the water. No one died, but it was reported
that the men clambered out of the canyon with nothing left but the

clothes they wore, "and by means of ladders made from driftwood, they reached once more the outer world." Two decades later, Frank Brown drowned near this spot during the railroad survey with Stanton. He actually died just below the rapid, in a riffle, but Soap Creek got the credit in campfire stories. River runners reported a drop of anywhere between twelve and twenty-five feet, a stomach-lurching plunge in the rapid's first fifty yards.

By 1927, somebody had successfully run every big rapid in the Grand Canyon except for Soap Creek. It was almost part of a boatman's religion to avoid the place. That year, Clyde Eddy and his boatman Parley Galloway (Nathaniel Galloway's son) ran it by accident, because they mixed up Badger Creek and Soap Creek and lined around the less dangerous rapid. Bessie and Glen Hyde must have traversed Soap Creek the following year in their ponderous, unwieldy scow, but since they never emerged from the Grand Canyon, nobody counted this a success. Holmstrom got the credit as the first to run it on purpose without flipping his boat. "It did not look so bad," he recorded in his diary. "Very large waves that would surely wreck things were on the left, but on the right [was] a little narrow channel, very swift . . ." He was right. By the end of the 1930s the rapid's character had mellowed. Sediment sifting into the channel had filled in the holes and softened the blunt force of the waves. Nevills, now, thought it was "wild looking" but not impossible to run. The boats only needed one person at the oars: Nevills judged it too great a risk to bring everybody through the rapid. He, Bell, and Gibson would row the boats downriver, and the two women and Reed would have to walk.

Clover and Jotter set off down the jumbled shoreline, picking their way along the foot of the talus, where boulders jammed their toes and snagged their clothing, and a misstep too close to the river could send one's shoes down into sucking sand. Meanwhile, at the head of the rapid, Nevills gave poor Gibson a pep talk. "You'll get your nerve back if you run it," he urged. Gibson looked close to fainting, but he swallowed hard and climbed into the *Botany*.

Nevills took the *Wen* through first. Safely at the foot of the rapid, he turned around to watch Bell make the run, followed by Gibson. The *Botany* was completely out of control, and Gibson "white as a sheet when he took off & shaking like a leaf." The women watched from their perch on the talus, Clover gripping the movie camera, holding her breath. Gibson hit every big wave and dashed through somehow, unable to wield the oars—paralyzed by fright, or by a jammed oarlock, or both. But he didn't capsize. There was a moment of stillness when the *Botany* came down to calm water. Then Gibson shouted to Nevills, "My nerves are okay now!"

🜄

THERE WERE MANY STORIES about the Grand Canyon. Some of them were true. Powell's crew had half-expected the river to plunge over waterfalls and disappear into underground tunnels for hundreds of miles at a stretch. His expedition proved this wasn't the case, but nightmare tales lingered. People said that if you traveled too deep into the chasm, you could look up at midday and see the stars. It was rumored that whole plateaus inside of the canyon had been cut off from the outside world for so long that primordial monsters still roamed there, relics of a ferocious past. The few scientific expeditions that had ventured inside—a few by river, the others on foot—came out with more fancy than fact. They spoke of a fabulously rich silver mine that nobody could find, and herds of feral horses no bigger than coyotes. They told campfire stories of a Petrified Man whose form shone out clearly from the canyon wall—and why not? The sculpted stone, sometimes, did look like it was trying to form living shapes, fluted into scales or fur by the constant wear of water. Strange squid-like things jetted their way inside the limestone, which was made of a million tiny sea creatures whose bodies had dissolved in the ancient ocean. Put an ear up against the wall, and maybe you'd hear the sloshing of the long-vanished waves.

Many people talked about the oppressive, claustrophobic feeling of the walls closing in overhead, blotting out sunlight, casting long purple shadows over the endlessly churning river. "The Grand Canyon of Arizona," wrote John L. Stoddard, "is Nature wounded unto death and lying stiff and ghastly, with a gash 200 miles in length and a mile in depth in her bared breast." That was one description in a collection of essays published by the Santa Fe Railroad in 1902. The book was meant to promote tourism, a plan that may have backfired, because none of the writers could agree on whether the Grand Canyon was gorgeous or horrifying. C. A. Higgins called it a "chaotic under-world, just emptied of primeval floods." Another visitor summed up his experience in a burst of feeling: "Horror! Tragedy! Silence! Death! Chaos!"

Jotter had dismissed these overblown descriptions before the trip. She told her father the Grand Canyon couldn't possibly be worse than the gray cliffs of Yosemite ("because the difference between three and five thousand feet can't be appreciated much as difference," she wrote.) Of course, there was a difference. In Yosemite she had slept safe on the gentle surface of the Earth and looked up at the mountains. Now, she was trapped in a mile-deep crack, with no way out but through. The boats drifted between deep red walls, which, when lit by morning sun, turned pale gold layered on rose. Windows and doorways opened high on the cliffs, as if built for gods or angels, bits of blue sky showing through. In some places, rocks were stacked as neatly as if by a bricklayer; in others, they made a disordered jumble, like a child's tower kicked to pieces. It was a place to overwhelm and bewilder the senses: fragrances so strong they had texture; colors so bright they rang like harp strings plucked by long, nimble fingers of sunlight.

One could be forgiven for thinking this was all there was to this place: stone, water, and sky. Also three little boats, suspended between these elements and wholly at their mercy. But Jotter made no mention of harrowing depths or ghastly colors in her journal. Her attention was all on plants. They clung to the talus slopes or fringed the river's edge, a sparse scattering of agave, yucca, and four-wing saltbush, with the occasional hackberry or redbud tree. The two botanists snatched up specimens whenever they could. They gathered samples of Mexican devilweed, tall green stems topped with white flowers which grew thickly on the cobble bars, and twining snapdragon (*Maurandya antirrhiniflora*), a plant with rambling tendrils and magenta blossoms shaped like pursed lips waiting for a kiss.

On the river, there were long stretches of slow water, split by rollicking rapids. Nevills's personal scale ranged from "a bit tricky" to "dangerous" to "damn rough!" but he had no more serious complaints about the crew. Gibson had faced his nightmares, and Bell proved a natural with the oars. Reed wasn't so adept, but he pitched in willingly on camp chores. He woke early to kindle the campfire and showed the others how to bury a can of beans in the hot coals before bed so it would be piping hot for breakfast. There were no more arguments. Jotter vented her feelings about Nevills's poor leadership by filling a whole page in her journal shortly after leaving Lee's Ferry, but outwardly she kept her composure. Nevills thawed enough toward Jotter to admit that she was a "good scout." Clover was relieved. She wrote that Jotter was "splendid in spite of those miserable days of whispering. We are trying to forget & forgive that."

In fact, they concealed their differences so well that the newer members of the crew seemed to have little inkling of the earlier unhappiness. "The gang could not have had wider interests," Reed mused, "and yet it seems to me that a band of friendship came to us that could not of come under any other circumstances."

On July 15, they pitched camp on a sandbar half-buried in driftwood. Bell created a table out of a twelve-foot piece of waterlogged lumber washed down from who knows where. The spot had an overhanging ledge to shelter them in a pinch, if it rained: the Redwall Limestone had appeared, pale white shelves stained crimson from iron oxides seeping down from the layers above. It had formed beneath a shallow sea more than 300 million years before, and fossil traces of sponges, sea lilies, and corals made a faded palimpsest within the stone.

It was Clover's turn to cook dinner while Jotter collected specimens. She scrambled up the talus slopes in search of plants. Apache plume (*Fallugia paradoxa*) was all over the hillside. Its pink, feathery flowers looked straight out of some fairyland, grafted to the end of dry, knobby sticks. Agaves were common, too, silhouetted on the ridges above her like astonished porcupines. She cut a few leaves from a particularly fine specimen with a twelve-foot stalk. *Leaves* was a misleading word. Agaves grew in rosettes of fleshy, blue-green swords, toothed all the way to the tips. Hualapai prize the plant for its heart, sweet as molasses when roasted in hot coals. In fact, a rare species of agave with long, lush leaves grows nowhere but the Grand Canyon, probably a cultivar, introduced and tended by Native people and planted close to roasting pits. *Agave phillipsiana* was unknown to Western botany in Jotter's time. The specimen she collected, *Agave utahensis,* is common in the Southwest. It is also called the century plant because people said it flowered just once in a century, a poetical exaggeration. The plant usually sends up a flowering stalk when it is between twenty and forty years of age. The big yellow blossoms turn the top of the stalk into a flaming torch for a few days or a week, drawing in a paparazzi of bats and buzzing bees. Then the stalk falls and the plant dies.

This agave was odd: it had red spines. Bright red, not the usual brown–burgundy color. *Curious*, Jotter thought. She looked closer. Then she realized that her hands were cut and bleeding. "The red was my contribution!" she wrote in her journal.

Night had fallen by the time she returned to camp. The others had eaten dinner without her. Jotter pressed her specimens in a light sprinkle of rain. Later she had a cup of hot tea and nibbled on leftovers, feeling sorry for herself. The cuts on her hands had scabbed over, her nails worn blunt and grimed from the day's work. Fine sand filtered into her clothing and hair. But that night, she dreamed of pressing plants in sleeves of newspaper. Clover, snugged beside her under the shelter of the overhanging ledge, heard her mutter, "It's just wonderful!"

"What is?" Clover asked.

"I made a wonderful collection," Jotter said. Clover realized she was talking in her sleep.

The rain cleared, but the air was sweltering even now, hours after the sun had descended behind the canyon walls. In the night, Clover woke with a start. A noise had startled her. Was the river rising? She climbed out of her bedroll and went to look. The river was rising, a little, but the boats were safely moored. She stood spellbound by the moonlight drifting down the cliffs, a play of silver light and deep shadow. Bell woke, too, and came to join her at the river's edge. They stood silent beneath the cold glow of the stars, watching the nearest rapid curl and froth, playful as an otter. Finally Clover crawled back into her bedroll, feeling her air mattress deflate by slow inches (she'd lost the plug some time before). "The night was so beautiful that I couldn't sleep," she wrote in her journal. She had been warned about the Grand Canyon: its oppressive walls and gloomy crags, and how the sound of water striking rock preyed on travelers' minds. She found, instead, a nameless beauty.

The two women woke before dawn, went for a swim, and then, tired of Grape-Nuts and hotcakes, made a mess of biscuits in a skillet for breakfast. They shot several rapids that morning and Jotter got an unexpected dousing when her boat struck a rock near shore and flipped her, head over heels, into the water. Just as well the weather was so hot. The Redwall Limestone now rose in a straight, shining, polished bulwark above them, riddled with arches, chambers, and rounded hollows where water had impudently scribbled its signature on the masterpiece of stone. Caves flickered with dancing blue light, driftwood wedged in their mouths like false teeth.

Thirty miles into the canyon, they passed Stanton's Cave, a round opening perched one hundred feet above the water. This was the place where Stanton had abandoned the river after three men drowned on his 1889 expedition. He stashed his supplies inside the cave and climbed to the rim in a desperate, wild-eyed scramble. Stanton was lucky. He had stumbled upon an ancient footpath, one of the few places a person could climb from river to rim. He had not been the first to see that dark, cool cleft in the wall as a refuge. By 1938, other river runners had ventured inside the cave and found twig figurines woven out of willow strands in the shape of four-legged animals. Some had tiny spears stuck in their sides. They may have been deer or mountain sheep, shorn of their horns, or perhaps long-necked horses. The figurines were the first signal to non-Native archeologists that the Grand Canyon had been in use by people at least three or four thousand years before; no surprise to Native peoples of the region, who knew their ancestors had walked those lands since time immemorial. Also in the cave were the bones of ancient horses, extinct ground sloths, and American cheetahs, as well as the dismembered skeletons of humpback chubs, monster fish with Quasimodo-like humps. Even the driftwood was intriguing: pieces of Western redbud and piñon pine washed down 35,000 years before, probably in a single massive flood.

The crew did not stop to see the cave. They had another destination in mind, a quarter of a mile downriver. Around 11 a.m., they dashed the boats sideways through a fast riffle, made a hard turn into an eddy, and floated back upriver to ground on a spit of sand. They had never stopped midday to collect plants before, but Clover insisted. Vasey's Paradise was special. Above them, freshwater springs leapt out of the limestone and unraveled long, twisting ribbons. At a glance they could see the dominant species: Western redbud, scarlet monkeyflower, and "gobs" of poison ivy. Clear rivulets of water chattered and burbled from beneath this verdant tangle, licked with streamers of algae and moss and more beautifully arranged than any ornamental garden. Powell had looked at this spot with a geologist's eyes, describing the sun-struck fountains as "a million brilliant gems," but he named it after a botanist, George Vasey. Vasey never boated the Grand Canyon, nor saw the place that bore his name. Clover and Jotter were the first botanists to make a catalog of the plants there for Western science.

Adiantum capillus-veneris (Southern maidenhair fern)
collected from Vasey's Paradise in the Grand Canyon. *Catalog*
#1582138, courtesy of the University of Michigan Herbarium,
Clover & Jotter collection, used by permission

They picked their way gingerly over the spray-slick stones. Plants
in this place reveled in water. The monkeyflower (*Mimulus cardina-*
lis) grew in clumps covered with blossoms that resembled ruby-red
slippers for very tiny feet. Here, too, were wooly clumps of Stans-
bury cliffrose (*Cowania stansburiana*), its flowers fragrant and creamy
white. There was a thicket of horsetail and a mat of watercress (*Ror-*
ippa nasturtium-aquaticum), an edible plant with a taste like peppery
lettuce. Mosses and ferns sprang up wherever spray touched the rock.
One variety, the side-fruited crisp-moss (*Pleurochaete squarrosa*), grew
in tight, kinky curls until it got damp, and then unfurled into yellow

stars. Longleaf brickellbush (*Brickellia longifolia*) grew out of cracks in the limestone, its roots in a hidden spring, its narrow leaves and white blossoms hung upside-down as if drunk on their own heady fragrance. Clover and Jotter sampled everything except the poison ivy (*Rhus radicans*), which lay in green hummocks over rocks printed with the silver tracks of snails.

Steps away from the springs, the desert reasserted itself: hedgehog cacti, spiky agave, and shrubby Mormon tea. This was a world that followed none of the neat rules Clover and Jotter had learned in botany textbooks. Clover was familiar with the work of C. Hart Merriam, who had come to Arizona almost fifty years before to work out his theory of "life zones." Merriam believed that the continent of North America could be divided into seven distinct zones, each with a particular distribution of plants and animals. He had used the San Francisco Peaks, an extinct volcano directly south of their present location, as a living laboratory.

Merriam's ideas had been powerful early in the century. He was born to an elite, well-connected family with a stately country estate in New York. As a young man, he had the freedom to roam the fields and woods and pursue whatever hobby he chose, which turned out to be killing and stuffing as many birds as he could. Like many nineteenth-century naturalists, Merriam trained to be a doctor. But in 1885, Congress authorized a section of ornithology (and later mammalogy) within the U.S. Department of Agriculture, and Merriam became its first director. As Asa Gray labored away on *Flora of North America,* Merriam undertook a similar survey of birds and mammals—a work so ambitious, in fact, he was destined never to complete it.

On July 26, 1889, Merriam showed up in Flagstaff with his wife, Elizabeth, his assistant, Vernon Bailey, and a cook. As an expedition, it lacked grandeur. They set up camp at the base of the San Francisco Peaks during the worst time of the year. The oppressive summer heat was livened only by terrifying thunderstorms and roiling flash floods. On one ill-prepared venture to the Painted Desert, the springs marked on their maps turned out to be dry, and they spent three days without water before limping into a Hopi village, Oraibi, to beg for melons and goat's milk. Later, Merriam and Bailey rode up the San Francisco Peaks as far as the horses would go, then clambered the rest of the way over treacherous scree. Spanish explorers had named the peaks Sierra Sinagua, "mountains without water," but Hopis knew better: snow clung to the shadows even in late summer, so they called it "the Place of Snow on the Very Top."

Merriam made careful notes of the plants and animals he saw on these forays. He thought the San Francisco Peaks could be used as a microcosm of North America as a whole. A day's hard hike from the Peaks to the desert mimicked, biologically, the trek from Canada to Mexico. At the very top, nothing grew but the hardiest of flowers, like the pygmyflower rockjasmine, a modest white bloom that could also be found in Greenland, Iceland, and other realms in the icy north. Below that came the timberline zone of bristlecone pine, gnarled and twisted from fighting the ever-present wind. Then came the spruce–fir forest, then mixed conifers—similar to the forests of Canada—and then the unbroken woods of ponderosa pine that skirted the peaks. Beneath this was a "Lilliputian forest" of piñon and juniper trees, which grew right up to the rim of the Grand Canyon. And then, at last, the desert: "the vast stretches of burning sand," as Merriam described it, "the total absence of trees, the scarcity of water, the alluring mirage, the dearth of animal life, and the intense heat, from which there is no escape."

Merriam's ideas weren't entirely new: he built on the work of the famed German naturalist Alexander von Humboldt, who had developed a similar concept about the relationships between plants and climate using a mountain in Ecuador as his model; and Hopis had their own names and rigorous classification system for the environmental zones in the Grand Canyon. Still, scientists received Merriam's seven "life zones" with enthusiasm. This was better, by far, than simply hacking North America into Eastern, Central, and Western provinces, as naturalists had done before. It also reflected how plants and animals evolved to fit their environments, a practical application of Darwin's theory. But criticisms soon arose. Merriam had focused only on temperature and ignored other factors that could influence a plant or animal's range. Cavalierly, he applied his life zones to the entire North American continent, even though fieldwork made it clear that they worked well only in the mountains of the western U.S.

Clover's trip downriver was an ideal opportunity to probe Merriam's life zones for flaws. She had dropped about a thousand feet in elevation since leaving Green River and would descend another two thousand if she made it to Boulder Dam. She now felt the life zone concept was useful in the Grand Canyon "only a broad way." Too many other factors shaped the distribution of plant life: the nearness to water, the texture of soils, the angle of sunlight, the browsing herbivores. She sampled moss one moment, plucked cactus pads the next.

Merriam's work, perhaps because of its flaws, sparked a lively conversation among botanists and ecologists. If temperature alone did not define the pattern of life on Earth's surface, what did? A more holistic view of climate fit better with observations, including rainfall and snowfall, evaporation and transpiration, and the changing seasons. But even this wasn't enough. In some places, soil overrode the importance of climate: deep sand dunes and rocky outcroppings. In others, water ruled: coastal marshes, mires, and bogs. There were physical processes like erosion and deposition, and biological ones like competition, predation, migration, and extinction. Disturbances—fires and floods—played a role. It was like a series of locked gates, and only those plants and animals with the right key—the right adaptations—could pass. The world wasn't made up of neatly defined zones, but rather circles within circles, with blurred boundaries and interlocking parts. Simple, elegant theories gave way to messier ones.

Merriam stuck with his life zones until his death in 1942, but he had come close to recognizing their flaws when he descended into the Grand Canyon during his 1889 expedition. A sore knee prevented him from hiking all the way down to the river, but what he saw puzzled him. The life zones seemed crowded into narrow, rapidly changing bands. Tiny forests clung to talus slopes, and springs interrupted the desert with frantic explosions of moss. At 1 a.m., he hiked back to the rim alone, holding a gun in one hand and a dead skunk in the other. Black as iron gates, the walls closed in. "The way seemed without end," he wrote in his journal. "The higher I climbed the higher the walls seemed to tower above me." He could say nothing about the Grand Canyon with any certainty. It was "a world in itself," Merriam wrote, "and a great fund of knowledge is in store for the philosophic biologist whose privilege it is" to study it.

CLOVER AND JOTTER had no time for philosophy. They had barely an hour to spend at Vasey's Paradise. "We collected furiously," Jotter wrote in her logbook, heedless of a light rain. Bell and Gibson, meanwhile, stripped down to shorts and showered beneath one of the waterfalls. By noon the men were waiting hungrily for lunch. Clover suggested mildly they get out the canned food and cold biscuits (left over from breakfast) and feed themselves. But when the two women finished putting up their samples in newspaper, they found the rest of their crew "waiting big-eyed & expectant under a rock."

In a rare moment of impatience, Clover wrote, "We have spoiled them completely."

They left Vasey's Paradise and went on, deeper into the canyon. The walls rose in tiers, stretching back to a jagged skyline. High gaps on the cliffs looked like keyholes, and when the angle was just right, the sun's rays fumbled through like a skeleton key turning in a lock. Their clothing grew disheveled, despite frequent use of Clover's sewing kit. The women wore their overalls rolled up to the knees; the men had their shirttails untucked or wore no shirts at all. "We are wet all the time," Clover wrote, "so the less on the better." The river had dropped a good deal. All of them grew more comfortable with running rapids, and Nevills felt it necessary to try to scare them back into caution with horror stories of what lay around the next bend.

This worked on Reed so well that he couldn't sleep the night before they reached President Harding Rapid, until Clover calmly said, "I imagine when we get to them, they'll just be another rapid."

They were now more than forty miles downriver from Lee's Ferry, and the plant life was changing as the climate grew hotter and drier. Honey mesquite (*Prosopis juliflora*) appeared, a shrubby tree with minuscule leaves and sweet-tasting beans tucked into rattling seed-pods. The tough, teardrop-shaped seeds wouldn't sprout unless they were battered by floodwaters or half-digested by an animal, thus ensuring they would spread far and wide. They were helped, too, by Native inhabitants of the canyon, who cut some trees for firewood but spared the ones with the sweetest-tasting beans; such management blurred the lines between the wild and the domestic.

Mesquite mingled on the talus with catclaw acacia (*Acacia greggii*), also called wait-a-minute bush, because of the way its curved thorns snatched at passersby. Strawberry hedgehog cacti (*Echinocereus engelmannii*) grew in thick rosettes straight out of the cliff walls, as if pinned up like wreaths. Prickly pears dangled long stringers of paddle-like leaves from the tops of boulders, Rapunzel-like, trying to escape their towers on ropes of knotted green hair. Prickly pear (also known by its Spanish name, nopal) has edible pads and fat, oval fruits, sweet to the taste, if one does not mind magenta-stained fingers and a sticker or two. Clover and Jotter had cataloged several species so far, some spineless but covered in tiny, near-invisible bristles, some with yellow flowers, others vivid cerise. "Their existence seems to be precarious," wrote Clover, "since they are usually found half-buried in sand or lodged between boulders." Near President Harding Rapid, *Opuntia engelmannii* appeared for the first time, with unusually large pads and plum-colored fruits. Indigenous residents of the canyon may have brought this type of prickly pear up from the south and deliberately tended the plants as a pleasant addition to meals.

There was plenty to collect while the men ran the boats through the rapids, but Clover seemed a little bored with her safe, landbound role. At President Harding Rapid, she dared Bell to hit a big rock on purpose and tip over so she could get a photograph. He did dart the boat thrillingly close to a boulder and had to apologize to Nevills afterward for his recklessness. Ashamed of herself, Clover wrote in her journal that she never dreamed he would try it.

Muav Limestone rose out of the river, gray and striated: a slip of time sending them back to the Cambrian Period, more than 500 million years before, when multicellular life began to flourish and struggle out of the fecund sea onto a barren shore. Bright Angel Shale appeared beneath it, crumbling horizontal layers of purple and green. It was now nearly impossible to climb from the river to the rim, but a crack in the sheer Redwall wedged with broken timbers showed where Ancestral Puebloans, long ago, built a precarious road. The crew floated below the open mouths of cliff dwellings and sifted through pebbles for arrowheads and sherds. Their fingers startled up tiny toads. Deer watched their passing from dark thickets of mesquite, ghosting away through the tight weave of spiny branches. Below the boats, the dark water concealed its secrets. Hard to believe, but there were fish in that river: fish with leathery skins and torpedo-shaped bodies evolved to withstand endless sandblasting, and monstrous minnows that grew to the length of a man and weighed one hundred pounds. Clover, in the back of her journal, began to scribble a poem:

> *How can I write so you will understand,*
> *Who have not heard the raging devil roar . . .*

But the canyon's strangeness seemed to slip away from the strict, formal lines, and she concluded in despair: "the subject will probably be beyond me."

They ran twenty-five miles on July 17, "a good days Run in any mans Language," scribbled Reed in his diary, and then punctuated the entry, as he always did, with the thankful words: "All Safe." The Tapeats Sandstone emerged at river level, dark rock fractured into horizontal lines, flaky as well-made pastry. Lying on top like serpentine dragons, fast asleep, were petrified flows of travertine, a spiky stone made from calcium carbonate precipitating out of water. They passed the Confluence sometime that afternoon, where the Little Colorado River emerged from its own canyon on the left and bent around its delta to join the Colorado. The waves turned choppy and coffee-brown where the two rivers met. Tumbled stones, rounded by water, lay on the delta: azure and mauve, taupe and terracotta, some white and cracked like eggs ready to open, others like blunt black knives. The Confluence is a sacred place to the region's tribes. Zuni send spiritual offerings down the Little Colorado to the Grand Canyon, the home of their ancestors. Hopis say nearby is the place of emergence, where all humankind climbed into this world, the Fourth World, through the hollow stem of a reed, and spread over the Earth, leaving footprints and broken pottery to mark their journeys. Hopi youth make a sacred pilgrimage to the Confluence to gather the salt that seeps out of the sandstone, pressed from an ancient sea and crystallized into gleaming stalagmites. They bring the salt back to the mesas east of the Grand Canyon, where, they say, their people settled at the center of the earth.

Nevills deemed the place a poor campsite, so they drifted on to the head of Tanner Rapid. Up until this point the river had hoarded its vistas, a notch here or a bend there revealing some startling view of sky—or merely another cliff, higher and farther away than the first. Now, as if regretting its stinginess, the landscape rolled back. Red round hills sloped down to the water, and beyond them, in every direction, one could see layers of strata stacked, tilted, and jumbled, wedding-cake-style, if a wedding cake oozed travertine and spit boulders. To the south, the round cylindrical bump of the Desert View Watchtower stood on the highest ridge, blue with distance and furred with juniper trees. They camped in a cove at the head of the rapid, found a handy jam of driftwood, and set it ablaze. Nevills had arranged this signal with the Park Service: a single bonfire meant "everything okay," a double bonfire meant "send help." It was a fine sight, the fire roaring and crackling beside the dark waters of the

river, with a stormy sky above. They strained their eyes, looking for
some answering glimmer from the tower. There—perhaps that was
it—a quicksilver shine in the darkness. Or perhaps it had been a trick
of starlight. It was hard to be sure of anything, down here.

The women woke before dawn the next day, as usual. All was gray.
The air held a sense of impending rain. Their camp was tucked into
a great bend in the river, so the water curved away in both directions.
A pink mist lay over its surface in languid folds. Dark clouds hung
in the east, underbellies alight with gold ribbon and purple gauze.
Then the sun's first rays crossed to the opposite canyon wall and lit
the Watchtower. The world turned salmon. The light slid downward,
burnishing the somber gray cliff to a glow. The gibbous moon, waning now, had not yet set; broken-edged, it hung over the canyon. A
rainbow leapt from the cliff wall into the sky, one dazzling pathway
from earth to cloud. Jotter and Clover stood in their damp, wrinkled
clothes, nails torn to the quick, aching and bruised, lost for words.
It was their last day on the river before the layover at Bright Angel
Creek, where they could rest and resupply. One more day before hot
baths, fresh fruit, and letters—one day, and three major rapids.

Chapter Nine

A MOST UNUSUAL AND HAZARDOUS MEANS

A SMALL CROWD GATHERED ON THE SOUTH RIM of Grand Canyon National Park, near a cluster of telescopes pointed down into the mazy depths. The river below was small—so small—like a loose silver thread in a tapestry of stone. Three black leaves seemed to curl and wisp in the frothy whitewater of Hance Rapid. No, not leaves. Boats! "Here they come!" someone cried. The boats drove hard to the left side of the river and then dashed to the right. They seemed weightless and adrift. Was anyone guiding them at all?

It was late in the morning on July 18. The night before, the *Arizona Republic* had reported a lone signal fire at Tanner Rapid, believed by park officials to indicate that the Nevills Expedition was safe. They were expected shortly to pass under the Black Bridge and stop at Bright Angel Creek, barring any mishap in the rapids. It was a stormy sort of day, with dark-bellied monsoon clouds broiling on the horizon, threatening squalls of rain. The South Rim was busy. Visitor numbers had grown dramatically since the park's creation in 1919. At first, they mostly came by railroad, wealthy travelers who bought roundtrip tickets from "End of Track" to "Rim of Canyon" and stayed in the lavish El Tovar Hotel or the more modest Bright Angel Lodge. In 1926 the balance tipped to visitors coming by car, so-called "sage-brushers" who packed their Model Ts with camping gear and spent the night in tents. These visitors were mostly white. National parks still banned or segregated people of color, and Indigenous peoples could no longer hunt for food or gather plants on their homelands. Traditional land use became illegal, while tourism spiked. More than 330,000 people visited the Grand Canyon in 1938. There were developed campgrounds now, an employee dormitory, sewage and electric lines, a brand-new post office, and even plans for a school.

But the Grand Canyon's visitor numbers still trailed behind Yellowstone and Yosemite, the nation's oldest national parks, and also fell short of Mount Rainier, Acadia, and Shenandoah, with soft green slopes or blazing autumn colors. Twice as many people went to Rocky Mountain National Park, and even more flocked to the Great Smoky Mountains. It was odd, but the Grand Canyon hadn't been an easy sell to tourists. It wasn't like looking at the mountains of Yosemite or the geysers of Yellowstone, or any other national park in the United States. Nothing about it was predictable or even, really, picturesque. How could you paint a landscape defined by the absence of something—the sweeping away of a whole mountain to the sea?

The park's current superintendent, M. R. Tillotson, was an engineer by training. He was determined to increase visitor numbers, which had faltered after the stock market crash. Hundreds of day laborers went to work in the Depression years to make the park presentable. They added trails, built roads, cleared out old mining claims, and created campgrounds to cater to the middle class. Marketing materials gushed about the paved roads and hot dinners almost as much as the sublime scenery. Women could rent riding breeches and straw hats, should they find their clothing unsuitable for a desert hike. Naturalists gave talks each evening illustrated with motion pictures or lantern slides. Here, one could experience the wonders of nature and have a nice clam chowder dinner, followed by blancmange pudding with cream.

This was, after all, the National Park Service's mandate: to provide for the public's enjoyment. That's what it said in the legislation that established the national park system in 1916: "to conserve the scenery and the natural and historic objects and the wild life therein and to provide for the enjoyment of the same in such manner and by such means as will leave them unimpaired for the enjoyment of future generations." From the start, the Park Service sought to bring tourists in and (less consistently) to keep mining, logging, grazing, and dams out. But in the 1930s, a fierce debate arose within the agency's ranks about what, exactly, it was supposed to preserve. The debate centered on a single word of the agency's mandate: *unimpaired.*

🌿

DOWN ON THE RIVER, Jotter stood on a rocky outcropping with a churning sensation in her stomach. They had come safely through Hance Rapid, quartering the boats in a zigzag pattern, oblivious of the alarmed watchers on the rim. ("It's enough to chill one's blood!" Nevills noted in his diary.) At its foot they entered the Upper Granite Gorge, a canyon within a canyon. Here, the basement of the world lay exposed—upthrust stone pinnacles like crenellated castles built by an architect who used teeth and claws instead of tools. No banks or sandbars here, just shelves of rock, polished to a black shine on smooth surfaces, veined and clotted pink, with sweat lines of white quartz. Mesquite trees unrolled tattered green ribbons down the draws that split the stone, and agave and hedgehog cacti grew right out of the rock. Anyone prone to vertigo had no safe place to look. The cliffs strained skyward, ridged and runneled, fighting gravity and the fate of all mountains, so alive they might ripple and flinch like a horse in the midst of curvetting. The river plummeted downward, funneling toward infinity. No way to portage or line the boats here: they had to brave the whitewater. Hance and Sockdolager were behind them. Grapevine lay ahead.

Holmstrom had warned Jotter about Grapevine in particular. It must be run, he told her; you can't climb around it. Enter through a narrow, swift chute in the center, pull to the left, drop down the rapid and then turn the boat hard to the right—and don't let your nerves get the better of you. The warning played through Jotter's mind as she stared at the seething whitewater. The crew had moored the boats on the cliff and walked a little way downriver to study

Grapevine, edging along a precarious ledge. Sharp stones snagged their clothing and tricked their feet. They had to shout to hear one another over the roar of the rapid. Holmstrom estimated the rapid to be a sixteen-foot drop with numerous holes, "and as we looked it over," Jotter wrote in her journal, "I had the old before-the-exam feeling in pit of stomach."

The wind picked up while they studied the rapid; it teased white-tipped claws from the river. Clover and Nevills went first. They returned to the *Wen,* and Jotter went with them to collect the movie camera. Then she hastened back to where the others were waiting. Reed and Bell looked grim and worried, and Gibson sat with his head cradled in his hands. Jotter handed a cigarette to each of them and smoked one herself to soothe her jitters.

The *Wen* went through. The watchers on the cliffside, barely breathing, saw the boat appear and disappear in the waves. Grape-vine packed "more of a wallop than most," in Clover's words. The *Wen* crashed through a pourover, and Nevills, soaked and grinning, turned round right in the middle of the lashing current to say, "What will Bill think of this one?" Gibson and Reed were next. They left their vantage point and set off to the boats. Reed was nervous, but the gut-clenching terror he'd felt since coming to the river had eased. Hours earlier, just before running Hance, he thought he saw a friendly face smiling up at him from the turbulent current. The eerie glimpse had given him, he wrote, "much needed courage."

Jotter had not been gifted with a similar vision. She followed behind the two men, the movie camera a deadweight in the satchel swung over her shoulder. She was watching her feet on the perilous ledges, following the same track she had traversed before, but some-how, she missed the way and found herself six feet higher above the river. She glanced down. It churned, chocolate-brown, a frothy boil. The world tipped, and for one wild moment she teetered on the edge, about to plunge down, down, down—to be dashed on the rocks and pounded in the fearsome current, swept away, tumbled to pieces—and then the strap of the camera's bag snagged on a rock crevasse. It held. Jotter found her footing again and flattened her body against the wall, breathing hard. Her knees buckled and she didn't trust herself to walk. She was still there, a few moments later, when Bell came around a corner and caught sight of her face.

"Here," he said roughly, "let me carry that camera."

She handed it over without a word. They reached the *Mexican Hat* and climbed in. Jotter felt weak and shaky. Bell began to push the boat out into the current, and Reed shouted at him from the other boat: he had left his life preserver on the shore. They turned back. Bell snugged the straps in place and took up the oars again. The wind was strong, pushing the boat too far leftward, no matter how much Bell fought against it with the oars. Painfully, he pulled back into the main current, centering the boat on the tongue. But as they came through the first long drop into the rapid, the fickle wind gusted again and pushed them off-center. No time! They were headed for the hole on the port side: a dark yawn in the river leeward of a cresting wave that continually broke and reformed.

"Here we go," Jotter said to Bell.

"We're in for it!" he shouted back.

The boat turned crosswise. They swept toward the hole. Bell dug one oar, hard, into the water and the *Mexican Hat* swung round, bow pointed upstream, blunt stern facing the hole. They caught the edge of it and went swirling in, around, and through. *Now we're in the thick of it,* Jotter thought, and Bell was hauling on the oars, teeth clenched, face set downriver, half-blinded by spray. A wave on the right—they passed it by—and another hole on the left—this, too, missed by inches. Then they came up over a wave and the whole bottom of the *Mexican Hat* was visible to the watchers in the *Botany* and the *Wen* below as the boat tipped vertical.

And then they were through, down to the quiet water where the other boats waited, and Jotter let go her white-knuckled grip and began to bail water.

"We go on," wrote Clover, "thru restless water between sheer walls of black to reddish basalt streaked with white marble." It wasn't truly marble, but thick ropes of Zoroaster Granite interlaced with dark schist formed 1.75 billion years ago when life on Earth had not progressed beyond a single cell. The ribbons of pale pinkish stone were once living magma in the veins of the earth, now hardened, folded, and warped by tectonic convulsions, brought into the sunlight by the thin knife of the Colorado River. These rocks were the roots of mountains that had long since eroded away.

The walls closed in; the river narrowed. Blooming agaves stood like spears thrust into the tortured stone. Wind caught up fistfuls of sand to blind them. There were still rapids ahead, but nothing so large, and it came as a surprise to Jotter to look up and see the Kaibab Bridge stretched over the water. The suspension bridge had been hauled in pieces into the canyon and assembled in 1928. CCC crews painted it black, so it was also called the Black Bridge. It was the only way to cross the river without a boat for hundreds of miles. As they passed beneath its span, they looked up. Three journalists waved down at them from the bridge.

"Look as if you're glad to be landing!" one of them yelled.

Jotter wasn't glad, "because it meant people, fuss, and the end of a perfect day."

They grounded the boats just below the bridge on a broad sandbar, near where Bright Angel Creek hummed a cheerful tune of its own composition. The newsmen had brought their mail, apparently for the purpose of handing it round while running the cameras. "Smile! This is the right letter, isn't it?" they grinned at the women, who tucked the letters away to read later, in private. Compared to the isolation of the preceding weeks, this place seemed crowded; tourists could reach it by hiking or riding a mule down the steep trails from the rim, and Phantom Ranch nearby hosted overnight guests. The manager of the lodge issued an invitation for them all to come to dinner. Clover and Jotter found a few useful bushes to use as a screen as they changed into cleaner overalls, but they were not quite finished when the rest of their crew and a gaggle of strangers marched by. "Don't look!" Clover yelled, half joking, and at the

Lois Jotter in the *Mexican Hat,* beached on
a sandbar near Bright Angel Creek. *Grand Canyon
National Park Museum Collection #00593*

sound of her voice all her crewmates involuntarily turned their heads.
The women laughed about it as they made their way up to Phantom
Ranch together, behind the rest of the group.

They passed over a broad delta covered in prickly pear and mesquite to the edge of the creek, which ran over many-colored cobbles
between young cottonwood trees planted in rows. Phantom Ranch
was built on a flat spot on the canyon floor which had been used as a
campsite for hundreds of years. It had held kivas and pit houses, and
then, much later, tents for adventurous tourists. In 1922 the Fred Har-
vey Company began building a resort designed by the architect Mary
Colter. It now included a central lodge and dining room, a recreation
hall, and a handful of cabins made of rounded river rocks. Tourists
paid six dollars a night for a room. There was a brand-new mule
corral and a swimming pool fed from the waters of Bright Angel
Creek. Sycamores sheltered the rustic stone buildings, white-barked
and long-limbed.

Clover and Jotter waited at the lodge while the men showered and
shaved. They appeared in ones and twos, "in various stages of dress &
undress," as Clover put it. She stayed up late after supper, with several

of the others, to play pool and talk to the cowboys who crowded round their table. But Jotter, craving quiet, took Bell across the footbridge and walked a little way up the Bright Angel Trail. They returned by moonlight to their campsite by the river's edge, blew up their air mattresses, and boldly lay side by side, gazing at the summer constellations.

It took some time for Clover and the rest of the group to join them. They had lingered too late at the lodge, and it was pitch-black now. They missed their way and ended up at the corral, where the mules gazed curiously over the slats with whiskered noses and long-lashed eyes. In the end, they had to ask a couple of wranglers and their girlfriends for help. The whole group headed for the river, one flashlight between them. It made a faint yellow circle, skittering among the tree trunks and along the slippery stones. The visitors wanted to sit in the boats, safely grounded on the sandbar, and it was a while before the crew had their campsite to themselves again. Nobody was ready to sleep. They laid out their bedrolls or threw themselves down on the sand, talking idly as wind rustled the hollow-stemmed, tassel-topped reeds along the creek. Clover dug out her bottle of Four Roses and unscrewed the lid. Whiskey fumes mingled with the scent of clear water, damp leaves, and the pervasive stink of mule. They might as well kill the bottle this evening, Clover declared. She passed around a jigger to everyone except Nevills, who didn't drink alcohol. Under cover of the darkness, Jotter secretly poured hers onto the sand.

FOR GENERATIONS, a narrow footpath had wound from the Grand Canyon's south rim down stony switchbacks and into a green oasis supported by springs bursting from the limestone. Havasupai, whose feet wore the path, called it the Coyote Tail Trail, a reference to the brushy ends of spruce trees. They used the same word for the canyon's south rim, where the spruce grew thickly. In summer, they grew squash and melons in the canyon and tended orchards on Havasu Creek. In winter, they moved to the plateau to hunt for deer and cottontail and burn fragrant juniper fires. They had followed this pattern for centuries. Then, in 1893, the U.S. government turned much of their winter range into the Grand Canyon Forest Reserve.

Reserve supervisor W. P. Hermann wrote, "The Grand Canyon of the Colorado River is becoming so renowned for its wonderful and extensive natural gorge scenery and for its open clean pine woods, that it should be preserved for the everlasting pleasure and instruction of our intelligent citizens as well as those of foreign countries." He went on, "Henceforth, I deem it just and necessary to keep the wild and unappreciable Indian from off the Reserve . . ."

The government took measures to keep the Havasupai on the tiny reservation set aside for them in the lower canyon, an area twelve miles long and five miles wide at Havasu Creek. In 1928, park rangers drove the last Havasupai farmer from the oasis known as Indian Garden (now called Havasupai Gardens). The same year, the Park Service took control of the old Coyote Tail Trail, which had been renamed the Bright Angel Trail and operated as a toll road for tourists. Havasupai began to call the South Rim by a word that meant "where the train stops."

Clover, Jotter, and the rest woke before sunrise the next morning with plans to hike the Bright Angel Trail to the South Rim, bleary with the aftereffects of whiskey and less than five hours of sleep. Yet another breakfast of Grape-Nuts and canned grapefruit did not improve matters. They faced an eleven-mile trek to the rim, climbing more than four thousand vertical feet, a hike that the Park Service warned was only suitable for visitors in the "soundest physical condition." The crew could have posted letters and ordered fresh supplies from Phantom Ranch, so it's likely they decided to make the hike merely for the fun of it—all except Reed, who opted to stay behind and guard the boats. The plant press, stuffed with specimens, also stayed behind. Clover arranged to have it hauled up the Bright Angel Trail on a mule and shipped to Michigan.

To save themselves more than a mile of hiking, they crossed the river on a rickety tramway used by CCC crews to haul firewood from one side to the other, not much more than a large wooden crate suspended on a cable, two sides completely open to the air. Everyone crowded in, and then—zip!—the cable swung by gravity down toward the river's center. They could see the rushing water sixty feet below through the slats beneath their feet. Then—creak, creak, creak—an operator on the other side cranked a winch to jerk the cage the rest of the way across. The long climb down the twisting rope ladder must have been an adventure in itself.

Their route staggered upward through a crack—a fault line— down the canyon's vertical face. Halfway up the trail, they all collapsed gratefully in the shade of the cottonwoods at Havasupai Gardens and gazed drearily at the switchbacks cutting the canyon wall above them. A checklist of plants circulated to botany-minded tourists at this time suggested they look for Indian hemp or dogbane here (*Apocynum cannabinum*), a sweet-scented flower with healing properties and tough, fibrous stems, which Clover had found at several stops along the Green and Colorado rivers; but she had not brought her plant press and so she sampled nothing.

Her collection was becoming a curious record of how people had shaped the ecology of the Colorado River: some plants cultivated and used by Indigenous peoples, others introduced by people of European descent. Havasupai Gardens had been shaped by human hands for millennia, beginning with Ancestral Puebloans, Cohonina, and Havasupai. White entrepreneurs, having forced the Havasupai out, planted cottonwoods and fruit trees and dammed the creek to irrigate strawberry patches. The Park Service, following at their heels, made changes of their own. A herd of roughly two dozen American pronghorn ghosted through the cottonwoods, deerlike creatures that approached visitors on shy, dancing feet in hopes of something tasty to eat. The pronghorn did not belong there. The Park Service transplanted them from Nevada in 1924.

At this time, only about 650 pronghorns remained in Arizona, and 26,000 in the nation, though they once numbered in the millions, more numerous than bison. They grazed in bunches on the high mountain meadows, buff-and-black fur nearly indistinguishable from the grass until they turned their white rumps skyward in alarm and dashed away. These particular pronghorns had been scooped up as infants and bottle-fed cow's milk on a Nevada ranch. Fenced, they became "extraordinary helpless," one observer reported. Two fawns broke their necks on a headlong dash, unable to see the fence that contained them.

Park Service officials might have had their mandate to preserve wildlife in mind when they decided to bring a dozen young fawns to the Grand Canyon, each packed into a crate so narrow they could not "change ends in it." More to the point, the animals made a nice tourist attraction. The half-tame herd at Havasupai Gardens increased to twenty-eight by 1933, but then their numbers diminished. They were plains animals, and their best defense was flight. On flat ground they could top sixty miles an hour; some biologists believe they evolved this fleetness so they could outrun the American cheetah, a Pleistocene animal long since extinct. Boxed into the canyon, there was no safety in speed. New fawns were picked off by coyotes and bobcats.

In a survey of the fauna of national parks published in 1933, George Meléndez Wright criticized the experiment, noting that it would be better "if no alien member were introduced into the canyon." Not that he thought the pronghorn represented any real menace to native creatures, but they did not "measure up to the Park Service aim of presenting animal life in its natural habitat." Born to a Salvadorian mother and an American father, Wright was one of very few biologists who questioned the Park Service's focus on tourism. How could one preserve a place as "unimpaired" if no surveys cataloged the plants and animals that lived there before drastic changes took place?

When Wright started his career as a naturalist at Yosemite, he entered a Park Service that generally categorized animals as either tourist attractions or pests. At the Grand Canyon, bison crossbred with cattle grazed on the North Rim, a place where bison probably hadn't grazed in great numbers since the Pleistocene. Rocky Mountain elk roamed Arizona's high country, shipped from Yellowstone by railcar in 1913 to replace the native Merriam's elk, which had been hunted into extinction. Ring-necked pheasants dumped in the bottom of the Grand Canyon disappeared within months. The same fate met a group of Gambel's quail, desert birds with charming top-knots and tiny golden babies which had the general shape and atti-tude of popcorn kernels—barely a snack for a bobcat. Visitors to the South Rim could feed half-tame herds of wild deer by hand. To please the visitors (and hunters on surrounding lands), park officials and hired hunters shot any predator that might threaten the deer. By the early 1930s, predator control agents had killed nearly eight hun-dred mountain lions on the North Rim, twenty wolves, hundreds of bobcats, and thousands of coyotes. At the same time, rangers packed trout eggs and fry down the Grand Canyon's trails in aerated cans. In 1931, Tillotson bragged that all the "favorable trout streams" had been stocked with non-native fish. To feed the trout, fifty thousand shrimplike creatures known as scud were stuck in the moss in Bright Angel Creek.

Wright disapproved. He felt that the parks had been drawn like lit-tle chalk squares around pretty bits of scenery, without any regard for the ecological needs of the creatures who lived within them. He con-vinced the agency to let him carry out a survey of wildlife in national parks, funded from his own pocket. ("Am I a visionary or just crazy?" he wrote to a friend at the start of the project.) For the next three years, Wright explored the parks and made careful notes, assisted by two colleagues and his wife, Bee.

The resulting document, known as "Fauna No. 1," set forth a series of blunt recommendations. Parks should never interfere with delicate "biotic relationships" until a proper scientific investigation had been carried out. As much as possible, each species should be left "to carry on its struggle for existence unaided." Bears and deer should not be fed for entertainment. Non-native animals should no longer be moved around at whim. Predator control needed to end. (Even the rattle-snake, Wright wrote, "should not be condemned without fair trial.") Wright went further and advocated for restoring degraded habitat and reintroducing vanished creatures, work that had to be based on a clear understanding of what parks had looked like prior to the "violent changes" inflicted by people of European descent. Bilingual in Spanish and English, with roots in Central America, Wright understood that ecology could benefit not just from scientific research, but also from the knowledge of Indigenous peoples, who had acted as stewards and skilled land managers before the national park system came into being.

Wright freely admitted that his ideas about science-based land management weren't popular. As it turned out, he would have far too short a time to try to change his colleagues' minds.

THE CREW LEFT THE COOLNESS of Havasupai Gardens and straggled upward. Ocher handprints shone from the cliffs and the river fell away beneath them, lost in a fantasy of stone. By midmorning, pack trains carrying "dudes"—wealthier tourists—began to come down the trail, reeking of animal sweat. Jotter was annoyed by the protocol that shunted hikers to the side to make room for the mules. "Something about being mounted on a mule makes people feel superior," she wrote in her diary. The tourists grinned and teased them: "Do you think you'll ever get up?" The July heat beat down on the exposed switchbacks. Ravens circled above them, then below them as they climbed. There was hardly any shade, except for the stone rest houses recently built by the CCC. "I didn't mind the first 4 or 5 miles," Clover wrote in her journal, "but when I had gone 6 ½ I didn't like it." She was less than three miles from the top when she collapsed from exhaustion. She was embarrassed, but she couldn't go a step farther.

Nevills set off at a jog to request a mule to rescue her. The rest of the crew stumbled along behind him, Gibson and Bell doing their best to bolster Jotter's flagging spirits. At the top, they flung themselves down at Emery Kolb's photography studio. The sprawling wooden house and lecture hall overhung the canyon's rim at the head of the Bright Angel Trail. Kolb and his wife, Blanche, ushered them into the showers and prepared pitchers of iced tea and lunch.

Nevills and Kolb knew each other. Kolb had passed through Mexican Hat in 1937 and examined one of Nevills's boats, pronouncing it a sensible design. His opinion mattered. He was a veteran of river trips, having run the Grand Canyon in a movie-making venture with his brother Ellsworth in 1911 and again as head boatman of the Birdseye expedition in 1923. He also took part in the dramatic, doomed search for Bessie and Glen Hyde, the vanished honeymooners. Newspapers sought his opinion at least as often as the idolized Buzz Holmstrom. Unlike Holmstrom, Kolb had a flair for publicity. He made his living by lecturing, showing films, and photographing tourists who headed down the Bright Angel Trail on mule trains.

The Kolbs had a grown-up daughter, Edith, who'd had an adventurous childhood. At the age of sixteen, Edith hiked into the Grand Canyon to meet her father while the Birdseye expedition was waiting for a resupply via mule train. Edith talked her father into letting her run Hance Rapid. Birdseye, who knew nothing of the matter, turned around at the foot of the rapid and spotted her riding fearlessly on the stern as it hit the waves head-on. "She is surely a game girl," he wrote. The local newspaper, the *Coconino Sun,* wrote a story about Edith's adventure, calling her "the only white woman" who had ever shot a Grand Canyon rapid. A week later, La Rue's wife, Mabel, took a mule into the canyon down the Bright Angel Trail and rode a short way downriver in one of the boats, holding her hat the whole time because she did not have a hatpin. About her first sight of rough water, she wrote, "I felt that my hat was no longer of any importance, for perhaps I should never need it again." She enjoyed the ride, but Birdseye's men refused to take her any farther. "They said the next rapids would be too rough," Mabel wrote, "but I think they were afraid I would spoil the bad reputation of the Colorado River Rapids."

Little danger of that. Some newspapers now cited Edith Kolb's experience as proof that women *couldn't* shoot rapids; one man claimed that responsibility for the safety of "one of the fair sex" so worried Edith's boatman that he nearly capsized out of pure nerves. He used the story to justify a snide comment about the "handicap" Clover and Jotter presented to their crew.

Naysayers aside, the public greeted the arrival of the two botanists at the South Rim with unbridled enthusiasm. Clover, after she joined the others at Kolb's studio, was amused by the fuss. They all went to see Kolb's movie that evening (admission: forty cents), and Kolb introduced the "daring troupe" to the crowd. Afterward, they were kept busy signing autographs. Jotter, Gibson, and Bell finally slipped away in search of dinner. Grand Canyon Village was quiet after nightfall, tastefully decorated with twisted junipers arranged to showcase the rustic architecture and leave the majestic canyon views unimpeded. The trio talked their way into the dining room at Bright Angel Lodge at closing time; the men coaxed a reluctant waitress to put in their order (steaks all around) just before 11 p.m. Later, Jotter joined Clover in the room they shared at the lodge. They had both forgotten to bring pajamas. They undressed and slept "raw" in the heat. After so many nights sleeping out under the stars, Jotter wasn't particularly grateful for a real bed—"our little rat trap," she called the room, "which cost us too much per night."

In a backhanded compliment, the Associated Press reported that all members of the expedition—including the women—had "borne up well." The article described Clover and Jotter as badly sunburned, the skin peeling from their hands and faces. Botany was not mentioned.

JOTTER ESCAPED her stifling room early the next morning to lounge on the terrace, write postcards, and peruse the thick stack of mail she'd received at Phantom Ranch. "My dear," one letter began, "it took my breath away a minute ago when I realized I could write just 'Lois Jotter' on an envelope and it would get to you!" Her friends and family had written to her with a mixture of envy and terror. Imagination filled the gaps in the news coverage. Some friends pictured a roiling river with whole trees threatening to smash up the boats; others imagined, half playfully, a wilderness of alligators and man-eating bears. An uncle in Chicago offered his congratulations and then promised a good scolding the next time he saw her: "You have no idea how much sleep we lost thinking of you risking your life on that treacherous river just for some new weeds," he wrote. "You could have had all the weeds you wanted out of my garden just for the asking."

They were supposed to hike back to the river that day and resume the journey, but Nevills, who had spent the night with the Kolbs, agreed to a delay so they could all be interviewed for an NBC broadcast that afternoon. He also invited Kolb to come along for the rest of the trip. They didn't need another boatman, but perhaps Nevills realized that Kolb's presence could only benefit his efforts to drum up publicity. The broadcast was set for 3:15 p.m. Jotter and Clover amused themselves by exploring the park and eavesdropping on tourists who wondered out loud whatever had happened to those people who were lost on the river. "Oh, they were found," Jotter assured them, without saying who she was. Some mistook her for a local resident because of her deep tan and asked if she recommended the three-dollar tour or the six-dollar one. She didn't know.

It was a windy day, with a long, low cloud bank lying across the distant North Rim, and loose puffs of cloud scudding through the canyon below their feet like ships in full sail. Neither Clover nor Jotter attempted to scribble down any kind of description of the Grand Canyon as seen from the rim—the buttes and pinnacles and ravines jumbled together in a hazy, dimensionless wonderland, now roseate, now purpled in shadow. Perhaps they felt, as one writer suggested, "where the Grand Canyon begins, words stop." Or perhaps it all seemed rather passé after having experienced the canyon from the perspective of the river.

Most tourists believed that because the Grand Canyon was pretty and inaccessible, it was pristine. The National Park Service encouraged these romantic perceptions. In 1928, Horace Albright, then director of the agency, wrote an article in the *Saturday Evening Post* titled "The Everlasting Wilderness," in which he described parks as places "preserved forever in their natural state," ignoring centuries of stewardship by Native Americans as well as the Park Service's own policies. At the time, the agency's idea of leaving the landscape "unimpaired" actually favored a kind of pruning of the scenery, in which anything unsightly—predators, wildfires, insects—was stamped out as quickly as possible, and anything desirable—elk, deer, and other "friendly" wildlife—was encouraged to increase.

This approach gave rise to some embarrassing situations. In 1924, the U.S. Forest Service, which managed much of the forested land north of the Grand Canyon on the Kaibab Plateau, published a report warning that the range was so overrun with deer they were in "imminent danger of extinction through starvation." The Forest Service and Park advocates wanted to shoot the deer or crate them up and ship them to anyone who paid for a railway ticket; the state of Arizona objected. In the middle of this "red-hot controversy," as one newspaper termed it, a man named George McCormick offered to herd as many as eight thousand deer into the Grand Canyon, force them to swim the Colorado River, and drive them up the other side. At a bargain price, too: only $2.50 a head. McCormick told the newspapers that it wouldn't be any harder to drive deer than cattle, because, having never been hunted, the deer were practically tame.

Everyone was eager for the "deer drive," which made the national papers. McCormick took a group of cowboys to the North Rim that December and hired more than a hundred Navajos and Paiutes to do the herding. A camera crew was there, and so was the famous novelist Zane Grey, "roughing it" with a Japanese chef, personal valet, and three assistants. In the middle of a blizzard that swallowed up trees fifty feet away in ghostly swirls of white, the riders whooped and hollered, clanging bells to chase the deer toward the canyon's rim, where McCormick had rigged up a chute out of white sheets to funnel them to the trailhead.

A game warden named Jack Fuss described the result later: the lead buck caught one glimpse of all those sheets hanging on chicken wire, and "whamo! Back he went."

Newspapers kindly blamed the snowstorm for the failure of the Great Kaibab Deer Drive, but Grey set the record straight; it was all down to "the total unexpected refusal of the deer to herd." Grey suggested that the Forest Service was to blame for the deer explosion by killing all the mountain lions, and advised simply allowing the cougars to return. Whether the Kaibab deer story is, indeed, a cautionary tale about predator control is up for debate; ecologists still argue about what caused deer numbers to rise so dramatically. The deer grazed every leaf, blade, and tree down to a nub and then their population crashed as, evidently, they starved to death.

Despite the public failure of the deer drive, the Park Service pursued the idea of relocating deer in a smaller way. From 1927 to 1931, the agency caught sixty fawns and trucked them from the north side to the south. Wright strictly opposed this experiment. He understood that the Grand Canyon was a natural barrier between related forms of life; it was a place to witness evolution in action, as species on either side diverged in a process known as allopatric speciation. The most famous example was the Kaibab squirrels on the north side, with white tails and black bellies, and the Abert's squirrels on the south side, with gray tails and white bellies. To meddle with these natural processes, Wright said, was to "invite disaster."

Grand Canyon Village was soon overrun with "friendly little deer." They made a charming tourist attraction, crowding the train station to beg candy out of visitors' pockets. One newspaper article gushed, "they'll come right up to you, kiss your face if you ask them," and eat cigarettes right out of your hand, looking "grateful and happy" for the treat. Cigarette-munching deer hardly fit the image of parks as "everlasting wildernesses." In his second wildlife report, published in 1935, Wright explored the inherent contradictions in the Park Service's mandate to preserve landscapes and open them up to public enjoyment—"ice and fire," in his words. To reconcile the two goals, he wanted the Park Service to stop doling out cheap thrills—penned bison, fed bears—and instead encourage visitors to seek out "the story of the endless change and struggle and the marvelous interrelations of all living things."

Wright may have been the first person within the Park Service to clearly articulate the idea that "unimpaired" meant keeping healthy, functioning ecosystems intact. He saw cougar-gnawed carcasses, charred grasslands, and beetle-chewed trees not as unsightly blemishes but as natural and necessary processes in the evolution of a landscape. His ideas were radical, but his words so earnest and persuasive that he succeeded for a time in influencing policy. The Park Service adopted his recommendations in a hesitant, piecemeal fashion in the early 1930s, ending predator control (at least on paper) and halting the intro-duction of non-native species, except for sportfish. In 1934 the agency adopted "Fauna No. 1" as their official wildlife policy and put Wright at the head of a new Wildlife Division. His success was short-lived. Two years later, Wright died in a car wreck in New Mexico, on his way to inspect a proposed national park.

$$\Downarrow$$

CLOVER AND JOTTER GATHERED with the rest of the crew outside El Tovar Hotel for the live NBC broadcast. Superinten-dent Tillotson was there, and a reporter named Arthur Anderson who drove up from Phoenix. He roped off an area outside the hotel especially for them. As it was radio, it didn't matter much what the women wore for the occasion—at least, they must have thought so. Clover was dressed neatly in slacks and a checkered blue shirt, but she'd opened her collar and rolled up her sleeves against the heat. Jot-ter wore her khaki overalls on top of a vivid blue shirt. They might have chosen their wardrobes differently had they known that Ander-son would offer his listeners a detailed physical description of them both, right down to their bare, sunburned arms.

"Good afternoon!" Anderson exclaimed into the microphone at

3:15 p.m. "We're standing on the very brink of the Grand Canyon of Arizona." His voice fell into the peculiar staccato cadence favored by radio and TV broadcasters at the time as he described how the whole world seemed to fall away, "and we feel as though we're witnessing some weird dream." After a lavish landscape description, Anderson turned to his first guest, Tillotson.

"Mr. Tillotson," he asked, "is it the usual thing to have visitors to your park arrive by boat?"

"Certainly not," said Tillotson in sharp, clipped tones. The usual visitors, he explained, "come by automobile, by rail, by airplane, by stage, by horseback, and by almost every conceivable means. . . . We purposefully do not, however, encourage parties to come by the route that Mr. Nevills has just used. This, for the reason that the Colorado is known to be one of the most dangerous and treacherous rivers in the world." His voice rising with urgency, Tillotson hurried on. "I know it well and most unfavorably. I should say that even the most experienced boatmen and those with the best possible equipment would have only a fifty-fifty chance of completing the trip successfully." The trip was neither safe nor sane, he said, and anyone who attempted it not only put their own lives at risk but also risked the lives of rescue parties, consumed the park's budget, and took rangers away from their usual duties. "Mr. Nevills and his party," Tillotson finally wound down, "certainly chose a most unusual and hazardous means of reaching the park, and just as certainly I would not advise anyone to follow their example."

It was not easy to recover from such a beginning. With considerable aplomb, Anderson asked Tillotson to clarify exactly where the Grand Canyon was located, a source of confusion for his national audience, and then turned to Clover. "How has the trip been so far?" he asked.

"It certainly hasn't been monotonous, with plenty of excitement and some danger," Clover replied in her husky, melodious voice.

"Would you say that other women would like it, enjoy it?" asked Anderson.

Clover hesitated. "I think some women might enjoy it," she said after a pause. "There's a great deal of hard work that goes with it."

"And you would say just offhand that it's not a pleasure jaunt?"

So softly she might have been speaking to herself, Clover answered, "No, it certainly isn't that."

Clover went on to speak about the botanical collection. She was sure they had collected at least two species of cacti unknown to Western science, but when she began to offer up the Latin names of the genera to which they belonged, Anderson interrupted her, laughing: "I was just a little bit afraid of that," he said. "To us they are still cacti!" Jotter's turn was next. She told a story about accidently making penuche (a simple kind of fudge) with pancake flour instead of sugar. She had an infectious laugh. Gibson, who followed, lacked her boisterous confidence, and spoke in a self-deprecating tone of his struggles to take color movies. He blurted out that he preferred to set up his tripod on the sandbars instead of taking pictures from the boats, and worried for the rest of the day that people would think him a coward. It probably didn't help that Anderson responded, "I certainly hope that you enjoy and live through the rest of your trip." Gibson was disconcerted. Even the interviewer seemed caught off-guard. "That was rather a mean remark," he acknowledged and then quickly turned to Bell.

"You're very much of a veteran on rivers," Anderson said. "How does this Colorado River through the Grand Canyon compare with other rivers on which you've sailed?"

"There's absolutely no comparison," Bell said in his lazy drawl. "Ah've handled boats on rivers and lakes and lagoons and oceans, and Ah think it has all the features of all of 'em rolled into one, plus a few more."

Kolb got a quick word in—he'd accepted Nevills's invitation to accompany the expedition the rest of the way—and then Nevills gave a detailed description of the Cataract boats with crisp, careful enunciation. By this time, Jotter and Gibson were doing their best to control hysterical giggles. Solemnly, Anderson wished them all luck: "We're sure they're going to need it."

The broadcast ended. Anderson told Clover she had a beautiful voice for radio. *Baloney,* she thought, unmoved by the flattery. The crew posed for photos and then went to a buffet dinner in Tillotson's home. Jotter lived up to her self-proclaimed reputation as a klutz when she knocked into a polished bookend of petrified wood and sent it, plus all the books, clattering to the floor. For her, the evening was awkward and terribly tedious. She was tired of all the "fuss & feathers," and not looking forward to a second stuffy night at Bright Angel Lodge. Clover wasn't happy, either. She intensely disliked Tillotson. Perhaps his dour introduction on the NBC broadcast had raised her ire, but whatever explanation she wrote in her journal, she later erased all but the harsh comments, "I can't stand him. Utterly without sympathy with humans."

There is no indication that Tillotson and Clover discussed her botanical research. It was just the kind of survey Wright had wanted the Park Service to conduct; Clover's data on the type and extent of exotic species along the river corridor surely would have been useful information. But the Park Service had largely lost interest in carrying out Wright's vision for science-based management. In 1938, the agency had plenty of landscape designers, engineers, planners, and architects on staff, but fewer than a dozen biologists. The focus remained on tourism and recreation, and the complexities of ecology, conservation, and preservation were left behind.

This made no sense to Jotter. Just before the river trip, she wrote to her father to express her astonishment over a newspaper article that treated conservation as a new idea. "Amazing!" she wrote, and then, to underscore the sarcasm, added four more exclamation points. But Jotter was in a privileged position when it came to ecological philosophy. During her time in the Yosemite Field School, she had made personal connections with biologists who had known Wright and supported his way of thinking. More profound was her father's influence. E. V. Jotter had worked at the Forest Products Laboratory in

Wisconsin during Aldo Leopold's tenure as assistant director there. In April 1938, Leopold stood in front of a group of civil engineers and spoke boldly about the complex consequences of human technology, including dams. Our tools, Leopold proclaimed, "suffice to crack the atom, to command the tides. But they do not suffice for the oldest task in human history: to live on a piece of land without spoiling it." In years to come, Leopold would forcefully articulate the need for a land ethic, which "changes the role of *Homo sapiens* from conqueror of the land-community to plain member and citizen of it." No wonder Jotter so hotly dismissed the notion that she had come to the Colorado River to "conquer" it. She was a botanist and the daughter of a forester, surrounded by conversations about the utility and beauty of trees. She did not know how rare this was.

They lingered late at the South Rim the next day, with much "milling and fooling around," in Clover's words. Jotter, too, felt impatient to get back to the river. They met the adventurous Edith Kolb over lunch. Not until late afternoon did the crew, with the addition of Emery Kolb, start down the seven-mile South Kaibab Trail to the river. It was rather like descending a staircase built by a mad carpenter, but on the plus side, they wouldn't have to turn around and hike back up again the way most tourists did. There were some benefits to coming by boat, after all, whatever Tillotson might think. Clover and Jotter did not have time, as they hurried downward under the rays of the setting sun, to collect plants, though they must have eyed them along the trail. There were more exotic species growing along the South Kaibab than they had found at the river's edge, no doubt a result of the foot traffic: sow thistle and curly dock, even straggling sprigs of oats, which must have dropped out of a mule's nosebag and sprouted. Squally wind snatched at their clothes. Clouds funneled into the chute formed by the canyon's walls and gathered in a panicked mass. Now and then, thunder cracked like hooves on stone.

The press reports on their departure were more muted than they had been at Green River or Lee's Ferry. Reporters thought the crew seemed to be in good spirits and perfect harmony. They had traveled more than four hundred miles without death or serious injury and seemed quite confident of reaching Boulder Dam within two weeks. Still, journalists did their best to stir up concern for the party's fate. The river had dropped below 20,000 cfs, still at flood stage and quite normal for the time of year. Back at Green River, newspapers had been full of dire warnings about the high water, but now they found equal fault with the lower level. A reporter wrote that the crew was expected to find the rapids between Bright Angel and Boulder Dam nearly impassable because of the rocks sticking through. Holmstrom couldn't be reached for comment, but he'd said before that low water was more dangerous than high.

"Even if members of the party succeed in emerging from deep canyon walls," the article went on with deep skepticism, ". . . they will have to pull their boats over 116 miles of water in a hot Nevada sun before they reach Boulder Dam."

At the bottom of the South Kaibab Trail, near sundown, they encountered a tourist who recognized them from the press clippings. "Say," he said to Jotter, "was there dissention in the party or were those two fellows who quit just yellow?" Furious, Jotter could only reply with an emphatic *no*, but later that evening she wrote to Kay Hussey (with instructions to publicize as widely as possible), "Gene was definitely not a quitter. He wasn't scared of rapids, handles a boat beautifully. Same holds true for Don Harris. I think the world of him!" There was nothing else she could do in defense of her former companions, but she remained angry at Nevills for not speaking up on their behalf.

To her father, she wrote only praise of the boatmen, and amusing anecdotes about the autograph hunters and press hounds—nothing about a near-disastrous tumble off a cliff to be saved by the strap of her camera bag. "Now, remember, Father," she concluded, "if we are late it's because we're taking our time getting around some rapids." Clearly, she didn't want a repeat of the frenzy stirred up by their late arrival at Lee's Ferry.

Night fell. The storm broke at last, and fat raindrops clattered on the cobbles with a sound like a distant stampede. Clover and Jotter lay awake in the cozy darkness—they'd been given cots in a government cabin—and listened to the men rustle around outside, rigging canvas shelters. The squall passed. A quarter moon peered round the clouds, half in shadow. "The canyon is lovely, Kay, and not particularly terrifying," Jotter confided to her friend by letter. She went on, "We're being lionized pretty badly and as you say the emphasis has been on"—here she sketched a small circle with a cross below, used by botanists to indicate the female sex—"rather than on Botany."

The final leg of the trip had begun.

Chapter Ten

A HUNDRED PERSONALITIES

THEY RAN RAPIDS EVERY DAY, BIG ONES. THE river hurtled between dark, glassy walls of schist, stone torn and reformed by the tectonic forces that broke up whole continents long ago. At Granite Falls, the current dashed hard against the right-hand cliff and then swept on in a series of tossing waves before parting around an island midriver—a tricky run. Nevills was halfway through when he felt the port-side oar slip its ring. The boat spun in a circle and swept side-on toward the cliff. Nevills stood up. Gripping the loose oar, he prepared to fend off the collision. Then a caprice of the current stopped the boat "as if with brakes." The oar juddered off the cliff and rammed, hard, into his stomach. His knuckles slammed into the rock and came away bloody. For a horrible, confused, churning few minutes, he was trapped. The oar kept him pinned against the bow, the river on one side, the cliff on the other, each striving against the other with Nevills's helpless body and the splintering boat stuck between.

Then he worked free and the boat jerked back into the current again at frightening speed. Breathing a quick prayer, Nevills made for a cove and gained its shelter. Jotter, watching from the shore, only saw that Nevills had been tossed about, but she admired how deftly Bell handled the rapid. He seemed to guide the boat merely by shifting his weight.

Jotter had high hopes of being allowed to run a rapid herself—she'd only been allowed to row the boat in calm water—but Nevills wouldn't allow it. In her logbook, she blamed Kolb's presence, complaining that Nevills wanted to show him how safe he was as a leader. Nevills did not mention the request in his journal but wrote that he considered Jotter "too reckless." Perhaps it was her habit of sitting up on the stern in rough water.

Nevills frequently ordered the women to walk while the men took the boats through a rapid, out of concern for their safety. Clover and Jotter complied, but privately thought running the river was less dangerous than collecting plants, with sheer walls to scale and things that stung or stabbed in every corner. Clover wrote of stumbling wearily through the "terrible black hornblende granite gneiss" with more feeling than precision. She was more exact in naming the plants. She picked up desert tobacco (*Nicotiana trigonophylla*), its pungent leaves a centuries-old remedy for sickness, and turpentine broom (*Thamnosma montana*), a citrus-scented shrub that spent most of the year leafless. Bentgrass and bluestem grew on the sandbars, and cacti were everywhere: hedgehog, fishhook, and prickly pear. Near Granite Falls, Clover collected an *Opuntia* that looked similar to a beavertail prickly pear, but its pads were longer and yellow-green in color. She wrote *Opuntia longiareolata* in her journal and marked next to the name *sp. nov.*: new species. It would be vital to get a sample to Michigan and confirm her suspicion.

They paused just before reaching Hermit Rapid. A big explosion wave—where the current dashed hard against a vertical wall of whitewater, twenty-five feet high at his estimate—made Nevills wary of running it. He decided to make camp and take a fresh look in the morning. This was the spot where a movie-making crew in 1927 had nearly met with disaster. The Pathé–Bray Company of Hollywood wanted to make a fictional adventure film called *The Pride of the Colorado,* or possibly a romance called *The Bride of the Colorado.* The company hired La Rue as a river guide and sent a camera crew to film dramatic background scenery. La Rue had left the U.S. Geological Survey in disgrace. He couldn't stop talking about his plans for a whole series of dams on the Colorado River, with Glen Canyon Dam as the centerpiece. La Rue's bosses warned him not to discuss "controversial matters" related to the Colorado River Compact anymore, but La Rue ignored them. In 1927, he gave the USGS an ultimatum: grant him a six-month leave of absence to go with the Pathé–Bray Expedition, or he would quit. Very well, replied his superiors; your resignation is accepted.

Shepherding around a bunch of cameramen for a ridiculous Hollywood movie must have felt like a letdown to La Rue after all his big plans. The male lead was John Boles and the heroine was played by an actress with the improbable name of Rose Blossom. The actors couldn't be risked on the river, so they weren't part of the expedition. The movie's climax was filmed at Hermit Rapid, where the crew sawed a boat almost in half and rammed it repeatedly against a rock until it broke. A boatman named Frank Dodge, who had grown up in Hawaii and had gone on the 1923 Birdseye expedition, was Boles's stunt double. A Navy man named Owen Clark stood in for Blossom, dressed in a long skirt, stockings, and a blond wig. Clark was on the bow and Dodge was rowing when a wave capsized the boat—a real wreck, instead of the fake one they hoped to film. Tangled in his wig, Clark was trapped under the boat and emerged bleeding from a head wound. Maybe the blood wouldn't show on black-and-white film?

The movie was never released, either because silent films lost popularity to "talkies" or because the acting was so bad. An advance review in *Photoplay* mentioned none of the actors' names but instead proclaimed, accurately enough, that the movie starred the Grand Canyon. "Nice scenery," the review went on, "but the picture offers little story interest."

La Rue never returned to the USGS. He continued his work as an engineer at a private consulting firm, which failed during the dark years of the Depression. His long dream of damming Glen and Grand canyons was over. At least, it seemed that way.

NEVILLS DECIDED TO LINE the boats around Hermit Rapid after all, where poor Clark, a.k.a. Blossom, a.k.a. the bride of the

Left to right: Elzada Clover, Norm Nevills, Lois Jotter, and
Lorin Bell line the boats around an explosion wave in
Hermit Rapid. Photograph by Emery Kolb. *Courtesy of Special
Collections, J. Willard Marriot Library, University of Utah.
Used by permission of Northern Arizona University*

Colorado, had narrowly escaped death by drowning. The decision
produced good-natured complaints from the crew, but the task was
done in just under two hours. They sweated and struggled, unaware
that they had become movie stars of a sort themselves that day, as
Pathé News had just released its film about their adventures. Some
theaters played the newsreels on an endless loop, so city folks could
escape the summer heat and their dreary offices at any time and
be transported to another world. "Scientists Brave Death in Rapids"
was the segment's title, and there were the boats launching from the
sandy shoreline of Lee's Ferry. Cut. Two tiny figures tossed in the
slate-gray water. Cut. A quick glimpse of the lettering along a boat's
prow. McFarland had taken plenty of footage of "camp life," but
none of these peaceful scenes, apparently, made it into the newsreel,

nor did any images of the women doing botany. The short, silent film was all about the rapids.

The next eleven miles were full of splashy rapids, one after another. Rubble slopes on both sides of the river made half-hidden coves, tucked amid piles of sharp boulders topped by sharper plants. At the head of Serpentine Rapid, Nevills pulled the *Wen* into a cove on the left, intending to stop and look it over. Reed and Gibson in the *Botany* crowded in behind. There wasn't much space, and their boat jutted into the river's current. Last in line, the *Mexican Hat* turned toward them, Bell at the oars, Jotter balancing lightly in the bow with a rope in her hand, ready to step ashore. But they were coming in too fast. Bell hesitated: it was either ram the *Botany* or turn back to the river. He swung the boat into the current again. There was no time to square up to the rapid's tongue. Bell spun the boat, hard, to face the blunt stern downriver, and in the same moment Jotter crouched down and tightened her grip. A hole opened in the river and swallowed the boat.

It was out of sight so long that Reed, watching from the cove, felt his heart stop for a beat or two. Then the *Mexican Hat* bobbed up and crested the wave that curled at the downstream edge of the hole, Bell and Jotter drenched but unharmed. Reed turned to Nevills in relief.

"We might as well go," he said, and nudged his boat into the current. The three boats reunited at the foot of Serpentine, "no worse for the wild ride," Reed wrote, "except to ship much water." It must have been partly out of fear that Nevills later blistered Bell for not following orders. Jotter got her share of criticism, too, even though she had no control over the boat. "Lois is a dangerous one to have on a trip," Nevills wrote, "as she has no judgement whatever."

Bell was injured. He had ruptured something during a bad run of a rapid several days before, and the pain now intensified so much he could barely sleep that night. There was nothing to give him but whiskey and a small dose of morphine. The next day, Gibson took over rowing the *Mexican Hat,* and Jotter joined Reed in the *Botany.* Reed was pleased. He felt he had barely gotten to know Jotter—they had been isolated in separate boats, busy with different tasks—and now he poured out praise: "a wonderfully good companion," he wrote, "sensible, but jolly and a great tease."

Downriver from Serpentine, barrel cacti (*Ferocactus acanthodes*) erupted on the canyon walls, some taller than a grown man, others toddler-high. Backlit by the sun, their thorny crowns became haloes. Some types of barrel cacti bent their heads southward to track the sun, but these ones were more apt to curve like commas to hold against the steep slopes. Sometimes they swelled so round in the middle they tore free and tumbled down under their own weight. Their resemblance to casks or barrels had tricked more than one desert traveler into imagining a pool of fresh water inside. A 1933 botany paper suggested that one could obtain a cool drink "if the top is cut off and the contents well stirred with a stick," but the insides weren't easily stirred; the pulp had a marshmallow texture and, to anyone unaccustomed to it, an acrid, stomach-twisting taste.

"The vegetation is changing a great deal," Clover wrote in her diary, barrel cacti and prickly pear now dominant, with plenty of little cylindrical hedgehog cacti and catclaw acacia mixed in. She had always intended to explore the side canyons in search of rarer plants, but there hadn't been time. On July 24, however, they stopped at midday to make the short climb to Elves Chasm, up a slot canyon where a creek leapt down a series of pools and cataracts. Travertine splashed the stones, like buckets of spilled paint, sharp underfoot except where the burbling water had polished it to a porcelain shine. The crew ate lunch here, grateful for the shade, and the women collected plants. They found broadleaf cattail (*Typha latifolia*) for the first time on the trip, and twinleaf bedstraw (*Galium watsoni*), another new species. They also cataloged beargrass (*Nolina microcarpa*), an eccentric cousin in the lily family, a circle of green blades. Clover grew ambitious and decided to collect samples of algae, filling jars with slippery green gobs to be studied later under a microscope. She left them in the bailing bucket to stay cool in the water, and Nevills, wanting to use the bucket not long after, tossed them all overboard. He apologized to Clover when she discovered the loss, but she felt churlish about it and wasn't inclined to forgive him. She hadn't come just for an adventure. Getting her specimens back to Michigan was the thing that mattered most to her, after getting out alive.

Charcoal names written on an overhang at Elves Chasm offered a litany of the river runners that had come before: Galloway, Eddy, and Dodge. They added "NEVILLS EXPEDITION '38" and went on. In the middle of the day the canyon became a furnace, and they turned their faces into any little breeze, seeking relief. But it rained most afternoons, cold drenching showers that blew up all of a sudden and passed in moments. Sated with rainwater, cacti swelled like whiskey barrels about to burst their rings. Their path followed the bends and curves of the river; cardinal points lost meaning. One day the sun rose downriver of their camp, the next, on the upriver side. Sunrises and sunsets became matters of stone and subtle light, blue chased from the cliffs back into the sky, coralline colors flooding in. Clover learned that even boating the Grand Canyon could become, somehow, routine: wake early, make breakfast, press plants, run rapids, cook dinner, sleep, repeat. Tired as she was, she couldn't rest until the day's specimens had been put up in paper and logged in her notebook, always with a terse notation—"bushy," "ratty," "common," "rare"— or sometimes a longer note on the color of the flower or condition of the soil. She filled page after page in her diary with descriptions of plants. Jotter, exhausted, stopped writing in hers altogether.

$$\psi$$

"LORD, WHAT COUNTRY," Clover wrote in her journal their fourth day out from Bright Angel. The river curved here in a great sinuous arc around the Great Thumb Mesa. Rumor had it that tiny wild horses roamed there: "no larger than coyotes," wrote park ranger Bert Lauzon, "with rabbit tails and mule ears and other peculiarities to startle the beholders thereof." Six months earlier, in January, three rangers had gone into the canyon to investigate these stories. A sorrel stallion and his band of mares ghosted ahead of them for three days before they were lassoed and dutifully measured from hooves to withers and ears to tail. They proved to be ordinary in every way except for their exotic living conditions. Had the rangers listened to their Havasupai guides, they might have saved themselves the trip; Havasupai knew these "sand rock horses" were the descendants of the ponies brought to the canyon by their great-great-grandfathers.

Still, stories of evolution run amok enthralled Grand Canyon visitors. In 1937 the American Museum of Natural History funded an expedition to Shiva Temple, a mesa rising more than a thousand feet above the Grand Canyon's floor on the north side of the river, supposedly unvisited by humans since the last Ice Age. The expedition members intended to study the plants and animals there, to see if they could trace divergences in their evolution. This was not entirely a silly question; populations did diverge from one another in isolation. But the media seized on stories of a "lost world" and an "island in the sky" filled with primeval forests and ancient monsters, where "life is as untouched by man as it was millions of years ago." *Popular Science Monthly* ran a story about the expedition illustrated by drawings of dinosaurs.

The idea that species could go extinct was still a relatively new one. In the nineteenth century, giant mammoth bones, tiny ammonites, and other fossils upended the traditional view of nature as fixed and unchanging, and naturalists warned that not only could species wink out of existence, but humans could be the cause. These troubling ideas met with plenty of resistance. Though extinction, like evolution, was a settled fact of science by the 1930s, the Shiva Temple Expedition seemed to tap into some buried wellspring of belief that, somewhere out there, primordial beasts still roamed, untouched by time. The Grand Canyon was the last possible holdout for this hope in the United States: so isolated, so little known, so full of hidden wonders.

The scientists left on September 13 and hiked to the top of Shiva Temple, where they found nothing more startling than a cheerful cadre of chipmunks. They also found plenty of evidence of human visitors, from stone arrowheads to tin cans. The latter had been left by Kolb to embarrass them. He had climbed up a few days before with his daughter, Edith, and his employee Ruth Stephens, determined to upstage the museum party (which also included a woman). Kolb's "expedition" remained secret for some time, and the museum scientists wrote up their findings with no mention of tin cans. Their paper in *Nature* dwelled on the arrowheads, which they thought might prove useful for showing that early Indigenous peoples had lived in North America at the same time as the ancient horses and giant ground sloths of the Pleistocene. There was nothing more remarkable to report except the enormous number of mosquitoes.

Clover had followed the Shiva Temple media coverage with dismay. She had just made her plans to boat the Colorado River with Nevills, and, above all, she wanted their expedition to be science-focused and dignified. The Shiva Temple Expedition was "much ado about nothing," and Clover told Nevills she wanted nothing to do with such "lurid ballyhoo and exaggerations."

Nevills promised to keep out anything sensational. Clover hadn't reckoned on the press considering the presence of women in the party as sensational all by itself.

$$\Downarrow$$

OCOTILLO (*FOUQUIERIA SPLENDENS*) appeared, growing out of the limestone terraces, a plant also known as candlewood or desert coral. It resembled a bundle of walking sticks until the rainy season, when rows of green leaves erupted along the long stems and a spray of red flowers exploded from the tips, trumpet-shaped to fit the beaks of hummingbirds. The leaves, alternating with spines, average an inch in length. Desert plants know that leaves are liabilities. They lose precious water every time the pores open to perform photosynthesis, sucking in carbon dioxide to transform into sugars. Ocotillo doesn't bother with leaves in the dry times; it carries out photosynthesis on its greenish stems instead. Mesquite trees adapted in a different way: they grow minuscule leaves in pairs along stems, barely big enough to make decent confetti, and turn them slantwise to the sun during the day to minimize evaporation.

The crew poses in the boats in lower Grand Canyon.
Clockwise from top: Lorin Bell, sitting, Lois Jotter,
standing with the tall stalk of a blooming agave, Bill Gibson,
standing, Dell Reed, Elzada Clover, and Norman Nevills.
Photograph by Emery Kolb. *Courtesy of Special Collections, J.*
Willard Marriot Library, University of Utah. Used by
permission of Northern Arizona University

But cacti know the real trick. Sometime in the last 35 million years, they rolled up their primordial leaves into spines, the most daring fashion accessory of the season. Multipurpose, too: a useful defense against nibblers, and a kind of sunshade and air-conditioning system in one. In the absence of leaves, photosynthesis moved to the green, leathery skin. Here another innovation took place: cacti learned to

keep their pores (known as stomata) closed during the day, to prevent moisture from siphoning away into the unforgiving sky. They
open their pores only during the cool hours of the night, squirrel-
ing away pockets of carbon dioxide, and complete the task of making sugar during the day. They also store water under their waxy
skins and quickly grow networks of tiny roots after rain to siphon up
moisture. One good storm can sustain a cactus through several years
of drought. For all this, cacti can be extravagant too, coming out in
showy blossoms in shades of cerise, gold, and crimson as gaudy as any
high school prom dress.

Clover and Jotter couldn't have known all this (the details of cactus
photosynthesis wouldn't be worked out for decades). But in cataloging plants that thrived in extremes, they were adding to the general
picture of evolution and adaptation, tracing the subtle threads of a
tapestry that had been in the making for 3.5 billion years. They could
see that plants weren't immune to the influence of people, not even
here. At Havasu Creek, where a rivulet of aquamarine water came
shying down a twisting slot canyon, Clover cataloged her first sample
of wild grape (*Vitis arizonica*), a species cultivated and harvested by
Native peoples for its sweet purple fruits, and growing in heaps and
hummocks along the water's edge. Like the mesquite, desert tobacco,
prickly pear, and agave, this was a plant that did not neatly fit the categories of wild and tame.

The creek's blueness was tempting—like a piece cut from the
sky. Jotter, Bell, and Gibson alternately swam and waded a little way
upstream to enjoy the cold water, but the creek was deep and swift
and Clover struggled to follow them. She was frightened when the
current snatched her and flung her hard against one of the boats. She
returned to her plant collecting while the others played. She longed to
follow the creek's windings up to the Havasupai village, where, Kolb
told her, big cottonwood trees grew. In fact, Havasupai remembered
a time when few cottonwoods grew there, but, confined to the tiny
reservation in winter instead of traveling to the plateau, they had been
forced to tend the trees like a crop. Every three years, a family lopped

all the limbs off their cottonwood tree, planted the new cuttings, and used the last cycle's cuttings for firewood to keep warm during the sunless, shadowed days. Neither Clover nor her companions seemed aware of the profound changes forced by the U.S. government upon the Havasupai people, or that the tribe was currently engaged in a decades-long lawsuit to regain a portion of their wintering grounds. Clover was interested in Indigenous peoples and cultures, and she once wrote regretfully of the "unhappiness" inflicted upon them by her ancestors, a too-gentle word for an ongoing campaign of genocide, relocation, and violent assimilation.

Five miles downriver from Havasu Creek, fat, warm drops of rain began to dimple the current. All seven of them were in the boats. They looked up. "I do not believe," Reed recorded, "that there is another place in the world where a storm looks as bad in the making as it does in the Grand Canyon of the Colorado." Black clouds boiled into the chasm of sky above them and, like an endless stream of spilled ink, blotted out the sun. Darkness fell. The rain came heavier, and when it hit the canyon's rims it rolled off into the air like smoke. Wisps of clouds poured from the rim like slow taffy, oozing down the drainages. The dimples on the river's surface turned to shimmers and froth, then to little fretting waves, slate-colored like the sky. They could see no place to take shelter on the short, steep skirts of boulders that flanked the river on either side, and so they rowed on, shivering in wet clothes as the temperature plunged. Thunder cracked. Thin, twisting waterfalls, silky brown, began to stream from the cliffs.

All at once, the sunlight found a way through the curtain of falling drops—it bent, sparkled, flashed, and reflected a sudden arc of color: ocher, amber, jade, indigo, violet. No, not one rainbow: two of them, a double arc that shimmered strangely close in the thick haze of rain. It leapt from wall to wall, a tenuous, tantalizing bridge. A moment more, surely, and they would find themselves plunged into that illusory world of color, transported out of the Stygian depths into—what? They forgot to feel the cold and wet, forgot hunger and exhaustion.

Then Gibson broke the reverent silence with a curse: he didn't have color film in his camera.

The shining glimpse vanished. Rain fell in cold, beating sheets. Hastily, they turned the boats toward the cliff. They had to get off the river, though there was no good place to land. They anchored as best they could to the slick stones and picked their way through the darkness and mud to the canyon wall and flattened themselves against it, desperate for the little warmth the rocks seemed to hold. Everyone smoked a cigarette while they waited for the rain to ease.

THEY LEFT THEIR POOR SHELTER with the rain still sheeting down and found an overhanging ledge to make a campsite. Firewood was scarce, and they had nothing to burn but the slender, whippy branches of catclaw acacia. Nearby, they discovered the remains of an old folding boat and, unmindful of its possible historic importance, broke it to bits and used it to kindle their campfire. There was also an old miner's cache with a slip of paper marking the date 1902. The matches still worked, to their delight, and Gibson claimed the prospector's pick as a souvenir. But the can of condensed milk had long since dried up, and at a touch the beans went to powder. They ate dinner as the sunset flamed scarlet and citron, and Clover pressed plants before going to bed. She was surprised, the next morning, to wake to the breakfast call. Reed had helped Jotter cook so Clover could sleep late. He invented a fried biscuit which Clover kindly called "decorative," as it proved impossible to chew.

The canyon began to open up a little, and the sandstone layers reappeared, flaky Tapeats and blocky Muav at the river's edge. Here and there, dark basalt slid over the sandstone, broken into upright cylindrical crystals. The basalt was left over from the volcanic flows that once dammed the Grand Canyon, belched from cinder cones on the plateau above. It happened fast, geologically speaking. Waterfalls of lava, hissing and sputtering into the river, could harden into immovable monoliths within days. The river, stymied, pressed against these barriers, prying and poking, until a whole series of frustrated lakes filled the canyon. But within a few hundred years—the blink of an eye, in canyon time—sediment piled up behind the barriers and the river clawed its way to the top and attacked the dams like a putty knife on a sandcastle. The stone crumbled; the river cut its way through. Powell had noticed places where a narrow channel wormed its way through bulwarks of basalt, and other spots where the river had done its work so well that nothing remained except worn black patches. "What a conflict of water and fire there must have been here!" he exclaimed, tossing plain scientific observation to the side, as he so often did. "Just imagine a river of molten rock running down into a river of melted snow. What a seething and boiling of the waters; what clouds of steam rolled into the heavens!"

The Colorado turned redder as the days went on, as if the water held some memory of those long-ago rivers of fire. "Waves look funny dashing over us in their redness," Clover wrote; they were no longer white-tipped but a simmering, soupy umber. Kolb showed Nevills how to rig up ropes and stand up on the stern while running a rapid, just for the fun of it. Even Gibson tried it. He had become "a real river man," in Clover's words, " . . . standing up & riding on stern all morn- ing wearing nothing but his little 'What-have-yous.'" Clover herself still put on makeup every day, although now she treated it as a joke. After running a rapid, soaked to the skin and muddy, wearing a tat- tered old hat jammed down low on her head, trousers rolled up to the knee, and a man's shirt cut off at the elbows, she liked to dab on a bit of lipstick and powder and turn to Nevills to ask, "How do I look?" merely for the fun of hearing him reply, "Like hell!"

At Lava Falls, the women collected their first sample of *Larrea glutinosa,* also known as creosote bush or greasewood. It is a spindly bush with waxy leaves and bright yellow flowers that burst into white, fuzzy fruits the size of peas. After rain, a fragrance arises from its leaves, brisk and pungent, perfuming the whole desert with an intox-

Larrea tridentata (creosote bush) collected from
Lava Falls in the Grand Canyon. *Catalog #18620, courtesy of
the University of Arizona Herbarium, used by permission*

icating freshness. It isn't really a single scent but probably a potpourri
of dozens of different organic compounds twined together. Creosote
bush can reproduce by cloning itself—new shoots appearing in rings
around the original plant—and in this way, resurrects itself into a
lifespan that can last for thousands of years. It grows abundantly
on the talus slopes of the lower canyon, evenly spaced as trees in an
orchard because chemicals secreted from its roots warn other plants
to keep their distance. It hosts sixty species of insects, though nothing
but a jackrabbit can tolerate its taste.

Clover and Jotter collected plants while the men lined the boats
around Lava Falls. It was unthinkable to run it. In the space of a hun-

dred yards, the river dropped almost forty vertical feet; a boat could shoot through in twenty seconds or stay trapped in a hole and get battered to bits. George Flavell and Ramón Montéz had successfully run Lava Falls in 1896, but nobody in the crew knew their story. This was a pity, since unlike practically everybody else who had run the Colorado River, the two men had a marvelous time. Nevills decided he couldn't risk it. They laboriously unloaded the hatches, portaged the gear, and lined the boats down the boulder-strewn shoreline. Bell lost his footing once and was sucked down beneath a boat, and Nevills was limping badly by the end of it.

"Another trip," he promised himself, "& I will run every rapid in the river."

EARLY IN THE MORNING OF JULY 29, a small plane flew overhead, circled, dipped its wings, and shot away. Nevills was cheerful at the thought that the world would soon receive word of their safety; he expected to reach Lake Mead, and the end of the journey, within a day or two. But the moment set off a deep melancholy in Clover. "Can't even get away from the world here," she lamented. They still had rapids to run, but nothing too dangerous—"wide splashy affairs," as Nevills put it.

They were now in the stretch of river scoured by hopeless searchers ten years before, during the bleak December when Bessie and Glen Hyde failed to emerge from the canyon. Bessie was a small, dark-haired woman with an artistic temperament (she sketched and wrote poetry), diminutive next to her lanky husband. She was twenty-two when she married Glen, after a brief first marriage that ended in divorce. The Hydes shared a love of excitement and adventure, and the Colorado River had leapt into newspaper headlines following the 1927 expeditions by Clyde Eddy and the Pathé–Bray Company, both geared to generate as much publicity as possible. The couple launched at Green River, Utah, just as Clover and Jotter had done. They, too, had hiked to the South Rim partway through the journey and met Kolb there, and they had also been hounded by national news media, which reported in the same breath that Bessie was "scared to death" and also "enjoying every minute of the adventure."

There the similarities ended. Kolb and his brother Ellsworth had been among the searchers who tried to discover the fate of the missing couple. They located the Hydes' scow—a boxy boat one river runner had dubbed "a floating coffin"—drifting in the lower canyon, empty but intact. Bilgewater sloshed in the bottom. The sweep oars fore and aft were in place, as if relinquished mere moments before. The brothers searched inside for clues. Hiking boots. A moleskin coat. Bessie's camera, loaded with film. A sack of flour and a fully baked ham. Bessie's journal, damp, was tucked into the side of the boat. The last entry was dated November 30 and indicated nothing amiss. The Kolbs took what they could carry and let the little boat loose, which proved a mistake, since no one else could search the vessel and quench the wild rumors that soon arose.

Kolb told pieces of this story to Clover while they traveled, and she felt her spirits sink. Bessie Hyde had come so very close to completing the journey. Clover sensed that she and Jotter were about to receive all the fame and accolades denied to Bessie, and it depressed her. She felt ashamed to enjoy running the river so much when it had terrorized others who came before her. "It's a great river with a hundred personalities," she wrote, "but it is not kind."

They drifted along, unhurried. Clumps of desert mistletoe bright with berries hung in the mesquite trees, and here and there, a willow tempted them with the promise of shade. They spotted a bighorn sheep, which was unfazed by Bell's wild attempt to shoot it. Feral burros appeared on both sides of the river, skinny gray animals with untrimmed hooves and twitchy ears, breaking the tranquility with raspy bawls ("cheerful," wrote Clover, "if not musical voices.") The descendants of pack animals abandoned by miners, burros were the unofficial mascot of Grand Canyon National Park. Despite this, the Park Service shot them by the hundreds in the

1920s and 1930s, out of concern about overgrazing. Bell wanted to eat one for supper, but the others overruled him.

They camped that night at Diamond Creek. This was Hualapai land: they had left the park's boundaries behind some time before. A creek came down to the river here at such a gentle slope that a rough automobile road had been carved out alongside it. Here, eighty years earlier, Lieutenant Joseph Christmas Ives of the U.S. Army Corps of Engineers became the first white man on record to visit the bottom of the Grand Canyon. He had come upriver in a steamboat called *Explorer,* and when it broke on the rocks at Black Canyon, he'd kept going on foot. "The region last explored is, of course, altogether valueless," he reported. "It can be approached only from the south, and after entering it there is nothing to do but to leave. Ours has been the first, and will doubtless be the last, party of whites to visit this profitless locality."

What his Hualapai guides thought isn't recorded, but Ives was convinced that the Colorado River, "along the greater portion of its lonely and majestic way, shall be forever unvisited and undisturbed."

Opuntia bigelovii joined the changing plant life; it looked like a small tree composed entirely of short, fuzz-covered cylinders. Its English name, teddy bear cholla, isn't very apt, for the fuzz is really barbed spines, and the slightest tremor can cause a joint to drop off and stick tenaciously to fur or clothing. Its Spanish name, velas de coyote (coyote's candles), is better; bright sunlight can transfigure the cactus into a whole candelabrum of lit tapers.

Near here, Clover picked up a different species of cholla, *Opuntia tetracantha,* puzzled by its presence. It usually grew near Tucson, hundreds of miles to the south. It was a fluke, she thought, or perhaps a gradient of these cacti really did exist from south to north and nobody had found them yet. But even a botanical mystery couldn't shake her gloom. The men seemed to notice Clover's depression that night and helped her with a few little chores around the camp. This small example of kindness, combined with Clover's disappointment and fatigue, overwhelmed her, "& I retired to the shadows of our wil-

A break for a meal in the Grand Canyon. Left to right: Lorin Bell,
Elzada Clover, Lois Jotter, Dell Reed, Bill Gibson, and
Norm Nevills. Photograph by Emery Kolb. *NAU.PH.568.1560,
Emery Kolb Collection, Special Collections and Archives,
Cline Library, Northern Arizona University*

low tree & wept for no particular reason," she wrote. She didn't want
to leave the river. That was the explanation she wrote in her journal
for her "hysteria." (She put the word in quotation marks, perhaps to
indicate irony or amused self-deprecation. Doctors had, for centuries,
diagnosed women with hysteria whenever they broke out of society's
accepted norms; the word itself comes from the Greek for uterus.)
Later, Clover sat up with Jotter after nightfall and the two women
talked quietly while the others slept. Then she took a flashlight and
went to bathe in the creek in private and wash out the clothes she was
wearing—very nearly the only clothes she had left; she'd been forced
to borrow socks from Kolb when all hers went to holes. The water
and the solitude eased her spirits, until some rustle in the bushes put
her in mind, for no particular reason, of mountain lions. Once the
idea was in her head, it wouldn't go away. The shadows turned sinis-

ter, as did every snap and sway of the breeze in the branches. Mountain lions did prowl the area, and even jaguars were found that far north in the 1930s, before predator control agents drove them out of the Grand Canyon. But Clover's fear shamed her. She struggled into her clothes and hurried back to camp—"a coward," she wrote in her diary, "altho I knew there was no lion."

They all half-expected, the next day, to come round a corner and see the shining expanse of Lake Mead. Descriptions of the vast reservoir, the largest in the world by volume, gave this impression. But no such vista opened before them. They ran less than twenty miles, through a series of fast rapids that Reed described as "straight aways, half circles, and letter S." The fearsome Separation Rapid, where three of Powell's party had abandoned the river, seemed to have lost its bite.

That night, they signed one another's sun helmets, like high school kids with yearbooks. "It was a pleasant two months—and thanks for showing me so much," Jotter wrote to Clover, as if they'd merely gone on a cruise or a summer camping trip. Clover responded, "Enjoyed fighting Botany and the old Colorado with you," and signed it "The other woman."

They set about the usual camp chores, scrounging for mesquite branches to kindle the fire, preparing a meal out of their diminished supplies, and washing their silt-filled clothes in the silt-filled river. They had done it many times before. But something seemed to be missing. They kept listening for a sound that wasn't there. The limestone and sandstone terraces had pulled back from the river: the world seemed large and dark and cavernous. Reed was the one who figured it out. The river no longer roared. Wide and silent, it lapped with a languid, listless motion against the shore.

They had reached the slack water of Lake Mead.

Chapter Eleven

LONELY FOR THE RIVER

BOULDER DAM HAD BEEN COMPLETED TWO YEARS before, and the Colorado was still filling up the reservoir. A pamphlet circulated by the U.S. Bureau of Reclamation proclaimed that the dam had transformed "the surly Colorado, sulking in its canyons" into a "useful and reliable friend." The reservoir would provide hydropower and water to faraway cities and was also popular for boating and fishing. "It provides an avenue of easy access," the brochure boasted, "to stretches of the river which had been visited by only half a dozen daring expeditions before the dam was built." In 1936 the National Park Service, which had long opposed dams within park lands, became a kind of awkward godparent of Lake Mead. The reservoir couldn't be a national park or monument, since it was hardly "unimpaired," so Congress created a new category: national recreation area. The Park Service was good at recreation. Its emphasis on tourism had paid off in the questionable inheritance of a human-created lake. Lake Mead was now fifty feet below the dam's spillway; it would rise to capacity in 1941. Stressed by drought and water demand, it would never again reach that level of abundance except for one wet winter in 1983–84.

Barrel cacti, saturated and torn up by their roots, bobbed at the edges of the reservoir. Others still clung to the earth, submerged except for their crowns of spines. The boats drifted sluggishly, a mile per hour. A despondent feeling settled over the party. The rapids marked on Birdseye's map no longer existed, buried beneath slack water. The journey was over. Nothing lay ahead but a long, hot, dull slog to Boulder Dam, without the river's current to help them along. All day they traded turns at the oars, switching every half hour. Blisters rose on sweat-slick palms. They took a siesta around 2 p.m. in a patch of shade, napping, swimming, and scrubbing up the boats so they would look good for the news cameras. As she sopped bilgewater from the *Wen,* Clover overheard the men joking about the women doing all the work, using a derogatory term for Indigenous women. They also—not for the first time—teased her about her weight, pretending to laugh at how easily she could float. Clover kept up a veneer of good humor and joined the others in a little roughhousing, throwing wet rags and wild melons at one another.

That evening, they rowed up a side canyon to spend the night in a sheltered spot. They had to keep well away from the banks because huge pieces of travertine, loosened by the rising reservoir, kept sloughing off into the water. They could find hardly any wood to burn. Nevills, foraging for brush, nearly stepped on a rattlesnake in the dark. Bell snagged the snake "behind the ears" and stuck him in an empty bacon can so they could get photographs in the morning.

The travertine proved uncomfortable to sleep on, especially if one did not have an air mattress to cushion the knobbles. Reed and Gibson both slept in a boat that night, their heads stuck out one side and feet out the other. Presumably only Oscar, the snake, was more unhappy about his sleeping arrangements, stuffed in a tin can with holes punched in the lid. Nevills piled rocks on top and nervously checked the can every few minutes with a flashlight.

Another plane circled them early that morning. They woke before dawn and rowed with blistered hands in the blistering heat, fighting for every mile. Beneath the sun-bleached boats, the water turned clear blue, no longer muddy and red. At 10 a.m., they decided to pull into a side canyon for an early lunch. "The boys swore violently when they found they had rowed only six miles," Clover wrote. They hadn't yet begun to eat when a distant buzzing echoed over the water. They all dashed to the water's edge and yelled, throats parched, arms waving.

There! A motorboat turned toward them, cutting curls of water out of the reservoir with its prow. Jotter, squinting against the glare, made out a familiar face at the helm.

Buzz Holmstrom had come to rescue them after all.

$$\Downarrow$$

IT HAD BEEN HOLMSTROM in the little plane they spotted that morning. He'd been watching for them from his post at Pearce Ferry. On his own trip, Holmstrom had stubbornly rowed across the reservoir for four days without help (the story went that he actually nosed his boat up against the dam), but none of them felt inclined to repeat this feat. They put the three boats in tow behind Holmstrom's and motored five miles to Emery Falls, a cataract tucked into a cove at Grand Wash Cliffs, which officially marked the end of the Grand Canyon and the beginning of Lake Mead.

A local newspaper reported a temperature of 139 degrees Fahrenheit, surely a mistake or an exaggeration, since that would smash the highest temperature record in the United States by several degrees. But it probably felt like 139 degrees out on the glare of the reservoir. Emery Falls must have been "quite high and pretty" at one time, Reed thought, but no longer; the reservoir had swallowed up the waterfall like a vacuum sucking up the end of a ribbon. Not far from the lakeshore, a dark cleft in the limestone beckoned with its promise of shade. Gypsum Cave was a famous spot among scientists at the time, only recently excavated by archeologists. Clover wanted to see it, but the short, steep climb proved too much for her. Holmstrom gave her a hand over the last big boulder and then she passed out briefly, probably from heat exhaustion.

The cave had been excavated in 1930 by a diverse Native American crew (Zuni, Pit River, Shoshone, and Washoe) under the direction of archeologist Mark Harrington. Accompanying them was Harrington's niece Bertha Parker, also known as Yewas, a twenty-three-year-old woman of Abenaki and Seneca descent. She had spent her childhood among archeological digs with her father, and Har-

The crew is "rescued" by Buzz Holmstrom on Lake Mead
near the end of their journey. *Courtesy of the Elzada U. Clover
Papers, Bentley Historical Library, University of Michigan*

rington hired her as a secretary. Parker cleaned, repaired, and cataloged the bones. When the paperwork was finished, she disappeared
into the multi-room cave with a headlamp, "worming her way into
the most inaccessible crevices," Harrington wrote with admiration.
In one such crevice, Parker unearthed an enormous skull. It belonged
to a Shasta ground sloth, a bear-sized animal that had gone extinct
ten thousand years before. Its bones lay among human-made objects:
ancient darts designed to be thrown by atlatls, bits of basketry, and
wooden flutes. Harrington concluded that humans and Pleistocene
animals had coexisted at the end of the Ice Age and wondered if the
sloths vanished because of overhunting. Later, scientists would put
precise dates to the bones and come to a different conclusion: humans
had made use of the cave hundreds of years after the sloths lived
and died there. Harrington was wrong about Gypsum Cave's history,
though he might have been right about the end of the Pleistocene
beasts. Scientists still point to overhunting as a possible cause of their
demise. As for Parker, she went on to document the Gypsum Cave
discoveries at the Southwest Museum in California, finally shedding
the title of secretary to become an archeologist and ethnologist.

Clover was interested in the cave's history, but she could find her
own obsession—plants—anywhere, even in the sloth dung that lit-
tered the floor. She recovered enough from her "swounding" (her
word for fainting) to identify ancient fragments of Mormon tea in
the dried dung. After exploring, everyone went back to Emery Falls
to swim and cool off. Soon a large motorboat appeared, stuffed with
thirty-some people, obviously looking for them. A blue banner fluttered on the boat's flagpole, displaying seven white stars around the
Buffalo Seal, the insignia of the U.S. Department of the Interior.
Journalists scribbled and cameras snapped as Gibson's wife flung
herself into his arms. Gibson's parents had come, too, and a Nevada
congressman.

"We had a long & beautiful ride in to Boulder Dam," Clover
wrote, with iced sodas, boxed lunches, and as much cold water as
they could guzzle. The expedition members crowded into the launch,

The crew arrives at Lake Mead. From left to right, top row: Dell Reed, Norm Nevills, Emery Kolb. Bottom row: Bill Gibson, Elzada Clover, Lois Jotter, and Lorin Bell. *Lake Mead National Recreation Area Archives Historic Photograph Collection, #1629*

and Holmstrom came too, handing his boat off to a friend. They put the three Cataract boats in tow, like ducklings bobbing along behind their mother. The painful miles that would have taken them days to row passed by in a blur. Clover only wished the journalists wouldn't lurk nearby, eavesdropping on her conversations and writing down every word. She was so exhausted that it took all her willpower to remain awake for the ride. At 8:30 p.m., they reached Boulder City. Cars packed the dusty, bare ground sloping down to the reservoir, and a crowd watched eagerly as the boat docked. A photographer took a picture, clearly posed, of Clover powdering her nose with a puff while Jotter held up a hand mirror. "What do you want to do first?" the reporters asked. Clover replied that she would like a glass of cold limeade and a plate of fried chicken. Jotter only wanted to wire her parents of her safe arrival. Dutiful daughter wasn't, apparently, what the journalists wanted; they pressed her to pick something else. Hesitantly, Jotter said she wouldn't mind buying a new hat (a more "ladylike" one, reported the congressman, "to replace the masculine

Lois Jotter and Elzada Clover at the end of their forty-three day
journey down the Green and Colorado rivers. *AP Photo/RJF*

sun helmet.") But when they reached the hotel, all plans for food, letters, and shopping were put on hold in favor of hot baths. "Both Miss Clover and Miss Jotter stated that they greatly enjoyed the trip," one newspaper recorded, "and announced they intended to make it again at the first opportunity."

It was strange to be off the river. In the hotel room they shared, Jotter carefully washed her face and hands and then asked, "Elzie, do you want to reuse this water?" The two women stared at each other a moment and then burst out laughing.

$$\psi$$

BOULDER CITY EXISTED because of the dam. Carefully planned under the supervision of the U.S. Bureau of Reclamation, the town had neat rows of Monopoly-like houses stuck out in a desert that received less than six inches of rainfall a year. It was located less than thirty miles from the heart of booming Las Vegas, Nevada, but its population in 1938 was only a few thousand people. Alcohol and gambling were illegal. Though it was built to house the dam's construction workers, some of whom were African American, city code prohibited Black people from living there until 1933. There is no record of a Black dam worker living there, perhaps because racism kept them from obtaining housing in Boulder City, or because prejudiced hiring polices meant that few Black people held jobs at Boulder Dam. As white women, Clover and Jotter had doors open to them that remained closed to others, including the doors of the elegant Boulder Dam Hotel.

Set facing the main street, the hotel was a graceful white building with private baths and air-conditioned rooms, popular among celebrities who came to see the dam, or needed a place to call home while they took advantage of Nevada's lenient laws on divorce. Jotter, Clover, and the rest didn't sit down to dinner until 11 p.m. The journalists reported that they ordered a "victory dinner of rattlesnake steak," an idea inspired by poor Oscar still stuck in the bacon can, but Clover, who was keeping detailed notes in her diary at this time, made no mention of any such thing. All she wanted was clean clothes, hot water, and a meal she didn't have to cook. They all ordered thick steaks and malted milks, and had seconds. Nevills didn't join them. He had dashed to a hospital in Las Vegas with Doris, alarmed over an abscess on her thumb. (The hospital in Boulder City had served only the male dam workers and did not treat women; it closed in 1935.) Around midnight, Jotter and the "boys" decided to go to Las Vegas for a night of carousing under the neon lights. Clover, disapproving, called it a "cockeyed project" and went to bed.

Jotter returned at 3 a.m. and slept soundly for two hours, waking up far too early and far too cheerful for Clover's state of mind. The two women ate breakfast together at the hotel. They must have perused the newspapers, curious to see how their faltering interviews the day before had been misquoted, embellished, or misconstrued. "Women Make Perilous Trip Through Colorado Gorges," declared the headline that morning, describing Clover and Jotter as "two Michigan schoolma'ams" with "copper-tanned cheeks." They had letters as well as press clippings to while away the time; envelopes addressed simply to "The Nevills Expedition" found a way into their hands. "Hurry back and don't do this to us again right away," a friend wrote to Jotter. "Can you just imagine what a weak sick feeling it was to go on the supposition you were safe, only because no wreckage had come floating down the river?"

After breakfast, Clover went to a beauty parlor. She was annoyed when three journalists tracked her there and snapped photos while she got her hair done. ("River Queens Seek Beauty," ran the next day's headline.) Then the whole crew gathered at the lakeshore to take stiff, posed photos in their boats for the *Los Angeles Times*. New people kept arriving to meet them. One of them was Frank Dodge, the boatman who had run the Colorado River with the Birdseye and Pathé–Bray expeditions. Clover thought he was an interesting person, but Dodge did not return the compliment. He dismissed Clover as a "spinster" and "a middle aged woman who lost her way in life." He was impressed by Jotter, though. She was a "nice buxsom gal," he told a friend, with "a good face, plenty smart." In a tone intended to bestow the highest praise he could think of, Dodge wrote that she would "make a fine mate for some explorer scientist."

It was an abrupt reawakening to the world above the canyon. They had left Green River, Utah, forty-three days before, and spent thirty-six of them on the water. All that time, their lives had been hitched to the river's rhythms. They had followed its contours, swallowed its silt, and slept to its murmurings. They would have to get used to the sensation of solid ground again, and the sight of the horizon. They would have to get used to a lot of things.

$$\psi$$

CLOVER SPENT A WEEK in Boulder City, most of the time in abject misery. She had no clear plans for the rest of her summer. Nevills remained in town but spent much of his time in Las Vegas watching over Doris's recovery. The rest of the party broke up on August 3. Reed and Kolb went to the South Rim. Gibson returned home to San Francisco. Jotter drove to California with Bell to collect yet more plants for the University of Michigan. She flirted lightly with Holmstrom before she left, saying he looked a bit like Cupid. Perhaps the joke referred to their difference in height, because he decidedly did not look like Cupid—Holmstrom once described himself as "a compromise between a mailman and a garbageman who has been lost in the woods for a couple of months"—but he took the teasing with good humor. Clover was amused by the little something-or-nothing between the two young people. But when Jotter left, her feelings began to prey on her. She went down to the pier just to feel the water rising and falling beneath the boats. Tears rose and threatened to choke her. She wondered when she would be able to run the river again. "I'm so lonely for it now I can hardly stand it," she wrote in her journal.

Holmstrom had a knack for appearing in the nick of time. One night he came to the hotel after dinner and rescued Clover from the unwanted attentions of a couple of tipsy female journalists. The next day, alone in her hotel room, she gave into anguish and wept. Then a call came from the lobby: Holmstrom was waiting for her. He had given his boat, the *Julius F,* a fresh coat of red paint and wanted her to see it. Clover splashed cold water on her swollen eyes and went to meet him. Holmstrom understood: he, too, had experienced a kind of "all-gone feeling" after leaving the Colorado. They devoured a box of candy together while poring over Clover's pictures of the river. Another time, they sat in Holmstrom's car and talked for hours, wrapped in a private world of their own. Amongst all the newshounds and autograph hunters, Holmstrom was the only person left in Boulder City who truly understood her feelings about the Colorado River. They were connected, somehow. The river tied them together.

Holmstrom told Clover he would be "eternally grateful" that he had met the expedition members. Clover sensed he was embarrassed by his former opinions about female river runners. "I'm sure that he had planned that the women would be terrible amazons," she wrote.

Clover spent the rest of her time preparing the plants for shipment to Michigan, sorting through her gear, and writing letters. She wanted to sell her photographs to *Life* but found to her dismay that Gene Atkinson had already sent them some of his, and they were of such poor quality that the magazine had given up on the idea. Nevills, meanwhile, arranged to sell the *Botany* to the Harbor Plywood Corporation, along with "a hundred or so" photographs and "exclusive release" of the story, for the enormous sum of $750. He had taken no photographs of his own, so he had to ask Bell, Gibson, Kolb, and Clover to share theirs. Clover seemed unaware of the larger deal when she wrote in her diary that Harbor Plywood would pay her $10 for several photographs. She refused, thinking the money too little for the risk she'd run to get them. Nevills did promptly pay his debts to Harris and Clover—he had borrowed money from both of them during the expedition—but when the details of the deal leaked to the rest of the crew, Jotter indignantly asked for a cut of the money. Nevills had, after all, rashly promised they would all share

in the financial rewards of the publicity, and the deal with Harbor
Plywood included everybody's life histories and a vague promise they
would all make frequent references to the hardiness of the plywood
boats. There is no record of Jotter receiving a reply. The *Botany* was
scrubbed, polished, and sent on a tour of department store windows
and small-town parades. Harbor Plywood told Nevills that the boat
always drew a crowd, and guests at a lumber dealers convention "fin-
gered it reverently as if it had been the Ark of the Covenant."

Clover visited Doris in the hospital and showed her movie reels
to the doctors and nurses. Later, she borrowed a projector from the
owner of her hotel so she could curl up on her bed and watch the
films in private. The rattlesnake coiled and snapped while someone
off-screen prodded him with a stick. Waves swallowed the boats and
spit them out again.

Doris left the hospital at last, and Nevills returned with her to
Boulder City to invite Clover to go with them to the South Rim. From
there, they would rendezvous with Bell in Tuba City before the Nevillses headed home to Mexican Hat. Clover agreed. They went to the
dock to load the *Wen* onto a boat trailer. The *Mexican Hat* would go
into storage, for now. Clover and Nevills performed what she called
a "sad little ceremony," taking the *Wen* out to open water for the last
time and then, with Clover at the oars, bringing the boat in to land.
Clover's blisters had healed, her hands soft again as she gripped the
leather-wrapped handles of the oars. She was dressed in white slacks
and high-heeled shoes, "so," she wrote, "it was hardly true to form."

All this time, Holmstrom had kept his plans to raft the Colorado River that autumn to himself. But when Clover found him to
say goodbye, the secret burst out of him. His partner, Amos Burg,
thought autumn was the perfect time for the trip, just as people all
over the country were returning from summer vacations and settling into their desks with a dull, unsatisfied feeling, eager for a
vicarious adventure. Burg planned to sell their film and make as
much money as he could: "I believe it will thrill the World." He
reassured Holmstrom that it didn't matter in the least that the Nev-

ills Expedition had succeeded. "After all," he wrote, "this is a big country and several expeditions could go down and still the markets wouldn't be scratched."

Clover was glad for his sake. "He is as lonely as I am for the river," she wrote. There was no reason to think that Holmstrom's plans would have anything to do with her.

⩗

THERE WERE MORE autograph hounds at the South Rim, where Clover spent the next two nights. Kolb hosted a private showing of Clover's films and asked her to address the crowd. She was annoyed with Kolb for playing up his role in the expedition; she thought he was deliberately making the rest of them sound like a "rattlepated bunch of greenhorns." At least in private conversations, however, Kolb admitted that the so-called "women's work" of botany, cooking, and camp chores had been more strenuous than anything the men had to do. He spoke warmly to Clover of his admiration for her courage and calm spirit.

Amid all the hubbub, Clover made an alarming discovery. The pressed plants she and Jotter had left at the bottom of the Grand Canyon had been mislaid. They had never been sent up the Bright Angel Trail by mule for shipment, as she'd arranged. The bundle contained every specimen between Lee's Ferry and Bright Angel, all the ferns and flowers from Vasey's Paradise, and at least one cactus Clover had thought was an undescribed species.

"Makes me furious & I am trying to have them traced," she wrote in her diary. She suspected that Nevills had misplaced them, and in the initial heat of her anger, she wondered if he did it deliberately to sabotage her. The two of them had planned to write a book together about the expedition, but Clover no longer felt excited by the prospect. "Doubt we can agree," she wrote. Nevills's desire to emphasize what Clover called "ballyhoo" finally caused her to snap. She would have to return to the University of Michigan without a good part of the collection she'd meant to get, and a fistful of ridiculous news reports—

exactly the situation she'd hoped to avoid. It was Shiva Temple all over again. Clover now felt that Nevills had not paid enough attention to the importance of their botany collection. Jotter, when she learned of the mislaid plants, felt the same; "he probably thought of them as dried up sticks," she wrote, "not regarding them in the way a botanist does: as sacred objects, a verification of his observations." Or hers.

Clover had her notebook, but some of the pressed specimens still needed to be identified, and they were meant to provide permanent proof of her conclusions about the river's ecology. This was why they had risked their lives. This was the reason for the late nights and early mornings, the cut hands and blistered feet. Now a third of their collection was gone. Had their efforts been for nothing?

With the mystery of the missing plants still unsolved, she left the South Rim with Nevills and Doris to visit Bell in Tuba City. He had returned from California to a good scolding from his family for his foolish decision to go down the river. Clover stayed there for some time, exploring the Colorado Plateau in Ed Kerley's unreliable truck, unperturbed by the idea of breaking down in the middle of nowhere (which happened at least once). She saw dinosaur tracks imprinted in stone and chatted with Navajos, with Bell as a translator. "Somehow I could not bear the idea of leaving the southwest," Clover wrote. Her misery found a reprieve when Nevills invited her and Bell to go down the San Juan River with a party of sightseers.

It was a peaceful eleven-day trip, the boats drifting languidly around the river's lazy curves beneath a bright August sky, the days muted and hot. "No danger here," Clover wrote, "but time to dream of that other river." They visited Rainbow Bridge again, this time during a swift summer storm that sent floodwaters raging down the side canyons and forced Bell and Clover to run for higher ground. "Wish you'd been along," Bell wrote to Jotter. It hadn't compared to the Grand Canyon, he said, but he had appreciated the chance to get to know Clover better—"a darned good sport and a very charming woman."

Afterward, Clover had no more excuse to linger. She had promised

the university she would go to Texas to do more botanizing. Her bedroll and camping gear were ready, but this time, contemplating long
days alone in the Río Grande Valley, she added a pistol to her pack.

$$\downarrow$$

BACK IN MICHIGAN, Jotter began her fall classes with renewed
enthusiasm for the work. She had earned some notoriety, a new experience. Strangers approached her to say, "May I take your picture?"
or "Will you sign this for me?" Fellow graduate students asked her to
give talks at their society meetings. She got used to speaking in public. But she still didn't think of herself as an adventurous person. The
whole thing had been Clover's idea, after all.

Clover returned to Ann Arbor in September. In her absence, Jotter had looked for a house they could share, but the rent proved too
high at any of the available places. Clover took a room at the Michigan Union, where faculty could order meals delivered to the door.
She reveled in the luxury of a Sunday breakfast in bed, but Jotter,
who joined her once or twice as an overnight guest, found it rather
uncomfortable, "what with spilling and crumbs." Jotter went back to
the ratty apartment where the botany and zoology graduate students
tended to congregate, so close to the Bell Tower they could hear it
chime loudly, on the hour, every hour, until midnight. The landlord
had a seedy reputation and liked to host wild parties. He stopped her
in the hallway one day, not long after her return, and asked, "Are you
still the same sweet girl, Lois?" Instantly she replied, "Even sweeter,
Mr. Sessions!" She did not report this conversation to her parents.

At least some members of her family seemed to feel that their Lois
had returned from the river with a few bad habits, or at least a boldness
she hadn't expressed before. At a Mennonite church meeting in Ohio
attended by her grandmother—a church so formal and old-fashioned
it had two doors, so that men and women could enter separately—
Jotter told the story of the runaway boat. "That darned boat," she said
playfully, and afterward, one of her aunts said in deep disapproval, "It
would have been better if you hadn't sworn in church."

Clover and Jotter showed their film footage and gave talks to public audiences at churches, women's clubs, and university luncheons, sometimes together, sometimes separately. "We had no feeling of egotism when we came out," Clover said to a packed auditorium of more than seven hundred people one fall day in Ann Arbor. She went on, "We felt that the river actually had a personality and we learned to be very respectful of it." The local paper reported afterward on Clover's darkly funny stories. When the lecture was over, an elderly woman approached Jotter to ask when she and Clover intended to go over Niagara Falls. (At this time, one woman and two men had survived going over the falls in barrels; it wasn't yet illegal to try.)

Jotter wore a special navy blue dress for these talks, with flowers and leaves embroidered on the skirt, appropriate for a botanist. Colonel Claude Birdseye himself introduced Jotter at one of her lectures, an implicit stamp of approval from the man who had initially disapproved of her plans to run the river. Jotter was abashed when Birdseye arrived in a tuxedo; her own dress was not nearly so formal. According to one observer, Jotter rather "played-down" the risk in her public talks. Jotter didn't think so. From the start, she had always pointed out that nothing about running the Colorado River was worse for women than for men.

Some astute members of their audiences recognized that there had been a danger unique to their gender, one not often spoken about openly in the 1930s. An older woman sidled up to Jotter after a talk. "Tell me," she whispered, "did anyone try to take advantage of you on that trip?"

Jotter was shocked. "Oh, no," she said.

"Well," the woman said, "they're men, aren't they?"

⇓

THE EFFECTS OF THE river trip continued to reverberate in the women's lives in unexpected ways. Not long after her return, Clover went to visit Thomas Lovering, the geologist, no doubt to swap stories about Arizona. Lovering happened to switch on the radio in the middle of an alarming broadcast. Aliens from Mars were attacking New Jersey! Lovering turned deathly white and rushed out to fill the gas tank of his car, telling Clover they ought to flee west. He was not the only one that night to mistake the radio adaptation of H. G. Wells's *The War of the Worlds* for a real news bulletin. But Clover sat calmly through the whole affair, until the announcer finally reassured listeners that the frightening story was fictional. "Maybe the waves did that to me," she wrote to Nevills the next day. "I believe it really would take a lot to make me excited any more."

Between classes and public appearances, the two women set to work writing up their findings. In the process, they repaired whatever wounds the expedition had left in their friendship. They never discussed the infighting that plagued the early days of the expedition, and if Clover's good opinion of Nevills was diminished after the fiasco of the missing plants, she kept it to herself. The specimens they managed to get back to Michigan were not of the best quality. Few of the flowers had been in bloom, and it had been difficult to properly preserve them or keep them dry during the hectic days of river running. The missing plants cast a cloud over their work. Had it really been worth it, risking their lives? Could they justify the danger and expense of the journey without a large part of the collection they had hoped to get?

It was a bad thought, that they would be remembered (if they were remembered at all) because they were women, not botanists. Clover's fears were realized when some of her colleagues gave her a hard time about taking the trip just for the excitement. Few people thought of their fieldwork as a serious scientific undertaking. The press reports were even more dismal. "Why should these women risk their lives in such a perilous exploit?" one writer opined. "The trip has been made before, hence there was little which another expedition could add to the geological and scientific knowledge of that marvel of nature. If the trip had to be made, there were men who could have taken their places, for the presence of women in the party was not essential to its success." The writer concluded that it was all

for adventure, and the sake of "conquering the unknown" and "sub-
duing the wilderness." Clover's name was misspelled, and the word
"botany" did not appear.

$$\Downarrow$$

IN EARLY SEPTEMBER, Jotter received an unexpected letter post-
marked from Wyoming. She opened it and found a single sheet of
torn-out notebook paper, filled with tiny, cramped writing that grew
steadily smaller as it went down the page in an effort to fit everything
in. "Dear Lois," the letter began, "Pardon that informal greeting but
it's the only way I know to start a letter . . ."

Holmstrom was on the river again, rafting from Green River,
Wyoming, to Lake Mead with Amos Burg. His letter was warm
with admiration, and his change of heart sincere. "I really think you
fit into the river life just as well as any man I know & a lot better than
some," he wrote.

Holmstrom's second trip down the Green and Colorado rivers
took more than two months. Jotter haunted his journey. He thought
of her in Cataract Canyon when he discovered an abandoned tin can
labeled "APPLS" in a feminine hand. He wanted to tell her about his
revolutionary system for removing worms from apricots. Her name,
and Clover's, shone on the canyon wall in white paint not far from
his own. He wrote to her at every possible stop. At Marble Canyon
Lodge, a letter was waiting for him. Jotter described an outfit she
wore for a publicity event, brown velveteen and blue silks. Holmstrom scribbled back, "I don't think I would like you as well that way
as all tanned & weatherbeaten & run down at the heels a little in an
old pair of slacks."

Then he confessed his own ragged appearance: his shoes had
given out and he hadn't taken a bath since he left Wyoming. "I'm
beginning to think perhaps women could really do some good on a
trip like this by keeping everyone cheerful & the general appearance
a little better," he said.

Holmstrom broke another record on that journey; he became the first person to run every rapid on the Colorado River between Wyoming and Lake Mead, including a few that shortly thereafter disappeared beneath the rising reservoir. Jotter, who kept in touch with nearly every one of her river companions, got a humorous letter from Reed on the occasion: "So that Buzz ran all of the rapids," he wrote, "never left one for me to be the first on, and here I had Lava Falls all staked out for myself." But there was no real envy. They all liked Holmstrom a great deal, and Jotter—unlike Clover—felt no pressing desire to return to the Colorado River.

On October 21, as the cottonwood leaves at Bright Angel Creek crisped into paper-thin circles of gold, Holmstrom pulled the *Julius F* ashore. Amos Burg, following in an inflatable rubber raft, fiddled with his movie cameras. The two men had picked up a companion along the way, a miner named Willis Johnson who had joined them at Green River, Utah. Johnson wandered away from camp, exploring, and chanced upon a curious artifact: a pile of newspaper stacked neatly on a rock. He went closer and found tongues of cactus sticking out of every layer. A forlorn prickly pear had thrust out a five-inch-long pad, reaching for the light.

He knew at once what he had found: Clover and Jotter's plant press.

Johnson rescued the abandoned press and "felt real proud" carrying it back to camp, to hand it into Holmstrom's care. The next day, Holmstrom lugged the awkward bundle up the Bright Angel Trail to mail to Michigan. A letter from Jotter was waiting at the top. Holmstrom wrote back to say he was so tired he could barely open the envelope. Almost as an afterthought, he squeezed in a note about finding their plant specimens in a "bad state of disrepair."

"She must have been a remarkable woman," Johnson said of Jotter later. "She probably didn't know that Buzz was in love with her. Some very strange things goes [*sic*] on in this world."

Jotter and Clover received the lost specimens with gratitude and delight. They sent some plants off to specialists for identification, while the rest went to the University of Michigan's Herbarium, as promised. Clover made plans to return to Arizona the following summer, and go by foot and horseback into the side canyons of the Colorado River to collect more cactus. But Jotter, absorbed in her thesis work and with no money to spare, declined the invitation to join her. Clover went back to Rainbow Bridge, Lee's Ferry, and Lake Mead, collecting plants from places that could be reached on foot. She hiked down the South Kaibab Trail again, sampling plants every half mile all the way to the canyon floor. And she did what she had longed to do the year before and visited the village of Supai to spend time among the Havasupai. In just over a month, she jotted down nearly five hundred more specimens in her Grand Canyon journal.

The desert tugged at Clover. "People wonder why I just live from one western trip to the next," she once wrote. "Everything is so big and timeless there. It makes so many worries and things here seem so petty." She returned to Arizona in the summer of 1940 and found an undescribed species of fishhook cactus in Havasupai Canyon, which she named *Sclerocactus havasupaiensis*. The following year, Clover and Jotter published a paper on the Grand Canyon's cacti in the *Bulletin of the Torrey Botanical Club*. It described four previously unknown cactus species picked up on their river trip: two hedgehogs, *Echinocereus canyonensis* and *Echinocereus decumbens*, one beavertail prickly pear, *Opuntia longiareolata*, and the smallflower fishhook cactus, *Sclerocactus parviflorus*. Clover sent a copy of the findings to Nevills and he wrote back to thank her. "But," he added, "I still have chills when I think of opening a hatch cover and getting harpooned by a cactus!"

Over the next three years, the women turned their attention to the rest of the plants. It was a relief to have the complete collection; they took pride in sampling at least one specimen for every cactus species observed on the river (though not so for other plants—at least, they skipped the poison ivy). They compiled a plant list, but went further than that. They took pains to interpret their findings, sorting through Clover's scribbled notes and constructing a picture of the river's ecology. The botany varied so widely it seemed almost pointless to discuss Merriam's life zones or Clements's climax communities. Instead, they made a chart of typical habitats and the plants associated with each:

moist sand, dry shores, rubble and boulders, springs and waterfalls, and talus slopes. The shoreline and the cliff walls experienced a near constant state of change. Landslides and floods tore plants into pieces, but also spread them downslope and downriver, to take root and try again. "Here is a case," the two botanists wrote, "where drought vies with flood waters in exterminating plants struggling for existence in a trying situation."

They concluded that the Colorado River through the Grand Canyon wasn't as important a corridor for plant migration as ecologists had previously supposed. They had found no Lower Sonoran species higher than Lee's Ferry: those endless deep gorges proved effective barriers. But plants did move around in the canyonlands in numerous complicated ways. Seeds fell off the high cliffs or stuck in the hooves of deer and bighorn sheep. Dismembered cactus pads washed down the river in floods and lodged between boulders, where they sprouted, only to be uprooted again. Clover and Jotter mused on that age-old question of why some plants thrived in a given place while others struggled or never sprouted there at all. They speculated that ash, redbud trees, and certain grasses were relicts from a wetter climate. They noted that *Echinocereus* showed a preference for limestone, and *Opuntia* grew in crevices and pockets high on the cliffs. They wrote of the physical factors that shaped plant life: extreme heat, poor soil, altitude, rainfall, the angle of sunlight, the steepness of the slope. They discussed how mice carried pockets of seeds in their cheeks to higher locations on the canyon walls, where the uneaten ones managed to sprout. They never used the term "ecosystem," but nevertheless, this was the kind of study Arthur Tansley had had in mind when he invented the word; they were considering all the possible interactions of physical factors with living things along the riparian corridor. And there were hints, here and there, of how humans played a role: the feral burros and introduced cows, the exotic plants—seventeen species in all—and the unknown influence of Boulder Dam.

In 1944, Clover and Jotter published the complete plant list in the *American Midland Naturalist,* naming more than four hundred species. The paper would prove influential to generations of botanists and ecologists in the Southwest; it's been cited more than seventy times. Jotter was satisfied with the work. It justified the risks she'd run. Holmstrom had come to the rescue one last time. He wasn't a likely hero, the man who had despaired to hear of two women running the Colorado River. But he seemed to understand how much the plant collection meant to her. It was what he remembered about her years later: her love of growing things. "I was helping a fellow move today," he wrote to her. "His wife had a cactus plant which would have fallen off the truck if I hadn't grabbed it with my bare hands. Right then I thot of you."

Chapter Twelve

HEAVEN AS I GO ALONG

"THE OLD RIVER RUINS PEOPLE FOR SETTLING down doesn't it?" Clover wrote to Doris Nevills one day. "I'm restless as the deuce." After the river trip, it seemed such a letdown to return to formal clothes and textbooks. But it was difficult to come up with the time and money for another adventure. She had classes to teach and research to do. Then, there was the fact that most people seemed to remember her 1938 experiences because of her gender, not her skill in science. She wasn't interested in river running merely for sport: she wanted to botanize. It would be half a century before the right invitation came along, and then, it was Jotter who received it.

In that time, the Colorado River underwent several drastic transformations. The first was the number of river trips. Nevills was determined to capitalize on the 1938 publicity and establish a regular business. He kept the *Wen* for that purpose. The *Mexican Hat* went to Harris, as promised, for his share in building the boats. The two men were not on easy terms. Nevills wrote to Harris after the expedition ended to thank him for his "good sportsmanship," but later he changed his mind. "I felt that your leaving me at Lees Ferry, with me in a spot for boatmen—was tough," he told Harris resentfully. "Naturally it struck me as wrong." He demanded to know Harris's "real reason" for leaving, refusing to accept Harris's job as an excuse.

No love lost, Harris thought, but he had come to regret his decision, too. "Gee, pal," he wrote to Jotter, "I've wished a thousand times since I left Lee's Ferry that I had gone on with you."

Harris ran the Grand Canyon the next year in the *Mexican Hat*. Gibson had overcome his fears of the river so thoroughly that he went along, too, for an encore. It was Gibson's second and last journey down the Colorado River. He went back to San Francisco to edit his film, writing to Jotter, "Wonder if you get as home-sick for the river as I do?" But Harris ran wild rivers the rest of his life, traversing the Grand Canyon more than three dozen times. "The river water got in my blood," as he put it. As river running evolved, he used each type of boat in turn: from his original wooden Cataract boat to rubber rafts to fiberglass speedboats.

Harris took paying passengers down the river but never tried to create a major enterprise. For Nevills, however, the "boating craze" took off. He walked a fine line in his publicity, exaggerating the river's dangers while also promising perfect safety. "See the desert by water," was his motto. He invited Clover to accompany him on his next Grand Canyon trip—and Jotter, too, despite his earlier complaints about her recklessness. Both women declined, busy with teaching and perhaps (though they never said so) unwilling to go with Nevills again.

Nevills's second Grand Canyon trip, in the summer of 1940, started from Green River, Wyoming, and covered more than a thousand miles to Lake Mead. He applied the lessons he learned in 1938 to his publicity plans; this expedition also included two botanists, Hugh Cutler and Mildred Baker. Doris came along ("as she refuses to stay home," Nevills told a reporter). She and Baker became the first women on record to run the Colorado from the headwaters to the dam. Unkindly, Nevills downplayed Clover and Jotter's botanical work to make this expedition sound more important, saying untruthfully that the two women had specialized in cacti instead of collecting all kinds of plants. Reed went along on that expedition as a boatman for his second canyon run. His attempts to commemorate the 1938 trip with woodcarvings had left him unsatisfied, but he wrote to Clover that the trip had brought him "real riches"; his son reconnected with him after an estrangement of ten years after seeing the Pathé newsreel.

The National Park Service still tried to discourage river trips. "It is simply a dangerous stunt," one official wrote to a prospective river runner. A 1941 article in the *Salt Lake Tribune* voiced the widespread perception that the "facts and features" of the river's ecology had been thoroughly mapped, and expeditions downriver now pursued nothing but "thrills or dramatic obituaries." In 1949 the *Boulder City News* ran a grisly cartoon depicting the Colorado River as a waterslide, spiked with signs bearing the names of the people who had died on its waters. Two shadowy figures labelled "Nevills" presided at the top, beneath a skull-and-crossbones flag.

Despite such admonitions, increasing numbers of men and women ran the Colorado. By dint of unrelenting publicity efforts, Nevills positioned himself as the nation's foremost expert in whitewater. Lumber companies referred clients to him for boat-building advice, and officials with the Park Service consulted him about starting a permit system for river runners. Unsurprisingly, Nevills supported the idea of limiting Grand Canyon runs to a select few "concessionaires," and voiced his objections to rubber rafts and solo cruises. As for his own company, Nevills boasted that he would take anyone on a river trip between the ages of seven and seventy-one. All but one of his Grand Canyon trips included women.

Stories of female river runners did exactly what Holmstrom once feared they would do: they made the Colorado River seem less dangerous. "The Grand Canyon has been competently surveyed," wrote one Park Service ranger, "and exploring the Colorado River is becoming a national pastime, now that the ladies have taken up the sport." Better maps, better boats, and growing expertise made a Grand Canyon voyage less risky, and greater familiarity with the river's rapids and capricious moods had blunted the sense of peril. But sexism also played a role in the river's diminished reputation: if women could do it, how bad could it be? One writer with a whimsical turn of mind punned on the idea of "shooting" rapids just a few months after Clover and Jotter returned from their trip. "The river rats claim it is a horrible degradation to a first rate rapid to get shot by a woman," the article read, "and probably some of the big, strapping ones the girls only slightly wounded just curled up and died of shame."

In 1946, the *Saturday Evening Post* profiled Nevills in an article called "Fast-Water Man," heaping praise on his river expeditions as both safe and thrilling adventures. The writer rehashed the 1938 trip, describing Clover as the "first woman" to run the Grand Canyon. Jotter was forgotten. This may have been a relief to her, since the article's description of Clover was neither flattering nor true. "Elzada took all the river had to offer," it read, "collected some new cacti and went back to tell boys and girls about plants. But something besides desire for rare cacti had driven her. In 1938 she was getting on. She had never married. Somehow, she felt, life was passing her by. She wanted at least one out-of-this-world adventure."

The story depressed and infuriated Clover. Her work as a respected university professor had been reduced to bedtime stories for children, and, instead of an accomplished scientist and explorer, she was depicted as an aging spinster with a life empty of meaning. How many times had she told a journalist her motivation was botany? Was it so hard to believe a woman might dedicate her life to science? Clover wrote to Jotter complaining about the "silly article" and said she wished for a report of the trip from *their* perspectives. Almost a decade had passed since the expedition, yet the public's version of events still disappointed her. Too many articles focused on death-defying drama or obsessed over the infighting in the expedition's early days. For her part, Jotter had grown more circumspect in her dislike of Nevills, and she respected her mentor's wishes to keep the irritations of the trip as much to herself as possible. When a historian came nosing for information about the "ill feeling" and asked to see her diary, Jotter told him coolly (and untruthfully) that she'd lost it.

"The idea of rehashing all that old stuff makes me sick," Clover told Jotter. What was needed was "a calm, true and dignified account of our trip which really was a grand adventure." But that seemed increasingly unlikely. The exaggerated stories dashed off by journalists during the expedition had hardened into an unmovable narrative, one that left science by the sidelines. After the *Post* story, Clover said, "I hoped that I would be out of print for the rest of my life."

⋁

HOLMSTROM CONTINUED to feel an all-consuming desire to be on the water. He never did show his movies of the Colorado River at the World's Fair. The scheme fell through, and he turned down subsequent offers of speaking engagements. "I'm plumb tired of talking about it," he wrote to Jotter, "and I'll bet you are by now too." To Clover, he was more philosophical about losing the chance to make some money from his river adventures: "I'm sure I've learned a lot in the last year and made a lot of good friends." He loved getting letters as he wandered from job to job, taking any kind of work that would let him camp out in wild country—mining, surveying, even drilling at potential dam sites on the Green and Colorado rivers. Whenever he received a letter (he told Jotter) he would carry it around in his pocket for a while, unopened, and sometimes take it out and hold it up to the light to try to make out the contents, and then put it back again, so that he could savor the experience as long as possible.

In 1939, proof of his change of heart, Holmstrom took an English-woman named Edith Clegg across the United States by river: the Columbia, Snake, Yellowstone, Missouri, Mississippi, Ohio, and Hudson. At first Holmstrom hadn't realized the client was a woman, and perhaps if he hadn't met Jotter and Clover, he would not have agreed. They left in late April and spent five months exploring the nation's waterways. Most of the rivers, Holmstrom felt, couldn't hold a candle to his beloved Colorado. He wrote to Jotter from Missouri, "don't like anything about this country—don't like mosquitoes, sandbars, heat, mud." He told Clover he wouldn't give ten cents for eastern Montana and the Dakotas together.

In New York, not far from Niagara Falls, they learned that Great Britain and France had declared war on Germany. President Franklin D. Roosevelt gave a speech on the radio, promising to keep the United States out of the war. A few weeks later, Holmstrom and

Clegg finished their explorations and she rushed home to England. Holmstrom went to Ann Arbor for a brief, hurried visit with Clover that autumn. He bought a new blue suit with his meager savings for the occasion, but was disappointed; Jotter was away. Clover shepherded Holmstrom around campus like a celebrity, and they daydreamed about going on a river trip together with people who truly valued the desert's beauty. Holmstrom went home to Oregon after that. In her next letter, Clover wrote cheekily that she hoped he had arrived safely and wasn't stuck on a cliff somewhere or buried under a landslide. It was clear the two of them had bonded over their love of wild country. "Funny," Clover wrote, "so many people are waiting for a reward in heaven. I am very doubtful about a heaven so like you I get my heaven as I go along."

The Imperial Japanese Navy struck Pearl Harbor on December 7, 1941, and the United States formally entered World War II the next day. Holmstrom enlisted in the U.S. Navy less than three months later. Navy life was an adjustment for him. He told Clover he sometimes got to thinking about camping and boating and felt unhappy, "but all that seems a long way off now." Clover sent him a care package while he was still in training in San Diego, and he wrote to her, "Somehow it made me think of rivers, canyons mountains and deserts. It made me think of sleeping out under the stars with a jagged skyline overhead and the roar of a rapid alongside"—and real, strong coffee brewed over a driftwood fire, not the stuff they served to soldiers that resembled coffee "only in color." He served on a ship in the South Pacific, then off the coast of England and France, returning once to visit his mother who worried he was "quite thin" and had a "deeply weary look in his eyes."

When the war ended in 1945, Holmstrom found work as a government surveyor and returned to the desert rivers he loved so well. He died on the Grand Ronde River in 1946 at the age of thirty-seven, apparently of a self-inflicted gunshot wound. Grief poured in from fellow river runners, along with bewilderment. Jotter found his death "incomprehensible," and her feeling was echoed by many others who knew Holmstrom's kindness, good humor, and respect for the land. Clover, in shock and sorrow, could only think that "the bigness of things" had caught up with him, while his mother, Frances, blamed the shadow of the war. She chose the words on her son's headstone from a poem by Robert Louis Stevenson: *Home is the sailor, home from the sea.*

TWO YEARS LATER, Nevills's life also came to an abrupt and unexpected end. In July 1949, he made his seventh and final run of the Grand Canyon. Soon after this, he struck a major deal with the Sierra Club to guide seventy-five people through Glen Canyon. By this time, policymakers had revived La Rue's old idea of building a dam there, just ten miles upriver from the site La Rue originally proposed. River runners had begun to realize they could lose the place. A 1945 report from the U.S. Bureau of Reclamation proposed building not only Glen Canyon Dam, but also two dams in the Grand Canyon called Marble and Bridge, on either side of the national park boundaries. Because this would waste all the whitewater falling steeply through the park itself, the proposal also included a forty-five-mile-long tunnel to divert the water to a power plant. The river that had carved the Grand Canyon would be no more, except for a trickle left for "scenic purposes." Gone were the days when people "sat helplessly by to watch the Colorado River waste itself or attempted in vain to halt its destruction," the report said. The river would be "utilized to the very drop" to convert the desert into "flourishing farms and beautiful homes."

Many in the tight-knit river running community hated the idea of losing Glen Canyon. The area had never been made into a national monument, but those who knew it rhapsodized about its loveliness. Nevills, however, was intrigued by the possibilities of tourism on the proposed reservoir. He even daydreamed about the water backing all the way up the San Juan River to Mexican Hat. "He loved the country and his enthusiasm was boundless—bad roads and all," remembered his second daughter, Sandra. The reservoir could put his little corner of the world on the map. The Sierra Club members he intended to guide down the river did not feel so sanguine about dams. It's hard not to speculate on how their influence might have changed Glen Canyon's fate, but the trip never took place. On September 19, 1949, Nevills and Doris got into their monoplane, the *Cherry II*, to fly to Colorado, where Doris intended to catch a commercial flight to California to see her family after the death of an uncle. Just after takeoff, the plane's engine died. Nevills banked and attempted to land. But the plane plunged downward into the gully at the end of the airstrip, crashed head-on into the cliff, and burst into flame. Nevills and Doris died instantly. He was forty-one years old, and his wife, thirty-five.

Some newspapers, reporting on their deaths, also predicted the death of Colorado river running. "It seems unlikely," wrote one journalist, "that any successors will find the fascination of the mighty canyons sufficient to outweigh the dangers and hardships." The writer added that even if successors did appear, dams would soon drown the river's secrets. Others, however, thought Nevills had popularized a new kind of sport that wouldn't easily fade. Eighty years had passed since Powell's first expedition, and historians could name just over one hundred people who had completed a Grand Canyon run. Roughly a third of those had gone on a Nevills Expeditions trip, including all of the women (who numbered just ten, including Clover and Jotter).

Nevills included women only as passengers. It was more a matter of good business practice than enlightenment. Ignoring his own record, he once wrote that "but one woman in a thousand is qualified for such an adventure," adding, "the Colorado river is no place for a timid clinging vine." It would be up to others to open the Colorado to female river guides, beginning with Georgie White in the 1950s. By the early 1960s, a dozen tour companies advertised commercial trips down the San Juan, Green, and Colorado rivers. Nevills Expeditions continued to thrive with others at the helm and ran wooden boats for another two decades after Nevills's death. The company exists today under the name of Canyoneers and still runs a historic Cataract boat alongside modern rafts.

The Nevillses' ashes were scattered over the canyonlands and a bronze plaque honors them at Navajo Bridge near Lee's Ferry. It reads, "They run the rivers of eternity."

∨

CLOVER'S JOB PROSPECTS did not improve after the expedition. One institution considered her too old; another dismissed her as young and inexperienced. Bartlett replied to these denials with cold disdain: he didn't really want to lose her. Clover remained at the University of Michigan. In April 1945, she went back to the Grand Canyon, where Park Service employees were tending rows of peas in Victory Gardens, not far from the canyon's rim. Clover got a permit and borrowed some equipment from the park's naturalist to go to Havasu Creek, promising to bring back some entomological specimens in exchange. She returned with vials of algae and handfuls of glittering dragonflies. She stayed at the Grand Canyon for several weeks, working side by side with the park's first paid botanist, Rose Collom. Collom was a self-taught botanist who, like Clover, liked to wander the wilds of Arizona in search of interesting plants. She was sixty-eight years old in 1939, when she convinced the Park Service to hire her. There's no record of what Clover and Collom talked about during their hours cataloging specimens; plants, probably, rather than the war. "In these troubled times," Collom once wrote, "when all the world is so upset, I think it rather steadies one to 'consider the lilies of the field . . .'"

Clover was still collecting plants at the Grand Canyon on May 7 when the Allies accepted Germany's unconditional surrender. The next day, nations around the world celebrated V-E Day, and ten days later, Clover left the South Rim and went to Lake Mead "to determine how formation of reservoir behind Boulder Dam has affected plantlife in Grand Canyon," according to the *Desert Magazine.* She had squeezed in a tour of the dam the day after the 1938 expedition ended in Boulder City and found it "almost too big & complicated to comprehend." Perhaps she began to wonder about the dam's effect on ecology that very day. Jotter was interested in this question, too. In a paper she presented on grasses and sedges of the Grand Canyon, she noted how the reservoir had drowned the vegetation. "One of the problems in prospect," she said, "is the marking off of certain areas along the rising waters, and the studying of the change of vegetation from year to year as the areas become affected by the greater proximity of the water." Perhaps this is the research plan Clover intended to carry out, but it seems the results of her investigation were never published. It would be left to other scientists, many decades later, to study the ecological effects of the Colorado River's big dams; that was the other transformation that caught up the river and left it forever changed.

Clover continued to travel, collecting plants from Guatemala, Haiti, and Mexico as well as the U.S. Southwest. She rose through the ranks at the University of Michigan to become curator of the Botanical Gardens in 1957 and Professor of Botany in 1960. She was the first woman in the botany department to earn a full professorship, and the first person to develop and teach a class at the botanical gardens, a popular undergraduate course that enticed many young men and women into botany. She invited students into her home for cider and donuts and took them boating on the lake. And she continued to give lectures on the Colorado River. She liked to show the movies at family reunions in Nebraska, where a gaggle of overexcited nieces and nephews would watch, enthralled, at the moving images projected on a white bedsheet. Students at the University of Michigan's Biological Station got the same treat. It was a tradition for professors to give a talk of some kind during the summer camps, but nobody could top Clover, either for her mastery of storytelling or for material. On the screen, the gray water churned. When the light struck it just right, it transformed to quicksilver, too blinding to look at, beneath the somber black cliffs of the canyons. Even in calm stretches the river seethed and simmered, and in the rapids, it turned to writhing coils, like a snake unwisely roused from its slumber. When the boats came tossing through, they looked no more suited to ride the river than a hot-air balloon was suited to reach the moon.

Echinocereus canyonensis (Grand Canyon claret cup)
collected from the Grand Canyon. *Courtesy of United States
National Herbarium, Smithsonian Institution, used by permission*

A former student said of Clover, "She never told us she was the
first lady down the Colorado—but we all knew." In fact, when the
topic arose, Clover was careful to say she and Jotter had been the first
non-Native women to boat the Grand Canyon. The river's long Indigenous history had made an impression on her.

None of the three Cataract boats ended up in the Smithsonian,
as Clover had once fantasized. Nevills donated the *Wen* to Grand
Canyon National Park, and Harris gave the *Mexican Hat* to the John
Wesley Powell Museum in Green River, Utah. The *Botany* somehow
made its way to Clover's home state of Nebraska and was pressed
into service when the Missouri River flooded in 1943. But something
did end up in the Smithsonian from the expedition, something that
mattered a lot more to Clover and Jotter: their plants. In 1952, the

University of Michigan transferred several of their pressed plants to the United States National Herbarium housed at the Smithsonian, including the type specimens of *Echinocereus canyonensis* and *Sclerocactus parviflorus*. They remain there to this day.

⇓

JOTTER'S LIFE WENT in a different direction. Three years after the river trip, while she was still working on her PhD research in Ann Arbor, a friend introduced her to a fellow scientist named Victor Cutter, Jr. Cutter's focus was mycology (the study of fungi) and he taught at Cornell University in Ithaca, New York. He was an avid hiker, angler, collector of plants, and lover of beagles, which he ran in field trials.

What followed was a "courtship by mail," as Jotter described it. In an early letter, attempting to convince Jotter to visit him in Ithaca, Cutter joked that no botanist could consider herself well educated until she'd seen Cornell, "and I know that in your heart of hearts . . . you desire to be known as a well educated botanist." Jotter, laboring over her PhD thesis and working part-time as a pharmaceutical botanist (drawing pints of blood from horses for research on vaccines), worried that she would have a tough time finding a teaching job in academia as a woman. If she married, it would be even harder. The Great Depression brought a spike in discrimination against women in the workforce, when fully half of U.S. states had laws against hiring married women. Some lawmakers went so far as to warn of the breakdown of civilization if married women were allowed to work. Despite this hostile atmosphere, Cutter tried to reassure Jotter about her future job prospects. Like a good scientist, he offered evidence: "All the depts. on this campus are seriously considering accepting only female applicants for assistants next year," he wrote. "There are several jobs still open at women's colleges in New England, such as Wheaton and Smith. If this does not add up to sufficient authority for my statement concerning the demand for women in science then I will send you some additional examples at the next writing."

Cutter added, by way of encouragement, "Obviously there are few young damsels of your age in the country which have had as wide and varied a training as you."

Jotter and Cutter married on October 24, 1942, in Ann Arbor. Clover hosted the pre-wedding bash, and the local paper, after a gushing column about Jotter's gown and bridal flowers, slipped in a mention of the women's journey down the Colorado River. The couple moved into an apartment in Ithaca, where the new bride finished her PhD dissertation. In 1943, she returned to Ann Arbor to defend her dissertation, six months pregnant with her first child. Now she was Dr. Lois Cutter. Hyphenated names weren't common in those days, but later in life she put "Lois Jotter Cutter" on her driver's licenses.

Gas and tire rationing hampered travel. Jotter Cutter and her husband took a bus from Ithaca to Ann Arbor and stayed with Clover to save money. The two women would see each other only rarely in the decades ahead. Jotter Cutter gave birth to a baby girl, Ann, in Ithaca later that year. She did not immediately return to teaching. She was a mother and a housewife now, stretching government-issued coupons and tending her Victory Garden. Her brother Walter enlisted in the Navy, but her husband was deferred for physical reasons from war service.

Jotter Cutter's son, Victor Cutter III, was born in 1950, after several miscarriages. Two years later, the family moved to Greensboro, North Carolina, where Victor Cutter became the head of the biology department at the Women's College of the University of North Carolina. He constantly advocated for girls and young women to pursue careers as research scientists. He died of cancer in 1962, when Ann was eighteen and young Victor just eleven. Jotter Cutter grieved not only for her husband, but for the scientific work that he would never complete. "I never truly understood those most trite words 'My better half' before," she wrote to a friend.

The following year, she took a job as an assistant professor in biology at the university. She filled her house with plants and her dinner table with lively conversation. Her home was a place to talk about botany, of course, but it was also a safe place for young women seeking counseling about sex and pregnancy, and for older couples in same-sex relationships who had few safe places to go. She became a mentor and teacher as well as a scientist. Carolyn Wyland, a former student, described her as "rock steady," full of wise counsel and quick to erupt into laughter. With a hard-won confidence, she could stand up in a classroom and lecture from memory without once looking at her notes. Trailing vines of clematis, collected by herself and her husband, draped over the house and turned it to a mass of leaves in summer. She liked to dig up plants from the garden and give them away. A friend, Linda Curtis, used to joke about those plants: "The things I got from the Cutters," she recalled, "were always really tough."

Glen Canyon Dam closed its floodgates that same year, 1963. A massive curve of cement, it looked like a pale crescent moon come to rest between the red walls of the canyon. By this time, it had become clear that the Colorado River did not have the abundant water once envisioned, just as Powell, La Rue, and others warned. The dam was an engineer's solution, a way to store the river's floods in wet years as a hedge against the dry, and prop up the terms of the Colorado River Compact. The reservoir behind the dam, christened Lake Powell, took seventeen years to fill—the second-largest reservoir in the country, after Lake Mead. It covered the glens and grottos of Glen Canyon, drowned Hite Ranch, lapped up to the brink of Rainbow Bridge, and backed slack water into Cataract Canyon, burying several of the rapids that had once terrorized river travelers. Almost immediately, the U.S. Bureau of Reclamation turned its attention to Bridge and Marble Dams, which were meant to be hydroelectric "cash register" dams to make money for massive water projects, such as piping water all the way from the Columbia River to slake the thirsty Southwest. But these schemes did not come to pass. Powerful environmental groups rallied against Bridge and Marble Dams and conspired with complex water politics to defeat them.

The world had changed. "Ecosystem" was now a household word, and people no longer wanted to conquer the Grand Canyon. They wanted to protect it. The field of botany, too, was swept up in these changes. It had fractured into specialties during Jotter's education, but now, as she reentered the workforce in the 1960s, botany was part of something bigger again: a new discipline called environmental science, born out of rising concerns about air and water pollution and the extinction of species. Jotter Cutter helped her university develop curricula for environmental science classes. She met Rachel Carson, whose 1962 book *Silent Spring* showed how scientific research could galvanize public opinion and spur changes in federal policy. All the while, she taught her two children to love science and the outdoors, and quietly championed women's equality. She was deeply concerned about people getting a good education in biology and botany. "I think my mother was way ahead of her time," her son Victor remembered. "The river trip was just an example of that."

She never said much to her children about her Colorado River adventures. But when Victor was four or five years old, he professed a sudden interest in filmmaking, and his mother dug into the closet and pulled out giant metal canisters containing reels of old silver nitrate film, no longer in use because of its tendency to burst into flame. She set up a projector and turned it on. The boats bucked and twisted; the river heaved. Entranced, Victor stared at the moving images. He had never seen anything like it: the only thing that came close, in his mind, was Hokusai's famous print of *The Great Wave off Kanagawa*.

Once, Clover came for a visit, and young Victor eavesdropped as the two women discussed botany. To his ear, it seemed they "talked in Latin half the time." The trip had changed their lives, and yet neither woman had run the Colorado River a second time. Jotter Cutter was a mother now—a widowed mother, at that—and didn't feel she could take the kind of risk she'd so blithely dismissed to her own parents at the age of twenty-four. Besides, by now the trip was "ancient history," and she didn't talk about it much "because I didn't want to seem a bore." Later in life, she had time and money to travel again: to Mexico, the Caribbean islands, and the Amazon rainforest. She preferred to see new places and new plants on every trip.

$$\downarrow$$

CLOVER RETIRED IN 1967 and was appointed Professor Emerita of Botany. "The superb cactus collection at the Botanical Gardens is her continuing monument," the Board of Regents announced. The collection reflected her love of travel and adventure: it included lady finger cactus from Texas, woolly torch cactus from Guatemala, and many other far-flung specimens. She had another monument: the many generations of students who passed through her classes and absorbed her deep passion for plants as if by osmosis. "She was always peeling the landscape for any plant of interest," a former student, Jane Myers, remembered. "There was no plant she wasn't interested in." Students faithfully memorized lists of plants, followed in her wake on field expeditions, and mucked about in the mud at the botanical gardens; no assignment was too far-fetched when it was commanded by Elzada Clover. "She kind of filled the room with her love of the subject," Myers said. "For her, it really was her whole life."

After her retirement, Clover moved to San Juan, Texas, to be close to family and the cactus she loved so well. "She really loved the desert," Jotter Cutter remembered, "not only for its plants, but also for the heat, the distances, and the beauty." Clover died on November 2, 1980, at the age of eighty-four. So it was her protégée, Lois Jotter Cutter, who at the age of eighty had a chance to go down the Colorado River as part of a scientific expedition one last time.

Chapter Thirteen

LEGENDARY

I N THE 1930S AND 1940S, NOBODY WAS THINKING about what happened to a river below a dam—nobody, that is, except for the engineers who determined how much water to release and when. Between 1938 and 1956—the year Grand Canyon National Park essentially banned "unauthorized boating"—just over two hundred people ran the Grand Canyon. Some years, nobody attempted it. But in 1960, more than two hundred people made the trip, and in 1970, the number was nearly ten thousand. This rise in river rafting coincided with a growing environmental consciousness among Americans. The Colorado was changing. It was impossible to ignore now that thousands of people rafted the river every year and camped on its sandbars. They couldn't help but notice how those sandbars had begun to disappear.

In those days, a person could stand on the little crescent of Kentucky bluegrass at the base of Glen Canyon Dam a few hours before dawn, look downriver, and see the dark water begin to rise. The hydroelectric turbines were going to work. Miles from any major city in a patch of lonely desert, one could watch the world wake up: neon signs in Las Vegas and the lights of Phoenix skyscrapers. By 9 a.m., the full-throated roar of the turbines had transformed sullen water to a cresting wave. This is called "hydropeaking"—the river's daily rise and fall in response to power demand. No longer was the Colorado hinged to seasonal rhythms: the spring pulse of snowmelt, the summer monsoon. Air-conditioned office blocks decided the pattern.

This new river never shrank down to a whisper during drought, nor did it rise to the fearsome, stone-eating deluges of the past. The water was always about 49 degrees Fahrenheit, no matter the season. It no longer froze in winter, and it wasn't warm in summer. The thick silt that had clogged throats and filled buckets on old river trips remained piled up far upstream behind the dam; the water now ran clear. Glen Canyon Dam was the last major dam built on the Colorado. The river never became the series of "quiet mill ponds" engineers and boosters had once envisioned. But nor was it the wild, untouched stretch of whitewater environmentalists wanted it to be. The Colorado was, in the words of geomorphologist Teo Melis, a "Frankensystem" of conflicting values and needs.

The National Environmental Policy Act signed into law in 1970 required federal projects to undergo an analysis of their effects on ecosystems, referred to as an environmental impact statement. It was too late to require such a statement for the construction of Glen Canyon Dam, but not too late to do one for its ongoing operations. The U.S. government requested this analysis in 1989. Three years later, Congress passed the Grand Canyon Protection Act, which ordered the U.S. Bureau of Reclamation to operate the dam in a way that protected "natural and cultural resources and visitor use," including the sandbars river rafters used for campsites.

So scientists needed to know how the dam had changed the river, which meant understanding how the river used to look. Researchers at the U.S. Geological Survey began to pore over photographs taken by Robert Brewster Stanton in 1890, comparing them to modern pictures of the same sites. Repeat photography was a relatively new technique. In the Grand Canyon, the work began with botanist Raymond Turner, who studied the riparian vegetation, and continued with Robert Webb and Teo Melis, who wanted to examine debris flows, the jumbles of boulders that formed the Grand Canyon's rapids. Webb and Melis soon discovered that the photographs opened a Pandora's box of questions: about the sandbars, the rapids, the grazing burros, and the exotic tamarisk trees. Not all these questions could be answered by a photograph. Webb, the scientist, began talking about the problem with Kenton Grua, a longtime river runner, and Diane Boyer, an archivist. In 1994, the three of them hit upon an idea. If they wanted to know what the Colorado River truly looked like before the dam, why not ask the people who had seen it?

$$\psi$$

IT WAS NOT THE FIRST TIME Jotter Cutter had been invited to return to the Colorado River, but she had never been tempted by appeals addressed to the "first woman" to run the Grand Canyon. This letter was different. It was printed on official U.S. Geological Survey letterhead, with "Research Project Office" in block letters across the top. The invitation was for a twelve-day rafting trip through the Grand Canyon to assess ecological changes. It was all about science. They wanted her to join because of her knowledge and skills, not her gender. She said yes.

"I am not sure if you realize how legendary you are in Grand Canyon history," Webb wrote to her in his next letter. "Your papers with Elzada Clover serve as benchmarks in botanical research along the Colorado River; I and many others have referred to them extensively in our continuing work." There was simply no other comprehensive plant list published prior to the closure of Glen Canyon Dam. Anyone who wanted to understand how the vegetation had changed—because of dams, exotic species, or any of the other human and natural influences at work on ecosystems in the past half-century—had to refer to Clover and Jotter's work.

The Old Timers Trip, as it came to be known, was funded by the Bureau of Reclamation's Glen Canyon Environmental Studies program. The thirteen "Old Timers" who joined the expedition had all rafted the Grand Canyon prior to the closure of Glen Canyon Dam. Besides Jotter Cutter, the group included two other women: Joan Staveley and Sandy Reiff, the daughters of Norm and Doris Nevills. Meeting them softened away any last lingering resentment Jotter Cutter felt toward Nevills. She now felt that the harmony of the

1938 trip had suffered simply from too many conflicting ambitions. It hadn't been possible to collect plants *and* animals *and* photographs *and* get safely and swiftly downriver. No surprise that they had struggled to get along. This trip would be different. Everyone had the same goal—to understand how the Colorado River had changed over the last half-century—and there would be plenty of time for stops and conversation. Jotter Cutter had some reservations about how sharp her memories would be, but her sense of humor hadn't dulled. In the paperwork she filled out prior to the trip, under "dietary restrictions," she wrote emphatically, "avoid Grape Nuts!"

She was active in several bridge clubs and had to explain that she would be gone for a couple of weeks. When they asked where she was going, Jotter Cutter hesitated. Few of her bridge-playing friends knew about her youthful adventures. Her mind flashed back fifty-six years to the nonsensical newspaper stories. "Oh," she said, "just camping in Arizona with friends."

One woman looked at her suspiciously. "Are you going to your old haunts?" she asked.

"Oh, no, not really," Jotter Cutter said. It wasn't exactly a lie. The Grand Canyon was hardly an old haunt, after all. She'd only been there one summer, a long time ago.

$\downarrow$

NAVAJO BRIDGE STILL SPANNED the canyon, but engineers no longer trusted the graceful metal archway to sustain the weight of modern cars. A replacement bridge, similar in style, leapt from one cliff and ended in midair, incomplete. Just beyond the bridge, a turn-off took travelers from the highway down to the river. Lees Ferry (spelled now without the apostrophe) was still the launch point for Grand Canyon trips. The same sunset-colored cliffs pulled back from the river, the blue sky unchanged, the green water unhurried. Only a botanist might notice that the willows were gone, replaced by gray-green tamarisk. Three big motorboats waited to be launched, homely and bulky with equipment. Beside them were two sleek dories and a smaller, boxier boat with the words MEXICAN HAT EXPEDI- TIONS painted on the side: a replica of a 1938 Cataract boat.

It could hardly have been more different than Jotter Cutter's expe- rience in Green River, Utah, fifty-six years before. No grizzled river rats stood at the river's edge to warn her to turn back. She com- mented on the food—much better—and the equipment: tents, pro- pane stoves, ice chests, watertight ammo cans, and sleeping bags, none of which she'd had on her first trip. She laughed when she saw the stack of folding chairs. Didn't the Grand Canyon still have rocks for sitting on?

The thirteen Old Timers, the scientists, and the river guides embarked from Lees Ferry on September 8, 1994. Jotter Cutter was the only representative of the 1938 botany expedition; of her former companions, only Don Harris was still alive, but he was too frail to go. Harris came to Lees Ferry to see the others off, however. Just for fun, he took the oars of the Cataract boat and brought it out into the calm water with Jotter Cutter perched on the stern, like the old days.

The river was greener than she remembered, the vegetation thicker along its edges, mostly tamarisk trees. Tamarisk had just begun to get a foothold in the Grand Canyon in 1938; Clover and Jotter's observa- tions had been among the first records of the exotic tree in the region. The Old Timers had mixed feelings about it, ranging from horror to philosophical acceptance. It formed dense thickets and swallowed up beaches, but it also offered shade and habitat for bugs and migratory birds. These kinds of conversations revealed why Clover and Jotter's plant list mattered: as a hedge against the human tendency to forget how the world used to look. This problem in conservation ecology now has a name: shifting baselines.

In the old days, plants hunkered down in sheltered nooks and eked out an existence between the twin threats of flood and drought. Now the big floods didn't come anymore, and the water's flow was steady and predictable. The barren strip of flood-raked sands on the river's edge had become a lush riparian forest—dominated by tamarisk, true, but also rich with seep willows, arrowweed, and desert broom. Marshy areas interposed with thick sheaves of cattails and reeds. Cottonwoods and Goodding's willows remained rare. There had never been many on the pre-dam river, and though the big floods no longer came through, ripping out the riverside vegetation, perhaps the tamarisk had too firm a hold, or else the abundant beavers kept the native trees in check.

Higher on the terraces, catclaw acacia and honey mesquite made thickets, shot through with brittlebush exploding with yellow flowers. Exotic camelthorn, too—a brushy plant originally from Asia with thorns long enough to fillet an unwary sandal. That was a species Jotter Cutter hadn't found on her first trip down the river. The Bermuda grass had spread since 1938, possibly from deliberate plantings near ranger stations or from golf courses in nearby towns. It made plushy mounds on the sandbars, as soft and inviting as in any well-watered city park.

The Grand Canyon was lush and green, but also very, very different. The scientists knew, from their study of the Stanton photographs, that many of the broad white beaches had vanished. Wind and water wore away the sandbars, and no new silty floods built them up again. They kept their observations to themselves, however. The trip, after all, was a kind of peer review, a test of their own conclusions. Unprompted, many of the Old Timers lamented the erosion. Bare sand had become jumbles of boulders or tangles of plants. The giant piles of driftwood were gone, burned in bonfires by early river runners. Even the sounds were different. They couldn't hear, in the night, the subtle song of sandbars calving away into the water. Sediment no longer scraped the sides of the boats in rhythmic, rasping lullaby.

Several Old Timers noticed the haze of air pollution and complained of noisy overflights from aircraft. But Jotter Cutter found one change decidedly for the better. The National Park Service had imposed regulations about trash and sewage disposal and limited the number of river rafters; no more would expedition members paint their names on the canyon walls.

The looming environmental impact statement offered a chance, maybe, to reverse some of the changes—to alter the operation of Glen Canyon Dam and thus partly restore the ecology of the Grand Canyon. The scientists involved in the Old Timers Trip had been deeply immersed in heated discussions about this possibility, arguing over what the river ought to look like. Bringing back the past wasn't all that simple. If they tried to restore a semblance of the pre-dam floods, they could lose the rich biodiversity of the new riparian corridor. These arguments could be fierce and frustrating, even among those who agreed that the demands of human societies ought to give, just a little, to the needs of ecosystems. But geomorphologist Jack Schmidt was struck by the way the Old Timers saw the Grand Canyon. Some of them had run it only once or twice, unlike modern river guides. Yet they had been profoundly changed by the experience. "These people remind us," Schmidt told an interviewer during the trip, "that the fundamental experience of this place is a place where you can have high adventure and really rich personal experiences. We all need to be reminded of that."

Jotter Cutter was certainly a living reminder of how to not take oneself too seriously. Time had not dulled her sense of mischief, and she still had a "whiplash smile, just popped up easy," in the words of the trip's physician, Tom Myers. Myers happened to be standing next to Jotter Cutter on the first night of the trip, at the campsite at Badger Creek Rapid, when some of the younger scientists began to geologize. It was natural, perhaps, to slip into a kind of rhapsody; the Grand Canyon did that to geologists. The conversation went on and on, people gesturing and tossing out words like "intrusion" and "unconformity." One by one, the Old Timers began to edge away, eyeing their sleeping bags. Finally only Jotter Cutter remained, her back ramrod straight, her expression rapt and attentive. *She's truly an academic,* Myers thought to himself. Then Jotter Cutter leaned over. "God," she whispered in Myers's ear, "are they ever going to shut up?"

$$\psi$$

THE DAM'S EFFECTS WERE COMPLEX. At Vasey's Paradise, the Old Timers stepped gingerly, unable to explore the spring as thoroughly as they might have wished, in part because poison ivy had taken over everything, but also because the spring was now home to an endangered species, the Kanab ambersnail, which lived only in a few small ponds in Utah and Arizona. The dime-sized, amber-colored snail benefited from Glen Canyon Dam. Without the threat of massive floods, its habitat, like the poison ivy's, had expanded from the spring all the way to the river's edge.

Water bugs hadn't fared as well in the post-dam river. Mayflies, stoneflies, and caddisflies glued their eggs to rocks on the river's edge, and when the water dropped in response to falling hydropower demand, the eggs dried out and died. Fish, too, suffered in the new conditions. Of the eight species of native fish in the Colorado River, four no longer lived in the Grand Canyon. If river managers agreed to tweak the pattern of flows released from the dam, fish and bugs could benefit, but other species, adapted to the new conditions, might be harmed.

There were other questions to debate, besides the management of dams. Should non-native plants along the river corridor be torn out and removed, and if so, which ones? What about the exotic trout stocked in the tailwaters below in the dam, valued for sportfishing but a threat to native fish? What restrictions should be placed on river rafters and tourists, particularly regarding visiting springs, caves, and other sensitive areas held sacred by the region's tribes? And what would happen to the Colorado River as the global climate warmed?

In 1938, scientists knew that human activity, primarily the burning of fossil fuels, had begun to thicken the atmosphere and heat up the planet. But it did not seem alarming at the time; one writer thought it might prove useful to delay "the return of the deadly glaciers." In 1994, scientists no longer felt so cavalier. A seemingly tiny change in the global thermostat could set in motion enormous events: stronger hurricanes, floods, wildfires, heat waves, and droughts. The hundredth meridian sketched by John Wesley Powell down the middle of the United States was shifting east, signaling vast new areas too dry for conventional agriculture. The "life zones" described by C. Hart Merriam in Arizona had begun to rearrange, plants and animals fleeing upward and northward to cooler climates, one windblown seed at a time. Climate change was calling into question, again, the definition of an ecosystem, and where humans fit in.

A week into the trip, Jotter Cutter took her turn in front of the video camera; all the Old Timers gave interviews about their river adventures. With the Colorado's roar in the background, she joked with her interviewer, Lew Steiger, about how Bob Webb had called her "legendary." Her kids had teased her about it, asking her how it felt to be a legend in her own time.

Steiger laughed along with her, but then added, "Well, you know, you *are* a legend!"

Jotter Cutter demurred. "Elzie really deserved it more than I did."

On this trip, there were no runaway boats, no nights spent alone at the river's edge. A long record of safe passage, by women and men alike, stretched before her. The guides were experienced; the equipment tested by time. The river's ebb and flow was predictable. In fact, the more she thought about it, the more she realized that nothing was the same—nothing but the canyon walls, the Kaibab, Coconino, and sheer Redwall rising above the river in beige, rose, and mauve, changing in color with the time of day and season yet indifferent to them. The river wasn't a wild place, not now. It was (depending on who you asked) a muscle of energy to turn hydroelectric turbines, a thousand-plus-mile-long ditch to deliver water to cities and farms, or a playground for tourists. Weather and climate still governed the pulse of the river, but not to the same extent. Its thrum of blood, its heartbeat, was squeezed to a different rhythm by the needs of people who lived hundreds of miles away, people who had never even seen it.

And yet, bighorn sheep still nosed their stilt-legged lambs down to the water to drink. Ravens still launched from the pinnacles, feathers so black they looked like holes cut into the sky. Debris flows and flash floods still tore down the side canyons and reshaped the rapids with rough, eager hands. Each morning the sun painted a masterpiece on the south-facing walls and then calmly scrubbed it out again. Every life hinged to the river, from the antlions on the sandbars to the real lions prowling the brush, all strove to eat, live, mate, and bear young, even as the mountains strove upward and the river strove to cut them down to the sea. What does "wild" mean, anyway? Not untouched by human presence, for even the plants—especially the plants—show how the canyonland's first inhabitants tended agave and prickly pear, coaxing them into new shapes. A wild place isn't one unchanged by humans. It's a place that changes us.

"What stands out about the canyon?" Steiger asked Jotter Cutter, as sunlight slanted gold and pink down the cliffs and the river fell into shadow. "Is it really different now?"

"I recognize that there [are] many individual small differences," she replied. "But the feeling that you get when you look up and see one high wall lit up, and the rest less so . . ."

Fifty-six years before, writing to her father to convince him to let her risk her life for a plant collection, she had told him that the beauty would surely make up for any discomfort she would feel. The discomfort and risk had lessened with time. The beauty was still there.

"Did this trip change you in any way?" Steiger asked at the end of the long interview.

"Oh, lots of ways," Jotter Cutter said, unconsciously answering the question her father had posed more than five decades before. She told Steiger that before the trip, she had been a scholarly person focused on academics, and, unlike Clover, not much of a daredevil—someone others might think of as "humdrum and not very exciting." She returned a minor celebrity, with a level of self-assurance she had never felt before. She'd had experiences others couldn't even imagine. After the Old Timers Trip, Jotter Cutter confessed her adventures for the first time to the women of her bridge club in North Carolina. Astonishment reigned. "If you ran out of clean clothes," one woman asked, "why didn't you just stop at a laundromat?"

$$\Downarrow$$

TWO YEARS AFTER the Old Timers Trip, in the spring of 1996, the Bureau of Reclamation opened the four bypass tubes at the base of Glen Canyon Dam. White waterfalls poured out of the tubes and raised a thunderous mist on the river. For a week, a flood of 45,000 cfs roared through the dam unchecked, the largest flood the river had seen since a very wet winter a decade before. It was an experiment, based on the conclusions of the Old Timers Trip and other scientific research showing that the river's sandbars had suffered from the lack of big floods. The water scoured out sediment from the riverbed and swirled it downriver, laying out new beaches.

The environmental impact statement had been published a year earlier, setting out options for the operation of Glen Canyon Dam. Thousands of people wrote letters in support of restoring the Grand Canyon's ecology, Jotter Cutter among them. The Secretary of the Interior signed off on the preferred alternative a few months after the 1996 spring flood and opened the door for more experimental high-water releases. In years to come, scientists and river managers would establish a formal program of beach-building floods and other kinds of releases designed to help native fish and aquatic insects—just the kind of science-based management which George Meléndez Wright had wanted, long before.

The experiments have many limits. The biggest flood on the river today is still small compared to the torrents of the past, and demand for water and hydropower often wins out over ecological needs. In the year 2000, a drought began in the Colorado River Basin that has not yet ended—the kind of long-reaching drought Powell and La Rue warned was possible, made worse by the warmer temperatures brought on by global climate change. In the summer of 2021, water levels in Lake Powell and Lake Mead plummeted to the lowest seen since the reservoirs were filled. The seven states that rely on the Colorado River now face a painful reckoning with legal agreements written at a time when all but a few ignored prophets believed that there would be plenty of water for all.

Despite these challenges, the program of experimental flows represents a profound shift in society's relationship with rivers. The old desires so prevalent in the early decades of the century to dam, drain, and control the Colorado are giving way to something more like love.

Many questions remain for the river's management. The debate is still unsettled on whether to embrace the Grand Canyon in its new state, changed by dams and exotic species but richly biodiverse, or to seek a return to the past—to the bleak, inhospitable place of water and stone that Clover and Jotter witnessed. Meanwhile, upriver, drought is now revealing parts of Cataract and Glen canyons that have lain underneath a reservoir for half a century. Forgotten bits of history—human and natural—emerge from the muck. It's a time to rethink the old laws and policies that govern the Colorado River, and to imagine new kinds of futures in which human desires don't subsume a river's needs. The work ahead requires the participation of scientists, community members, and Indigenous wisdom keepers. It demands an accurate knowledge of the past, and a clear-eyed understanding that no landscape is unchanged by people, nor any person unchanged by the land.

Jotter Cutter returned from her second river trip with "a feeling of renewed life," in her words. She wondered, now, how she had stayed away from the Grand Canyon for so long. She continued to take an eager interest in the Colorado River, corresponding with river runners, amassing stacks of newspaper clippings, and writing letters to federal

Lois Jotter's pith helmet, a souvenir of her 1938 river trip,
bearing the signatures of her companions. *Photo by author.*
*NAU.3D.2018.35, Lois Jotter Cutter Collection, Special Collections
and Archives, Cline Library, Northern Arizona University*

agencies to advocate for conservation. She died on April 30, 2013, at
the age of ninety-nine. She kept, her entire life, two souvenirs of her
1938 river trip: the match case Holmstrom gave her, and the yellow
pith helmet scribbled with the signatures of her companions. The ink
is faded now, the names barely legible. But Holmstrom's words stand
out boldly from the rest, as if perhaps someone traced them afresh in
the intervening years. They read: "To the girl who proved me badly
mistaken."

Epilogue

A WOMAN'S PLACE

LOIS JOTTER'S MATCH CASE MADE ONE MORE TRIP down the Colorado River.

In the fall of 2021, while researching this book, I rafted the Grand Canyon with a botany crew tasked with weeding out exotic species. I carried Jotter's match case in a zipped pocket the entire way. It had passed to her son, Victor, who gifted it to me. It still contained a few brittle matches that, for all I knew, Jotter had put there during her 1938 journey.

I took Clover and Jotter with me in other ways, too. The waterproof river guide in my gear had been drawn from the same topographic maps they used. The dedication in my botany field guide, *River and Desert Plants of the Grand Canyon,* paid homage to them. In a way, the crew and I were continuing the work begun by Jotter and Clover: to name, catalog, understand, and protect the Colorado River's plants. Sometimes I felt their presence so strongly that I turned round at the foot of a rapid, half-expecting to see a ghostly Cataract boat cresting a wave.

What would have happened, I wondered, if Clover and Jotter never ran the river—if they had listened to the critics and doomsayers, or to their own doubts? They brought knowledge, energy, and passion to their botanical work, but also a new perspective. Before them, men had gone down the Colorado to sketch dams, plot railroads, dig gold, and daydream little Swiss chalets stuck up on the cliffs. They saw the river for what it could be, harnessed for human use. Clover and Jotter saw it as it was, a living system made up of flower, leaf, and thorn, lovely in its fierceness, worthy of study for its own sake. They knew every saltbush twig and stickery cactus was, in its own way, as much a marvel as Boulder Dam—shaped to survive against all the odds.

A woman on a boat is, thankfully, no longer headline news, and a twenty-four-year-old botanist camping alone on a sandbar for a night is unlikely to stir the Associated Press into a frenzy. Women have rowed boats down the Colorado River since the 1950s; today, roughly a third of commercial river guides in the Grand Canyon are women. But women in wild places still face hostility and dismissal, and worse. In 2016, Grand Canyon National Park ended its River District, which patrolled the canyon to enforce rules and offer emergency assistance, in response to widespread sexual harassment by male employees against female river guides. Less severe, but more frequent, are the casual stereotypes Clover and Jotter faced in 1938. "You absolutely do not need to cook every night—or any night," advises a modern blog for women on river trips.

The same challenges that Clover and Jotter confronted decades ago remain barriers for women in the sciences today. In the United States, half of all bachelor's degrees in science, engineering, and mathematics go to women, yet these women go on to earn only 74 percent of a man's salary in those fields. A recent study found that it will be another two decades before women and men publish papers at equal rates in the field of botany, a field traditionally welcoming to women. It may take four decades for chemistry, and three centuries for physics. Stereotypes linger of scientists as white-coated, wild-haired men, and they limit the ways in which young people envision their futures. In a famous, oft-replicated study, 70 percent of six-year-old girls, asked to draw a picture of a scientist, draw a woman, but only 25 percent do so at the age of sixteen.

Yet women have always been scientists. It is my hope that recalling this past can change the future, building a world in which anyone who wishes can run rivers, climb mountains, study plants, build rocket ships, and fight for a deeper understanding of the planet on which we live. Clover and Jotter's names are still remembered in the botany and river running communities. A hedgehog cactus with pink flowers and dense spines that grows in New Mexico is named Clover's cactus (*Sclerocactus cloverae*); it's now under consideration for endangered species protection. River rafters in Cataract Canyon, rediscovering places once buried beneath Lake Powell and now revealed by drought, informally call two side canyons Clover Canyon and Jotter Canyon, in a stretch of river known as Botany Aisle. Scientists raft the Grand Canyon every year, carrying a plant guide shaped in part by Clover and Jotter's findings.

Their story matters. It adds to the unfolding record of how life, human and nonhuman, finds ways to flourish even in the most unlikely of circumstances. Like others before them, Elzada Clover and Lois Jotter valued their curiosity about the world more than their presumed place within it. They go ahead and, like stars reflected on the river, show the way.

ACKNOWLEDGMENTS

WITH GRATEFUL THANKS TO THE FOLLOWING PEOPLE:

My agent, Laurie Abkemeier, and my editors, Matt Weiland and Huneeya Siddiqui, for their steadfast belief in this book, as well as copyeditor Allegra Huston and the entire team at W. W. Norton for ushering this story into the world.

The readers who reviewed this manuscript, in whole or part, and offered guidance and corrections: Sarah Boon, Nikki Cooley, Ash Davidson, Antonia Malchik, Tom Martin, Teo Melis, and Erin Zimmerman. Any errors are my own.

My intrepid research assistants during the time of coronavirus, Cymelle Edwards at Northern Arizona University and Roxanne Pinsky at the University of Michigan.

Paul Mirocha, for another excellent map of the Colorado River.

The Atavist Magazine published my longform article "The Wild Ones" in October 2019, which grew into this book. My thanks to the team that worked to improve that story: editors Jonah Ogles and Seyward Darby, factchecker Adam Przybyl, and copyeditor Sean Cooper.

My writing has received much-appreciated financial support at various times in the form of grants and prizes from the Ellen Meloy Fund for Desert Writers, the Arizona Commission on the Arts, the Bill Desmond Writing Award, and the Thomas Lowell Travel Journalism Award.

The relatives, friends, and former students of Elzada Clover and Lois Jotter: especially Victor Cutter III, who trusted me with his mother's story, and Linda Curtis, Marilyn Findley, Kenneth Majors, David Mastie, Jane Myers, and Carolyn Wyland. Maxine Schatz of the Nemaha Valley Museum connected me with members of the Clover family.

Sandy Nevills Reiff, for sharing her insights about her father and mother's adventures; and Greg Reiff, who kindly answered my questions about Cataract boats.

The many historians and archivists who made this book possible by their careful curation of historical documents, especially Sam Meier and Peter Runge at Northern Arizona University Cline Library. Sam gave countless hours to curating the documents in the Lois Jotter Cutter Papers, and Peter jump-started this book at the very beginning. Documents, photographs, and audio files were made available by staff at the University of Michigan, University of Utah, Southern Utah University, Utah State Historical Society, Huntington Library, Library of Congress, Sherman Ginsberg Film Library, Peru State College, Mission Historical Museum, University of Arizona Herbarium, Smithsonian Institution, Natural History Museum of Utah, Glen Canyon National Recreation Area, Lake Mead National Recreation Area, and Grand Canyon National Park. Tom Martin, Richard Quartaroli, and Mara Rockliff supplied copies of historical documents, and Kim Clarke pointed the way from Michigan. Many other people answered obscure questions for me; they are named in the end notes.

The experts who have shaped my thinking about Colorado River history and ecology, including Diane Boyer, Nikki Cooley, Coleen Kaska, Ted Kennedy, Rebecca Lawton, John Fleck, Teo Melis, Tom Myers, Jason Nez, Emily Palmquist, Jack Pongyvesa, Wayne Ranney, Sarana Riggs, Brian Richter, Octavius Seowtewa, Jack Schmidt, Larry Stevens, Karen Underhill, and Richard Valdez. Wendy McBride and Kenneth Heil answered my cactus questions, and Meg Flynn and Mike DeHoff described the lost (and now returning) rapids of Cataract Canyon. I am especially grateful for the Intertribal Centennial Conversations group and their efforts to educate others about the Indigenous history and spiritual importance of the Grand Canyon.

The river crew: Dan Hall, Mike Kearsley, Melissa McMaster, Amy Prince, and Greg Woodall. Thanks for showing me the ropes.

Kevin Fedarko, for encouragement and enthusiasm at every stage of this project.

The many teachers and mentors who instilled in me a love of science, writing, and history, especially: Kevin Schindler, for geeking out about science history; Debra Marquart and Alison Hawthorne Deming, for lessons on writing that continue to resonate; Melanie Lenart, for my start in science journalism; Susan Aiken, for a fantastic college course on women in literature; Tom Wilson, for ushering me through my environmental science degree; Madeline Kiser, por las cartas y poemas; Kelly Crane and Cris Santa Cruz, for strengthening my passion for literature and history, and Cathrine Wiegert, for handing me books in which princesses rescued dragons and had adventures of their own.

All the wonderful women writers I know, especially Ash Davidson, who kept these words safe for me while I was on the river; Kate Petersen, for evening walks and extraordinary cakes; and Sarah Boon, Antonia Malchik, Kimberly Moynahan, Kim Steutermann Rogers, and Erin Zimmerman, for their encouragement and many lively conversations about science writing.

Gus Delgadillo, for his stories of the old days.

My self-proclaimed number one fans, Ruth Burke and Brenna Dixon.

My godparents, Dick and Lois Shelton, without whom I would not be a writer.

My parents, Ken and Karen, and my amazing family: Jessica, Eddie, Sofia, Mateo, Kasondra, Chris, Gia, and Zion, who motivate, inspire, and uplift me, who read drafts, critique sentences, and, at all hours of the day and night, answer my questions about everything from the symptoms of heat exhaustion to the habitat of mountain lions to the likely range of a .22 pistol.

The cat, Gandalf, for many unsolicited additions to the text.

My husband, Chris, road trip companion, archival assistant, builder of bulletin boards, and maker of mochas. I could ask for no better partner on the rivers ahead.

Lastly, my deepest thanks to Elzada Clover and Lois Jotter, whom I will never meet. They told their stories and preserved their memories so that new generations of women and girls could be inspired one day.

A NOTE ON SOURCES

The events of the 1938 river trip have been drawn primarily from the journals of Elzada Clover, Lois Jotter, Norm Nevills, Don Harris, and Dell Reed. Most of these journals exist in multiple versions. I have made use of all of them but favored the original handwritten copies. Where accounts of the journey differ, I have generally favored Clover and Jotter's perspectives. Dialogue in this book is quoted directly from original sources whenever possible. In some cases, I have reimagined the exact wording from situations recalled by those involved.

Letters and newspaper articles were sourced from the manuscript collections listed below. Also, articles can be found in https://chroniclingamerica .loc.gov, www.newspapers.com, and the U.S. Bureau of Reclamation's Hoover Dam Historical Collection.

I have used, throughout the text, the 1938 nomenclature for plants. Some of the Latin names have changed, or the plants in question have been split or lumped into different categories. I have written Indigenous place names only in English translation because they are not mine to give. For more on Indigenous connections to the Grand Canyon, I refer readers to "The Voices of the Grand Canyon" story map hosted at www .grandcanyontrust.org.

These notes offer a guide for further reading; they are not a comprehensive list of my sources.

Manuscript Collections

Buzz Holmstrom Collection, 1935–44, NAU.MS.311. Special Collections and Archives, Cline Library, Northern Arizona University, Flagstaff, Arizona.
Elzada U. Clover Papers, 1938–44. Bentley Historical Library, University of Michigan, Ann Arbor, Michigan.

Harley Harris Bartlett Papers, 1909–60. Bentley Historical Library, University of Michigan, Ann Arbor, Michigan.

LaPhene "Don" Harris Papers, 1938–98, ACCN 2881. Special Collections, J. Willard Marriott Library, University of Utah, Salt Lake City, Utah.

Lois Jotter Cutter Papers, 1938–2007 [manuscripts], NAU.MS.69. Special Collections and Archives, Cline Library, Northern Arizona University, Flagstaff, Arizona.

Norman D. and Doris Nevills Papers, 1890s–1953, MS 0552. Special Collections, J. Willard Marriott Library, University of Utah, Salt Lake City, Utah.

Norm Nevills Papers, 1908–49 [manuscripts], NAU.MS.317. Special Collections and Archives, Cline Library, Northern Arizona University, Flagstaff, Arizona.

Otis R. Marston Papers, 1870–1978. Huntington Library, San Marino, California.

USGS Old Timers Collection [manuscripts], NAU.MS.358. Special Collections and Archives, Cline Library, Northern Arizona University, Flagstaff, Arizona.

Expedition Journals

Elzada Clover's journal, parts one and two [original], 1938, Elzada U. Clover Papers, Box 1.

Elzada Clover's journal, Green River to Lee's Ferry [revised], 1938, Norman D. and Doris Nevills Papers, Box 29, Folder 2.

Dell Reed's journal, Lee's Ferry to Boulder Dam [transcript], 1938, Otis R. Marston Papers, Box 283, Folder 31.

Don Harris's journal, Green River to Lee's Ferry [original], 1938, LaPhene "Don" Harris Papers, 1938–98, Mss B 1053, Box 1, Folder 1, Utah State Historical Society, Salt Lake City, Utah.

Don Harris's journal, Green River to Lee's Ferry [transcript], 1938, LaPhene "Don" Harris Papers (University of Utah), Box 1, Folder 1.

Lois Jotter's journal [original], 1938, Lois Jotter Cutter Papers, Series 1, Box 1, Folder 2.

Lois Jotter's journal [annotated], 1938, Lois Jotter Cutter Papers, Series 1, Box 1, Folder 3.

Norm Nevills's journal [original], 1938, Norman D. and Doris Nevills Papers, Box 27, Folders 3–10.

Norm Nevills's journal [revised], 1938, in *High, Wide and Handsome: The*

River Journals of Norman D. Nevills, ed. Roy Webb (Salt Lake City: Utah State University Press, 2005).

Botany References

Elzada Clover and Lois Jotter, "Cacti of the Canyon of the Colorado River and Tributaries," *Bulletin of the Torrey Botanical Club* 68, no. 6 (June 1941): 409–19, https://doi.org/10.2307/2481651.

Elzada Clover and Lois Jotter, "Floristic Studies in the Canyon of the Colorado and Tributaries," *American Midland Naturalist* 32, no. 3 (November 1944): 591–642, https://doi.org/10.2307/2421241.

Kristin Huisinga, Lori Makarick, and Kate Watters, *River and Desert Plants of the Grand Canyon* (Missoula, MT: Mountain Press, 2006).

Jack L. Carter, Martha A. Carter, and Donna J. Stevens, *Common Southwestern Native Plants: An Identification Guide,* 2nd ed. (Silver City, NM: Mimbres Publishing, 2009).

Oral Histories

Joan Nevills Staveley, oral history interview with Stephanie Capaldo, October 26, 2005, Ecological Oral Histories Course Collection, NAU. OH.2005.111.11, Special Collections and Archives, Cline Library, Northern Arizona University, Flagstaff, Arizona.

Joan Nevills Staveley and Sandra Nevills Reiff, oral history interview with Lew Steiger, September 12, 1994, NAU.94.100.15–16, U.S.G.S. Old Timers Collection [oral history interviews].

LaPhene "Don" Harris, oral history interview with Gary Topping and Linda Thatcher, May 16, 1998, LaPhene "Don" Harris Papers, Box 1, Folder 6.

Lois Jotter Cutter, oral history interview with Lew Steiger, September 14–15, 1994, NAU.OH.94.100.22–25, U.S.G.S. Old Timers Collection [oral history interviews].

Articles, Books, and Interviews

Prologue: STRANDED

600 miles: Elzada Clover, "Danger Can Be Fun," *Michigan Alumnus Quarterly Review* 45, no. 14 (Winter 1939): 104, Elzada U. Clover Papers, Box 1.

Taylor quote: Edward T. Taylor, "Renaming of the Grand River, Colo.," in *Hearing*

Before the Committee on Interstate and Foreign Commerce of the House of Representatives (Washington, DC: Government Printing Office, 1921), 14, 6.

277 miles: Randy Moore and Kara Felicia Witt, *The Grand Canyon: An Encyclopedia of Geography, History, and Culture* (Santa Barbara, CA: ABC–CLIO, 2018), xxxviii.

A dozen expeditions: Richard Quartaroli, "Dock's Data of Navigational Numbers: The First 100 Grand Canyon River Runners," *Boatman's Quarterly Review* 22, no. 3 (Fall 2009): 21–23.

Chapter One: ON THE BORDERS OF PRECIPICES

Clover's biography: Her death certificate and headstone give her birth year as 1886, though census records also indicate 1885 or 1887 as possibilities. Sources: Ancestry. com; FamilySearch; William Cook's *The Wen, the Botany, and the Mexican Hat* (Orangevale, CA: Callisto Books, 1987); Kenneth Majors, phone call with author, February 5, 2020; Jane Myers, phone call with author, October 23, 2020; Jane Myers, "A handful of teachers become compelling memories," *Ann Arbor News*, December 14, 1980, https://www.mlive.com/ann-arbor/.

Influenza pandemic: Peter Spreeuwenbeg, Madelon Kroneman, and John Paget, "Reassessing the Global Mortality Burden of the 1918 Influenza Pandemic," *American Journal of Epidemiology* 187, no. 12 (December 2018): 2561–67, https:// doi.org/10.1093/aje/kwy191. Also: Niall P. A. S. Johnson and Juergen Mueller, "Updating the Accounts: Global Mortality of the 1918–1920 'Spanish' Influenza Pandemic," *Bulletin of the History of Medicine* 76, no. 1 (Spring 2002): 105. The number of deaths in World War I is usually cited as 16–20 million.

History of botany: Elizabeth B. Keeney, *The Botanizers: Amateur Scientists in Nineteenth-Century America* (Chapel Hill: University of North Carolina Press, 1992); A. G. Morton, *History of Botanical Science: An Account of the Development of Botany from Ancient Times to the Present Day* (London: Academic Press, 1981); Sharon E. Kingsland, *The Evolution of American Ecology, 1890–2000* (Baltimore: Johns Hopkins University Press, 2005).

Women in botany: Vera Norwood, "Women's Roles in Nature Study and Environmental Protection," *OAH Magazine of History* 10, no. 3 (Spring 1996): 12–17, https://doi.org/10.1093/maghis/10.3.12; Wynne Brown, *The Forgotten Botanist: Sara Plummer Lemmon's Life of Science & Art* (Lincoln: University of Nebraska Press, 2021); Ann B. Shteir, *Cultivating Women, Cultivating Science: Flora's Daughters and Botany in England, 1760–1860* (Baltimore: Johns Hopkins University Press, 1996); J. F. A. Adams, "Is Botany A Suitable Study For Young Men?" *Science* 9, no. 209 (February 1887): 116–17, https://doi.org/10.1126/science.ns-9.209S.116; Wilson Flagg, "Botanizing," *Atlantic Monthly* 27, no. 164 (June 1871): 657; Emanuel D. Rudolph, "Women in Nineteenth Century American Botany: A Generally Unrecognized Constituency," *American Journal of Botany* 69, no. 8 (September 1982): 1351, https:// doi.org/10.2307/2442761.

Asa Gray: A. Hunter Dupree, *Asa Gray: American Botanist, Friend of Darwin* (Baltimore: Johns Hopkins University Press, 1959). Also: James L. Reveal, "Asa Gray and the

Botanical Exploration of the American West," *Harvard Papers in Botany* 15, no. 2 (December 2010): 309–16, https://www.jstor.org/stable/41761701.

Almira Hart Lincoln Phelps: Emanuel D. Rudolph, "Almira Hart Lincoln Phelps (1793–1884) and the Spread of Botany in Nineteenth Century America," *American Journal of Botany* 71, no. 8 (September 1984): 1161–67; Almira Hart Lincoln Phelps, *Botany for Beginners,* 2nd ed. (Hartford, CT: F. J. Huntington, 1833); Almira Hart Lincoln Phelps, *Familiar Lectures on Botany* (Philadelphia: J. B. Lippincott, 1865).

Plants in Rio Grande Valley: Elzada Clover, "A Vegetational Survey of the Lower Rio Grande Valley, Texas," *Madroño* 4, no. 2 (April 1937): 41–66, https://www.jstor.org/stable/41422215.

South Mission School: Clover's 1959 résumé, listing an "Indian mission school," comes from the faculty and staff files of the University of Michigan Bentley Historical Library. I've concluded that the school was really the South Mission School based on a search of newspaper archives and discussions with Cinda Nofziger (Bentley Historical Library) and Vernon Weckbacher (Mission Historical Museum). Articles quoted come from the *Brownsville Herald.*

Clover's college education: Susan Abrahams (Peru State College), email communication with author, February 24, 2020; Caitlin Moriarty (Bentley Historical Library), email communication with author, November 8, 2021; Margaret A. Nash and Lisa S. Romero, "Citizenship for the College Girl: Challenges and Opportunities in Higher Education for Women in the United States in the 1930s," *Teachers College Record* 114, no. 020305 (February 2012): 5–6.

Darwin: Charles Darwin, *On the Origin of Species* (1859), ed. Gillian Beer (New York: Oxford University Press, 2008). Relationship to botany: Erin Zimmerman, "How a Love of Flowers Helped Charles Darwin Validate Natural Selection," *Smithsonian,* February 12, 2019. Views of gender and race: Agustín Fuentes, "'The Descent of Man,' 150 years on," *Science* 372, no. 6544 (May 2021): 769, https://doi.org/10.1126/science.abj4606; Josie Glausiusz, "Savages and Cannibals: Revisiting Charles Darwin's Voyage of the Beagle," *Insight,* May 27, 2021, http://www.whatisemerging.com/opinions/savages-and-cannibals; Gil G. Rosenthal and Michael J. Ryan, "Sexual Selection and the Ascent of Women: Mate Choice Research Since Darwin," *Science* 375, no. 6578 (January 2022): 1–10, https://doi.org/10.1126/science.abi6308.

Plants in Utah: Elzada U. Clover, "The Cactaceae of Southern Utah," *Bulletin of the Torrey Botanical Club* 65, no. 6 (June 1938): 397–412, https://doi.org/10.2307/2481220.

Indigenous river running: Jason Nez, interview with author, January 10, 2019; Leigh J. Kuwanwisiwma, T. J. Ferguson, and Michael Yeats, "Öngtupqa: The Enduring Association of the Hopi People and the Grand Canyon," in *Reflections of Grand Canyon Historians: Ideas, Arguments, and First Person Accounts,* ed. Todd R. Berger (Grand Canyon, AZ: Grand Canyon Association, 2008); and Tom Martin and Peter Brown, "Before Powell? A Descent of the Colorado River through the Grand Canyon on a Tule Reed Raft," *The Ol' Pioneer* 32, no. 2 (Spring 2021): 10–12.

Chapter Two: HAVE YOU SEEN THAT RIVER?

Grand Canyon's formation: Wayne Ranney (geologist), email communication with author, October 19, 2019; Wayne Ranney, *Carving Grand Canyon: Evidence, Theories, Mysteries* (Grand Canyon, AZ: Grand Canyon Association, 2005); Mary C. Rabbitt, "John Wesley Powell: Pioneer Statesman of Federal Science," in *The Colorado River Region and John Wesley Powell* (Washington DC: Government Printing Office, 1969), 7, https://doi.org/10.3133/pp669A.

Age of the earth: Stephen G. Brush and Ellis Yochelson, "The Age of the Earth in the Twentieth Century," *Earth Sciences History* 8, no. 2 (1989): 170–82, https://doi.org/10.17704/eshi.8.2.1555205161r6pvu3.

Continental drift: Ronald Good, "The Botanical Aspects of Continental Drift," *Science Progress* 54, no. 215 (July 1966): 315–24, https://www.jstor.org/stable/43425689; Rama L. Rao, "Wegener's Theory of Continental Drift," *Current Science* 5, no. 9 (March 1937): 506–07, https://www.jstor.org/stable/24206530.

History of conservation: Dorceta E. Taylor, *The Rise of the American Conservation Movement: Power, Privilege, and Environmental Protection* (Durham, NC: Duke University Press, 2016), 295. Also: David Treuer, "Return the National Parks to the Tribes," *Atlantic*, May 2021, https://www.theatlantic.com/magazine/archive/2021/05/return-the-national-parks-to-the-tribes/618395/.

Clover's grant: Elzada U. Clover, "Project #R-40, Botanical exploration of unknown areas of Utah and Arizona," February 5, 1938, Horace H. Rackham School of Graduate Studies Records, Box 35, Bentley Historical Library, University of Michigan, Ann Arbor, Michigan. Also: Proceedings of the Board of Regents (1936–39), University of Michigan, https://quod.lib.umich.edu.

Roy Chapman Andrews: Carol Bird, "Don't Take A Woman When You Go Exploring," *Lincoln Star*, April 24, 1932; Isabelle Keating, "Woman Challenges Explorer Andrews," *Brooklyn Daily Eagle*, January 6, 1932; "Women Explorers," *Albuquerque Journal*, January 16, 1932; "Mr. Andrews Statement about Women Belied At Recent Dinner of Female Geographers," *Barnard Bulletin* 36, no. 26 (February 9, 1932): 1.

Atkinson's biography: Ancestry.com; Jeff Bessinger (Lakeshore Museum Center), email communication with author, February 27, 2020. Atkinson's only surviving writing about the 1938 trip is a letter to Harry Aleson, February 17, 1961, Harry LeRoy Aleson Papers, Box 17, Folder 7, Research Center of the Utah State Archives & Utah State History, Salt Lake City, Utah. Thanks to Valerie Jacobson for providing a copy.

First female rangers: Polly Welts Kaufman, *National Parks and the Woman's Voice: A History* (Albuquerque: University of New Mexico Press, 2006), 73, 83, 86.

Yosemite Field School: "Educational News," *School Life* 22, no. 7 (March 1937): 223; and M. E. Beatty, "A History of Firefall," *Yosemite Nature Notes* 13, no. 6 (June 1934), 41–43.

Buzz Holmstrom: Robert Ormond Case, "He Shot the Colorado Alone © SEPS" *Saturday Evening Post*, February 26, 1938, 8–9, 34–40; Vince Welch, Cort Conley, and Brad Dimock, *The Doing of the Thing: The Brief Brilliant Whitewater Career of Buzz Holmstrom* (Flagstaff, AZ: Fretwater Press, 1998); Brad Dimock, ed.,

Every Rapid Speaks Plainly: The Salmon, Green, and Colorado River Journals of Buzz Holmstrom (Flagstaff, AZ: Fretwater Press, 2003).

Deaths in Grand Canyon: Michael P. Ghiglieri and Thomas M. Myers, *Over the Edge: Death in the Grand Canyon* (Flagstaff, AZ: Puma Press, 2001), 140–41, 147, 184, 215, 292.

Chapter Three: A MIGHTY POOR PLACE FOR WOMEN

Dust Bowl: Thomas L. Stokes, "Dust Storms Come Back To Middle West," *Indianapolis Times*, February 27, 1936; Thomas L. Stokes, "Tugwell Hero To Citizens Of New Deal City," *Indianapolis Times*, February 20, 1936.

John Wesley Powell: Powell, *The Exploration of the Colorado River and Its Canyons* (1875; New York: Penguin, 1997); John Ross, *The Promise of the Grand Canyon: John Wesley Powell's Perilous Journey and His Vision for the American West* (New York: Viking, 2018); Frederick S. Dellenbaugh, *A Canyon Voyage: The Narrative of the Second Powell Expedition* (1908; Tucson: University of Arizona Press, 1991).

Cataract boats: Greg Reiff (relative), phone interview with author, January 24, 2022; Roy Webb, "Facing Your Danger: The History of the Cataract Boat," in *A Rendezvous of Grand Canyon Historians: Ideas, Arguments, and First Person Accounts*, ed. Richard D. Quartaroli (Grand Canyon, AZ: Grand Canyon Association, 2013), 29. Note: Montéz and Flavell also faced the rapids on their Grand Canyon expedition, but prow-first.

Plant collection methods: Wendy McBride (botanist), phone communication with author, December 27, 2021; Erin Zimmerman (botanist), email communication with author, July 22, 2020.

Intersection of three deserts: Ann Haymond Zwinger, *Downcanyon: A Naturalist Explores the Colorado River through the Grand Canyon* (Tucson: University of Arizona Press, 1995), 40.

Debris flows and river velocity: L. M. Highland et al., "Debris-Flow Hazards in the United States," U.S. Geological Survey National Landslide Information Center, 1997, https://pubs.usgs.gov/fs/fs-176–97; Meredith Hartwell (USGS), email communication with author, October 26, 2021. Thanks to the UGSS scientists who answered my inquiry about river velocity: David Topping, Paul Grams, Michael Moran, Joel Sankey, and Todd Wojtowicz.

Chapter Four: THERE GOES THE MEXICAN HAT!

Names of Colorado River: Taylor, "Renaming of the Grand River, Colo.," 17–18; Moore and Witt, *The Grand Canyon*, 171; Tori Peglar, "The Hualapai Bird Singer," Grand Canyon National Park Trips, March 9, 2018, https://www.mygrandcanyonpark.com/park/hualapai.

Colorado River flow: Stream gauge data downloaded from https://waterdata.usgs.gov/nwis. Thanks to Tom Martin for suggesting combining the Green River and Cisco gauges with a 24-hour time lag to estimate the flow at the confluence. The comparison is based on a concrete mixer capacity of 270 cubic feet. Anything over 15,000 cfs was considered flood stage on the pre-dam river, according to Ted Kennedy (USGS), phone interview with author, September 14, 2020.

Cataract Canyon: Robert H. Webb, Jayne Belnap, and John S. Weisheit, *Cataract Canyon: A Human and Environmental History of the Rivers in Canyonlands* (Salt Lake City: University of Utah Press, 2004). The description of the rivers' colors at the confluence is drawn from E. L. Kolb's *Through the Grand Canyon from Wyoming to Mexico* (1914; Tucson: University of Arizona Press, 1989), 129. Note: Different people counted the number of rapids differently; Clover likely got her number from Dellenbaugh.

Powell quote: Powell, *The Exploration of the Colorado River*, 206.

Steamboats: Toni Carrell, James E. Bradford, and W. L. Rusho, *Submerged Cultural Resources Site Report: Glen Canyon National Recreation Area* (Santa Fe, NM: U.S. National Park Service, 1987); Richard E. Lingenfelter, *Steamboats on the Colorado River, 1852–1916* (Tucson: University of Arizona Press, 1978), 106–10.

Ecosystem concept: Christophe Masutti, "Frederic Clements, Climatology, and Conservation in the 1930s," *Historical Studies in the Physical and Biological Sciences* 37, no. 1 (September 2006): 27–48, https://doi.org/10.1525/hsps.2006.37.1.27; Steward T. A. Pickett and J. M. Grove, "Urban Ecosystems: What Would Tansley Do?" *Urban Ecosystems* 12, no. 1 (2009): 1–8, https://doi.org/10.1007/s11252-008-0079-2; A. G. Tansley, "The Use and Abuse of Vegetational Concepts and Terms," *Ecology* 16, no. 3 (July 1935): 299–300, https://doi.org/10.2307/1930070; A. G. Tansley, "The Problems of Ecology," *New Phytologist* 3, no. 8 (October 1904): 196, https://doi.org/10.1111/j.1469-8137.1904.tb07347.x.

Chapter Five: A BEAUTIFUL PEA-GREEN BOAT

Ellen Thompson: Beatrice Scheer Smith, "The 1872 Diary and Plant Collections of Ellen Powell Thompson," *Utah Historical Quarterly* 62, no. 2 (1994); Helen H. Tindall, "Ellen Powell Thompson," *Woman's Journal* 42, no. 13 (April 1, 1911); Stanley L. Welsh, "Utah plant types—historical perspective 1840 to 1981—annotated list, and bibliography," *Great Basin Naturalist* 42, no. 2 (June 30, 1982): 133, https://www.jstor.org/stable/41711873; Dellenbaugh, *A Canyon Voyage*, 165, 195, 216.

Stanton surveys: Robert Brewster Stanton, *Down the Colorado* (Norman: University of Oklahoma Press, 1965); David Lavender, *River Runners of the Grand Canyon* (Tucson: University of Arizona Press, 1985): 22–23; Otis Reed "Dock" Marston, *From Powell to Power: A Recounting of the First One Hundred River Runners Through the Grand Canyon*, ed. Tom Martin (Flagstaff, AZ: Vishnu Temple Press, 2014), 121–22.

Historic Colorado River floods: Webb, Belnap, and Weisheit, *Cataract Canyon*, 55; E. C. LaRue, "Water Power and Flood Control of Colorado River Below Green River, Utah, Water-Supply Paper 556" (Washington, DC: Government Printing Office, 1925), 14, https://pubs.er.usgs.gov/publication/wsp556.

Tumbleweed: Maurice Grenville Kains et al., *The Russian Thistle: Its History as a Weed in the United States, with an Account of the Means Available for Its Eradication* (U.S. Department of Agriculture, Division of Botany, 1894), 12; James A. Young, "Tumbleweed," *Scientific American* 264, no. 3 (March 1991): 86.

Chapter Six: DELAYED

Nonsense botany: Edward Lear, *Nonsense Songs, Stories, Botany, and Alphabets* (Boston: James R. Osgood and Company, 1871).

Darwin quote: Darwin, *On the Origin of Species*, 360.

Eddy expedition: Clyde Eddy, *Down the World's Most Dangerous River* (New York: Frederick A. Stokes Company, 1929); Lavender, *River Runners of the Grand Canyon*, 66–76; Marston, *From Powell to Power*, 309.

Austin quote: Mary Austin, *The Land of Little Rain* (Bedford, MA: Applewood Books, 1903), 34.

Glen Canyon: C. Gregory Crampton, *Ghosts of Glen Canyon: History Beneath Lake Powell* (Salt Lake City, UT: Bonneville Books, 2009); Gregory C. Crampton, "Historic Glen Canyon," *Utah Historical Quarterly* 28, no. 3 (1960): 282; Katie Lee, *Glen Canyon Betrayed* (1998; Flagstaff, AZ: Fretwater Press, 2008).

Cottonwoods: Patrick Shaforth et al., "Establishment of Woody Riparian Vegetation in Relation to Fluvial Patterns of Streamflow, Bill Williams River, Arizona," *Wetlands* 18, no. 4 (December 1998): 577, http://dx.doi.org/10.1007/BF03161674.

Average low flows: John Fleck (University of New Mexico), email communication with author, January 4, 2022. The median low flow recorded at Lee's Ferry from 1921 to 1959 is around 5,000 cfs.

Dam surveys: Diane Boyer and Robert H. Webb, *Damming the Grand Canyon: The 1923 USGS Colorado River Expedition* (Logan: Utah State University Press, 2007); Walter B. Langbein, "L'Affaire LaRue," *WRD Bulletin* (April–June 1975); Eugene Clyde La Rue and Hubert Work, *Water Power and Flood Control of Colorado River Below Green River, Utah* (Washington, DC: Government Printing Office, 1925), 19.

Rainbow Bridge: For more on its spiritual importance, see Karl W. Luckert, *Navajo Mountain and Rainbow Bridge Religion* (Flagstaff: Museum of Northern Arizona, 1977).

Chapter Seven: HELL, YES! WHAT RIVER?

Making the desert bloom: "Boulder Dam," brochure, Lois Jotter Cutter Papers, Box 3, Folder 7; "How the great Colorado Desert is being made to blossom," *Los Angeles Daily Times*, January 1, 1905; William Merrell Vories, "Arizona," *Arizona Republican*, May 17, 1914.

Colorado River Compact: For a detailed analysis of the Compact and hydrologists' attempts to measure the river's flow, see Eric Kuhn and John Fleck, *Science Be Dammed: How Ignoring Inconvenient Science Drained the Colorado River* (Tucson: University of Arizona Press, 2019). Note: The Upper Basin got 7.5 million acre-feet of water annually; the Lower Basin got 8.5 million acre-feet. Because Arizona balked at the thought of splitting its share with California, the Lower Basin got the bonus 1 million acre-feet a year. Legal experts generally agree that this water comes from Arizona's tributary rivers, the Salt and the Gila. John Fleck (University of New Mexico), email communication with author, August 27, 2021.

Tillotson quote: M. R. Tillotson and Frank J. Taylor, *Grand Canyon Country* (Palo Alto, CA: Stanford University Press, 1929), 26.

Dutton quote: Clarence E. Dutton, *Tertiary History of the Grand Cañon District* (1882; Tucson: University of Arizona Press, 2001), 141.

Chapter Eight: PARADISE

Grand Canyon: Larry Stevens, *The Colorado River in Grand Canyon: A Guide*, 6th ed. (Flagstaff, AZ: Red Lake Books, 2002); Robert H. Webb, *Grand Canyon, A Century of Change* (Tucson: University of Arizona Press, 1996); Zwinger, *Downcanyon.*

Birdseye survey: Boyer and Webb, *Damming the Grand Canyon*, 56–59; "Fear District Explorers Lost in Flood In Colorado Canyon," *Evening Star* (Washington, DC), Sept 23, 1923.

Soap Creek: Robert Webb and Diane Boyer, "The Changing Rapids of Grand Canyon—Soap Creek Rapid," *Boatman's Quarterly Review* 14, no. 3 (Fall 2001): 6; Frederick S. Dellenbaugh, *The Romance of the Colorado River* (New York: G. P. Putnam's Sons, 1902), 320. Note: Kolb reported a fall of 25 feet; Flavell reported a fall of 12 feet.

Santa Fe Railroad book: *The Grand Canyon of Arizona* (Chicago: Passenger Department of the Santa Fe, 1902).

Agave phillipsiana: Wendy Hodgson, "Taxonomic Novelties in American Agave (Agavaceae)," *Novon* 11, no. 4 (Winter 2001): 410–16, https://doi.org/10.2307/3393152.

Stanton's Cave: Stanton, *Down the Colorado*, 89; Eleanora Roberta Iberall, "Paleoecological Studies From Fecal Pellets: Stanton's Cave, Grand Canyon, Arizona," master's thesis, University of Arizona, 1972, 4, https://repository.arizona.edu; Stephen C. Jett, "Grand Canyon Dams, Split Twig Figurines, and 'Hit-and-Run' Archeology," *American Antiquity* 33, no. 3 (July 1968): 341–51, https://doi.org/10.2307/278702; Douglas W. Schwartz, Arthur L. Lange, and Raymond deSaussure, "Split-Twig Figurines in the Grand Canyon," *American Antiquity* 23, no. 3 (January 1958): 264–74, https://www.jstor.org/stable/30246670; John-Paul Michael Hodnett and Vincent L. Santucci (National Park Service Paleontology Program), Microsoft Teams communication with author, June 17, 2022. Note: Yvette Running Horse Collin makes the case that the split-twig figurines in Stanton's Cave represent horses, in "The Relationship Between the Indigenous Peoples of the Americas and the Horse: Deconstructing a Eurocentric Myth" (master's thesis, University of Alaska–Fairbanks, 2017), 141–42, https://scholarworks.alaska.edu/handle/11122/7592.

Powell quote: Powell, *The Exploration of the Colorado River*, 238.

C. Hart Merriam: Wilfred H. Osgood, *Biographical Memoir of Clinton Hart Merriam, 1885–1942* (Washington, DC: National Academy of Sciences, 1947), 1–57; Keir B. Sterling, *Last of the Naturalists: The Career of C. Hart Merriam* (New York: Arno Press, 1977); C. Hart Merriam, *Life Zones and Crop Zones of the United States* (Washington, DC: Government Printing Office, 1898); C. Hart Merriam, "The Geographic Distribution of Animals and Plants in North America," *Yearbook of the U.S. Department of Agriculture* (1895), 206.

Ecological classifications: Andrea Wulf, *The Invention of Nature: Alexander von*

Humboldt's New World (New York: Vintage Books, 2015), 102–03, 148–49; Kuwanwisiwma, Ferguson, and Yeats, "Öngtupqa," 94–95.

Criticisms of life zones: Roderick P. Neumann, "Life Zones: The Rise and Decline of a Theory of the Geographic Distribution of Species," in *Spatializing the History of Ecology: Sites, Journeys, Mapping* (New York: Routledge, 2017); Rexford F. Daubenmire, "Merriam's Life Zones of North America," *Quarterly Review of Biology* 13, no. 3 (1938): 327–32, https://www.jstor.org/stable/2808379; Victor E. Shelford, "Life Zones, Modern Ecology, and the Failure of Temperature Summing," *Wilson Bulletin* 44, no. 3 (September 1932): 144–57, https://www.jstor.org/stable/4156104.

Merriam quotes: Arthur M. Phillips III, Dorothy A. House, and Barbara G. Phillips, "Expedition to the San Francisco Peaks: C. Hart Merriam and the Life Zone Concept," *Plateau* 60, no. 2 (1989): 15; C. Hart Merriam, "Results of a Biological Survey of the San Francisco Mountain Region and Desert of the Little Colorado, Arizona," in *North American Fauna* (Washington, DC: Government Printing Office, 1890), 37.

Indigenous connections to the Confluence: Octavius Seowtewa (Zuni), phone interview with author, April 13, 2021; and Jack Pongyesva, "Commemorating our Indigenous presence and sharing our true history of the entire Grand Canyon region," presentation, Hiking Guide Training Seminar, Grand Canyon, AZ, February 15, 2019.

Chapter Nine: A MOST UNUSUAL AND HAZARDOUS MEANS

Grand Canyon tourism: Stephen J. Pyne, *How The Grand Canyon Became Grand: A Short History* (New York: Penguin, 1998); Michael F. Anderson, *Polishing the Jewel: An Administrative History of Grand Canyon National Park* (Grand Canyon, AZ: Grand Canyon Association, 2000); David Scott and Kang Jae Jerry Lee, "People of Color and Their Constraints to National Park Visitation," *George Wright Forum* 35, no. 1 (2018): 73–82; *Grand Canyon National Park, Arizona* (Washington, DC: Government Printing Office, 1938), 8.

Debate over purpose of parks: Richard West Sellers, *Preserving Nature in the National Parks: A History* (New Haven: Yale University Press, 1997).

1.75 billion years ago: Stevens, *The Colorado River in the Grand Canyon*, 8. Note: The switch from single-celled to multicellular life is usually cited as having happened one billion years ago, but may have happened as early as 1.56 billion years ago, according to "Ancient origins of multicellular life," *Nature* 533, no. 441 (2016): https://doi.org/10.1038/533441b.

Phantom Ranch: Teri A. Cleeland, "The Cross Canyon Corridor Historic District in Grand Canyon National Park: A Model for Historic Preservation," master's thesis, Northern Arizona University, 1986, 47, http://npshistory.com/publications/grca/cleeland-1986.pdf; Robert W. Audretsch, "Phantom Ranch: Crucible of the Civilian Conservation Corps," *Journal of Arizona History* 51, no. 1 (spring 2011): 45, https://www.jstor.org/stable/41697338. Note: Clover and Jotter did not catalog cottonwoods along Bright Angel Creek, but they were almost certainly in place in the 1930s, according to Nancy J. Brian, Wendy C. Hodgson, and Arthur M. Phillips III, "Additions to the Flora of the Grand Canyon Region, II," *Journal of* *the Arizona–Nevada Academy of Science* 32, no. 2 (1999): 119, https://www.jstor.org/stable/40021305.

Havasupai people: Stephen Hirst, *I Am the Grand Canyon: The Story of the Havasupai People* (Grand Canyon, AZ: Grand Canyon Association, 2006). The Havasupai place names mentioned here come from Coleen Kaska (Havasupai), interview with author, February 15, 2019.

Havasupai Gardens: The National Park Service filed an application with the U.S. Board of Geographic Names to change the name to Havasupai Gardens in October 2021. As of this writing, the name change is not yet formalized. Joëlle Baird (Grand Canyon National Park), email communication with author, November 29, 2021.

CCC tramway: Nevills calls this a "Forest Service" tramway. I concluded it's the CCC tramway based on photo matching in NAU's Cline Library Special Collections and Archives. There are few details, so I've imagined what the crossing was like based on the Rust tramway (discontinued by 1938), described in *Phantoms of the Past: A Historic Walking Tour* (Grand Canyon, AZ: National Park Service), 2.

Pronghorn: Vernon Bailey, "Mammals of the Grand Canyon Region," *Nature Notes: Natural History Bulletin* 1 (June 1935), http://npshistory.com/nature_notes/grca/nhb-1c.htm; and Edward W. Nelson, *Status of the Pronghorned Antelope, 1922–1924* (Washington, DC: U.S. Department of Agriculture, 1925), 3–4.

George Wright: Jerry Emory and Pamela Wright Lloyd, "George Meléndez Wright 1904–1936: A Voice on the Wing," *George Wright Forum* 17, no. 4 (2000): 14–45, https://www.jstor.org/stable/43597720; Dayton Duncan, "George Meléndez Wright and the National Park Idea," *George Wright Forum* 26, no. 1 (2009): 12, https://www.jstor.org/stable/43598092. Wright's first survey: George M. Wright, Joseph S. Dixon, and Ben H. Thompson, *Fauna of the National Parks of the United States: A Preliminary Survey of Faunal Relations in National Parks* (Washington, DC: Government Printing Office, 1933). Wright's second survey: George M. Wright and Ben H. Thompson, *Fauna of the National Parks of the United States: Wildlife Management in the National Parks* (Washington, DC: Government Printing Office, 1935).

Rocky Mountain elk: Michael A. Amundson, "'The Most Interesting Objects That Have Ever Arrived': Imperialist Nostalgia, State Politics, Hybrid Nature, and the Rise and Fall of Arizona's Elk, 1866–1914," *Journal of Arizona History* 61, no. 2 (Summer 2020): 255–94, https://muse.jhu.edu/article/757911.

Pheasants and quail: Florence Merriam Bailey, *Among the Birds in the Grand Canyon Country* (Washington, DC: Government Printing Office, 1939), 26–27.

scud: Dean W. Blinn and Gerald A. Cole, "Algal and Invertebrate Biota in the Colorado River: Comparison of Pre- and Post-Dam Conditions," in *Colorado River Ecology and Dam Management, Proceedings of a Symposium, May 24–25, 1990* (Washington, DC: National Academy Press, 1991), 109.

Edith Kolb and Mabel La Rue: Boyer and Webb, *Damming the Grand Canyon*, 14–19, 131.

"words stop": George Wharton James, *The Grand Canyon of Arizona: How to See It* (Boston: Little, Brown, 1912), 7. The author goes on for quite some time after this statement.

Albright quote: Horace M. Albright, "The Everlasting Wilderness," *Saturday Evening Post*, September 29, 1928, 28.

Great Kaibab Deer Drive: Brad Dimock, "Jack Fuss and the Great Kaibab Deer Drive," *Boatman's Quarterly Review* 17, no. 2 (Summer 2004): 16; Neil Carmony, "The Grand Canyon Deer Drive of 1924: The Accounts of Will C. Barnes and Mike E. Musgrave," *Journal of Arizona History* 43, no. 1 (spring 2002): 58; "Kaibab Deer Herd Must Be Reduced Immediately," USDA Office of the Secretary Press Service, October 13, 1924, https://www.fws.gov/news/Historic/NewsReleases/1924/19241013 .pdf; "County and State Game Wardens Halt Deer Hunt to Give M'Cormick a Try," *Coconino Sun,* October 31, 1924; Zane Grey, "Zane Grey Tells Why Drive Failed," *Coconino Sun,* December 19, 1924.

Kaibab deer debates: Aldo Leopold, "Deer Irruptions," *Wisconsin Academy of Sciences, Arts, and Letters* (1943): 351–66; Dan Binkley et al., "Was Aldo Leopold Right about the Kaibab Deer Herd?" *Ecosystems* 9, no. 2 (2006): 227–41, http://www .jstor.org/stable/25470332; Margaret Moore (Northern Arizona University), email communication with author, March 29, 2021.

Cigarette-munching deer: "Kaibab Fawns Brought To South Rim Of Canyon," *Coconino Sun,* October 14, 1927.

NBC broadcast: "Nevills Expedition," narrated by Arthur Anderson, NBC Blue Network, July 20, 1938. Thanks to David Sager of the Library of Congress for providing a copy of the audio, and NBC for permission to quote.

Leopold quotes: Aldo Leopold, "Engineering and Conservation," in *The River of the Mother of God* (Madison: University of Wisconsin Press, 1991), 254; Aldo Leopold, *A Sand County Almanac and Sketches Here and There* (New York and Oxford: Oxford University Press, 1949), 204. Note: Leopold became assistant director of the Forest Products Laboratory in May 1924. E. V. Jotter worked there at least until October 1924, according to Julie Blankenburg and Amy Androff (Forest Products Laboratory), email communication with author, May 24, 2011.

Chapter Ten: A HUNDRED PERSONALITIES

Pathé–Bray Expedition: Lavender, *River Runners,* 66–74; Gregg Bachman and Thomas J. Slater, eds., *American Silent Film: Discovering Marginalized Voices* (Carbondale: Southern Illinois University Press, 2002), 106, 113; "Brief Reviews of Current Pictures," *Photoplay,* September 1928, 6.

Newsreel: Sadly, this film has not survived, but a catalog record includes a brief description. Lance Watsky (Sherman Grinberg Film Library), email communication with author, March 29, 2021.

Barrel cacti: Clover and Jotter recorded small barrel cacti growing above mile 110, but these were likely misidentifications of the many-headed barrel cacti (*Echinocactus polycephalus*), according to a footnote in Webb, *Grand Canyon, A Century of Change,* 247–48. For descriptions of obtaining water from barrel cacti, see William Temple Hornaday, *Camp-fires on Desert and Lava* (New York: Charles Scribner's Sons, 1908), 217–19; Steven J. Phillips and Patricia Wentworth Comus, eds., *A Natural History of the Sonoran Desert* (Tucson: Arizona–Sonora Desert Museum Press, 2000), 202–03; Vera Higgins, "Characteristic Features of Cacti," *Science Progress* 28, no. 110 (1933): 247, http://www.jstor.org/stable/43410831.

Little Horse Expedition: Bert Lauzon, "Little Horse Expedition Under Great Thumb [original diary]," January 15–25, 1938, and "The Little Horses and Other Fabulous Tales of Grand Canyon," Lauzon Family Collection, NAU.MS.238, Special Collections and Archives, Cline Library, Northern Arizona University, Flagstaff, Arizona.

Shiva Temple Expedition: Betty Leavengood, *Grand Canyon Women*, 3rd ed. (Grand Canyon, AZ: Grand Canyon Association, 2014), 69–76; Edwin Teale, "Explorers Hunt Prehistoric Animals In Lost Worlds," *Popular Science Monthly*, November 1937, 42–43, 138; "'Shiva's Temple', Arizona," *Nature* 140 (September 1937): 537–38, https://doi.org/10.1038/140537c0.

Cacti evolution: Jon Rebma and Donald Pinkava, "*Opuntia* Cacti of North America— An Overview," *Florida Entomologist* 84, no. 4 (December 2001): 478, https://doi .org/10.2307/3496374; Erika J. Edwards and Michael J. Donoghue, "*Pereskia* and the Origin of the Cactus Life-Form," *American Naturalist* 167, no. 6 (June 2006): 777– 93, https://doi.org/10.1086/504605; Mónica Arakaki et al., "Contemporaneous and Recent Radiations of the World's Major Succulent Plant Lineages," *Proceedings of the National Academy of Sciences* 108, no. 20 (May 2011): 8379, https://doi.org/10.1073/ pnas.1100628108.

Volcanic flows: G. Brent Dalrymple and W.K. Hamblin, "K-Ar ages of Pleistocene Lava Dams in the Grand Canyon in Arizona," *Proceedings of the National Academy of Sciences* 95, no. 17 (August 1998): 9744–49, https://dx.doi.org/10.1073%2Fpnas.95 .17.9744; Ranney, *Carving the Grand Canyon*, 138–39; Powell, *The Exploration of the Colorado River*, 274.

Creosote bush: B. E. Mahall and R. M. Callaway, "Root Communication Among Desert Shrubs," *Proceedings of the National Academy of Sciences* 88, no. 3 (1991): 874– 76, https://dx.doi.org/10.1073%2Fpnas.88.3.874.

Flavell expedition: George Flavell, *The Log of the Panthon* (Boulder, CO: Pruett Publishing, 1987).

Bessie Hyde: Brad Dimock, *Sunk Without a Sound: The Tragic Colorado River Honeymoon of Glen and Bessie Hyde* (Flagstaff, AZ: Fretwater Press, 2001); Leavengood, *Grand Canyon Women*, 45–58.

Burros: John Willis, "'On Burro'd Time': Feral Burros, the Brighty Legend, and the Pursuit of Wilderness in the Grand Canyon," *Journal of Arizona History* 44, no. 1 (spring 2003): 1–24, https://www.jstor.org/stable/41696750.

Ives quote: Joseph Ives, *Report upon the Colorado River of the West* (Washington, DC: Government Printing Office, 1861), 110.

Hysteria: Olivia Campbell, *Women in White Coats: How the First Women Doctors Changed the World of Medicine* (Toronto: Park Row, 2021), 100.

Jaguars: Jessica Moreno (wildlife biologist), interview with author, June 10, 2021.

Chapter Eleven: LONELY FOR THE RIVER

Gypsum Cave: M. R. Harrington, "Man and Beast in Gypsum Cave," *Desert Magazine* 3, no. 6 (April 1940): 4; M. R. Harrington, "The Mystery of Gypsum Cave," *Scientific American* 146, no. 1 (July 1930): 35; Anna Reser and Leila McNeill, *Forces of Nature: The Women Who Changed Science* (London: Frances Lincoln Publishing, 2021), 163–66.

Boulder City: Paul W. Papa, *Boulder City: The Town That Built the Hoover Dam* (Charleston, SC: History Press, 2017), 54; Michael Hiltzik, *Colossus: Hoover Dam and the Making of the American Century* (New York: Free Press, 2010), 317–18.

"risk their lives": "Brave Women," Archives/*Spokesman-Review,* July 21, 1938. Thanks to Jessica Bell for permission to quote.

Lost specimens: Brad Dimock, "Willis Johnson," *Boatman's Quarterly Review* 8, no. 3 (Summer 1995): 31. Note: It's unclear exactly where Johnson found the plant press; Jotter wrote that it was "off the Bright Angel Trail."

Sclerocactus havasupaiensis: Elzada U. Clover, "A New Species and Variety of Sclerocactus from Arizona," *American Journal of Botany* 29, no. 2 (February 1942): 172–73, https://doi.org/10.2307/2437447.

Botany findings: Clover and Jotter, "Floristic Studies," 591–642; Emily Palmquist (USGS), phone interview with author, March 31, 2021; Larry Stevens (Museum of Northern Arizona), phone interview with author, July 27, 2021.

Chapter Twelve: HEAVEN AS I GO ALONG

Clark quote: Neil M. Clark, "Fast-Water Man © SEPS," *Saturday Evening Post*, May 18, 1946, 30.

Holmstrom's final years and death: Welch, Conley, and Dimock, *The Doing of the Thing*, 265–70.

Nevills's final years and death: Nancy Nelson, *Any Time, Any Place, Any River: The Nevills of Mexican Hat* (Flagstaff, AZ: Red Lake Books, 1991); Gaylord Staveley, "Norm Nevills," *Boatman's Quarterly Review* 17, no. 1 (Spring 2004): 43; Sandra Nevills Reiff (relative), phone interview with author, August 20, 2021.

Female river guides: Louise Teal, *Breaking into the Current: Boatwomen of the Grand Canyon* (Tucson: University of Arizona Press, 1994).

Clover's 1945 trip: Traci Wyrick, "Louis Schellbach's Log Books: Part VI," *The Ol' Pioneer* 24, no. 3 (Summer 2013): 12; Traci Wyrick, "Louis Schellbach's Log Books: Part VII," *The Ol' Pioneer* 24, no. 4 (Fall 2013): 3.

Rose Collom: Richard D. Quartaroli, "The Grand Canyon Rose: Grand Canyon National Park's First Botanist, Rose Collom," in *Celebrating 100 Years of the National Park Service: A Gathering of Grand Canyon Historians: Ideas, Arguments, and First-Person Accounts,* ed. Richard Quartaroli (Grand Canyon, AZ: Grand Canyon Association, 2018), 50–55; and Richard Quartaroli, "Grand Canyon's Other Rose and First Botanist," *Grand Canyon River Runner*, no. 15 (Spring 2013): 12–13.

Clover's final years and death: "Elzada Urseba Clover: Memoir," in *Proceedings of the Board of Regents* (University of Michigan, June 1967), 628–29; Jane Myers (U–M alum), phone interview with author, October 13, 2020; David Mastie (U–M alum), phone interview with author, September 17, 2021; Kenneth Majors (relative), phone interviews with author, February 5, 2020, and January 24, 2022; Marilyn Findley (relative), phone interview with author, February 5, 2020.

Fate of the Cataract boats: Janet Balsom and Brynn Bender, "From Courtyard to Conservation: The Grand Canyon Historic Boat Conservation Project," in

Reflections of Grand Canyon Historians: Ideas, Arguments, and First-Person Accounts, ed. Todd R. Berger (Grand Canyon, AZ: Grand Canyon Association, 2008), 26.

Fate of the plants: Eric Schuettpelz (Smithsonian Institution), email communication with author, March 8, 2021; Michael Palmer (Matthaei Botanical Gardens), email communication with author, July 13, 2021. Note: A search for Clover's name in SEINet (https://swbiodiversity.org/seinet/) shows her specimens in multiple herbaria.

Lois Jotter's final years and death: Victor Cutter III (relative), multiple interviews with author, 2019–22; Carolyn Wyland (UNC alum), phone interview with author, November 15, 2021; Linda Curtis (UNC alum), phone interview with author, February 28, 2021; Tom Myers, "Farewell," *Boatman's Quarterly Review* 23, no. 3 (Fall 2013): 9–10.

Damming the Grand Canyon: For various perspectives, see Kevin Fedarko, *The Emerald Mile* (New York: Scribner, 2013); Russell Martin, *A Story That Stands Like a Dam: Glen Canyon and The Struggle for the Soul of the West* (Salt Lake City: University of Utah Press, 2017); Bryan Pearson, "Salvation for Grand Canyon: Congress, the Sierra Club, and the Dam Controversy of 1966–1968," *Journal of the Southwest* 36, no. 2 (1994): 159–75.

Chapter Thirteen: LEGENDARY

Old Timers Trip: Robert H. Webb, Theodore S. Melis, and Richard A. Valdez, *Observations of Environmental Change in Grand Canyon, Arizona* (Tucson: U.S. Geological Survey, 2002); Teo Melis (USGS), interview with author, July 2, 2021; Tom Myers (doctor), phone interview with author, July 20, 2021; Diane Boyer (archivist), phone interview with author, July 1, 2021; Lew Steiger (river guide), phone interview with author, August 13, 2021; Sandra Nevills Reiff (relative), phone interview with author, July 1, 2021.

River ecology: Jack Schmidt (Utah State University), phone interview with author, July 20, 2021; Larry Stevens (Museum of Northern Arizona), phone interview with author, July 27, 2021; Richard Valdez (fish biologist), phone interview with author, July 13, 2021; John C. Schmidt et al., "Science and Values in River Restoration in the Grand Canyon," *BioScience* 48, no. 9 (September 1998): 735–47, https://doi.org/10.2307/1313336.

River rafting numbers: Statistics from 1940–71: "Grand Canyon National Park Colorado River Users," Lois Jotter Cutter Papers, Box 3, Folder 7. Statistics prior to 1940: Quartaroli, "Dock's Data of Navigational Numbers," 24.

"quiet mill ponds": National Park Service, *A Survey of the Recreational Resources of the Colorado River Basin* (Washington, DC: Government Printing Office, 1950), chap. VII, https://www.nps.gov/parkhistory/online_books/colorado/chap7a.htm.

No other plant list: See table of plant lists in Mar-Elise Hill and Tina Ayers, "Table 1: Past Floristic Work in Glen Canyon NRA," in *Vascular Plant Inventory of Glen Canyon National Recreation Area* (Fort Collins, CO: U.S. Department of the Interior National Park Service, 2009), 2. Also: R. Roy Johnson, "Historic Changes in Vegetation Along the Colorado River in the Grand Canyon," in *Colorado River Ecology and Dam Management, Proceedings of a Symposium May 24–25, 1990* (Washington, DC: National Academy Press, 1991), 184.

Schmidt quote: Jack Schmidt, oral history interview with Lew Steiger, September 1994, NAU.OH.94.100.13–14, USGS Old Timers Collection [oral history interviews].

Aquatic insects: Theodore A. Kennedy et al., "Flow Management for Hydropower Extirpates Aquatic Insects, Undermining River Food Webs," *BioScience* 66, no. 7 (July 2016): 561–75, https://doi.org/10.1093/biosci/biw059.

Climate change: For the status of knowledge in 1994, see "Summary for Policymakers," in *IPCC Second Assessment Report* (Intergovernmental Panel on Climate Change, 1995), 19–24, https://www.ipcc.ch/report/ar2/syr/. The "deadly glaciers" quote comes from G. S. Callender, "Can Carbon Dioxide Influence Climate?," *Weather* 4, no. 10 (October 1949): 314, https://doi.org/10.1002/j.1477–8696.1949.tb00952.x. Also: Richard Seager et al., "Whither the 100th Meridian? The Once and Future Physical Human Geography of America's Arid–Humid Divide. Part II: The Meridian Moves East," *Earth Interactions* 22, no. 5 (March 2018): 1–24, https://doi.org/10.1175/EI-D-17–0012.1; Connor Nolan et al., "Past and Future Global Transformation of Terrestrial Ecosystems Under Climate Change," *Science* 361, no. 6405 (August 2018): 920–23, https://doi.org/10.1126/science.aan5360.

Experimental floods: Michael P. Collier, Robert H. Webb, and Edmund D. Andrews, "Experimental Flooding in Grand Canyon," *Scientific American* 276, no. 1 (January 1997): 82–89, https://www.jstor.org/stable/10.2307/24993568; John C. Schmidt et al., "The 1996 Controlled Flood in Grand Canyon: Flow, Sediment Transport, and Geomorphic Change," *Ecological Applications* 11, no. 3 (2001): 657–71, https://www.jstor.org/stable/3061108; Lawrence E. Stevens et al., "Planned Flooding and Colorado River Riparian Trade-offs Downstream of Glen Canyon Dam, Arizona," *Ecological Applications* 11, no. 3 (June 2001): 701–10, https://www.jstor.org/stable/3061111; E. D. Andrews and Leslie A. Pizzi, "Origin of the Colorado River Experimental Flood in Grand Canyon," *Hydrological Sciences Journal* 45, no. 4 (2000): 607–27, https://doi.org/10.1080/02626660009492361; *Record of Decision, Operation of Glen Canyon Dam, Final Environmental Impact Statement* (U.S. Department of the Interior, October 1996), Northern Arizona University Colorado Plateau Digital Collections. Note: The Long-Term Experimental and Management Plan (LTEMP) which formalized the flow experiments was finalized in 2012 and expanded in 2016; it is still ongoing.

drought: A. Park Williams, "Large Contribution from Anthropogenic Warming to an Emerging North American Megadrought," *Science* 368, no. 6488 (April 2020): 314–18, https://doi.org/10.1126/science.aaz9600; also: Elizabeth Kolbert, "The Lost Canyons Under Lake Powell," *New Yorker,* August 9, 2021, https://www.newyorker.com/magazine/2021/08/16/the-lost-canyon-under-lake-powell.

Epilogue: A WOMAN'S PLACE

Swiss chalets: Stanton, *Down the Colorado*, 152.

Female river guides: Nine of the sixteen Grand Canyon concessionaries had gender information for their guides available on their website or upon request. Data compiled by author in 2019, and independently confirmed by John Dillon (Grand Canyon River Outfitters Association), email communication with author, September 20, 2019.

Grand Canyon River District: A. C. Shilton, "Why Female River Guides Aren't Welcome in the Grand Canyon," *Outside,* March 30, 2016, https://www.outsideonline .com/outdoor-adventure/water-activities/why-female-river-guides-arent-welcome -grand-canyon/.

Cooking quote: Shaina Maytum, "Row Like a Girl: And Other Advice for Women on the River," *Duct Tape Diaries,* April 27, 2021, https://community.nrs.com/duct -tape/2021/04/27/row-like-a-girl-and-other-advice-for-women-on-the-river/.

Data on women in science: Richard Fry, Brian Kennedy, and Cary Funk, "STEM Jobs See Uneven Progress in Increasing Gender, Racial, and Ethnic Diversity," Pew Research Center, April 1, 2021, https://www.pewresearch.org/science/2021/04/01/ stem-jobs-see-uneven-progress-in-increasing-gender-racial-and-ethnic-diversity/; Luke Holman, Devi Stuart-Fox, and Cindy E. Hauser, "The Gender Gap in Science: How Long Until Women are Equally Represented?" *PLoS Biology* 16, no. 4 (April 2018), https://doi.org/10.1371/journal.pbio.2004956; and David I. Miller et al., "The Development of Children's Gender-Science Stereotypes: A Meta-analysis of 5 Decades of U.S. Draw-A-Scientist Studies," *Child Development* 89, no. 6 (March 2018): 1949–50, https://doi.org/10.1111/cdev.13039.

Clover's cactus: Kenneth D. Heil and J. Mark Porter, "Sclerocactus (Cactaceae): A Revision," *Haseltonia* 2 (1994): 31–33. As of June 2022, Clover's cactus is listed as "under review" by the U.S. Fish and Wildlife Service. For more: "Petition to List the Clover's Cactus (*Sclerocactus cloverae*) under the Endangered Species Act," WildEarth Guardians, May 29, 2020, https://pdf.wildearthguardians.org/docs/ Clovers-Cactus-Petition-Final-2020.pdf.

Botany Aisle: Meg Flynn and Mike DeHoff (Returning Rapids Project), Zoom interview with author, July 29, 2021. More info at https://www.returningrapids.com/.

INDEX